BASIC SCIENCE FOR FOOD STUDIES

Titles already published in this series:

Accounting in the Hotel and Catering Industry
Frank Wood and Peter Lightowlers

Titles to be published in this series:

Applied Science for Food Studies
V.L. Brownsell, C.J. Griffith and Eleri Jones

Mathematics for Catering Students
H.G. Davies

V.L. BROWNSELL BSc, PhD
C.J. GRIFFITH BSc, PhD
ELERI JONES MSc, PhD

BASIC SCIENCE FOR FOOD STUDIES

LONGMAN London and New York

Longman Group Limited
Longman House, Burnt Mill, Harlow
Essex CM20 2JE, England
Associated companies throughout the world

Published in the United States of America
by Longman Inc., New York

First published 1985

British Library Cataloguing in Publication Data

Brownsell, V.L.
  Basic science for food studies.
  1. Science   2. Food industry and trade
  I. Title   II. Griffith, C.J.   III. Jones, E.
  502'.4664   Q158.5

ISBN 0-582-41328-1

BSDCS7

Set in Linotron 202 10/12pt Times
Produced by Longman Singapore Publishers (Pte) Ltd.
Printed in Singapore

CONTENTS

Acknowledgements   x

CHAPTER 1 MEASUREMENT AND DENSITY   1
1. 1 Introduction   1
1. 2 Units   1
1. 3 Density   4
1. 4 Relative density   4
1. 5 Hydrometry   5
Questions   7

CHAPTER 2 FORCE, WORK AND ENERGY   8
2. 1 Introduction   8
2. 2 Force   8
2. 3 Work   11
2. 4 Energy   12
2. 5 Conversion of energy   16
2. 6 Conservation of energy   18
2. 7 Useful and non-useful work   18
2. 8 Power   19
Questions   20

CHAPTER 3 HEAT   21
3. 1 Introduction   21
3. 2 Heat and temperature   21
3. 3 Measurement of temperature – thermometry   22
3. 4 Thermal capacity   26
3. 5 Change of state and latent heat   27
3. 6 Effect of pressure on the boiling point of a liquid   29
3. 7 Effect of additives   30
3. 8 Energy value of foods   30
3. 9 Methods of heat transfer   30
3.10 Microwave cooking   35
3.11 Evaporation and humidity   35
3.12 Refrigeration   37
Questions   38

CHAPTER 4 ELECTRICITY   40
  4. 1 Introduction   40
  4. 2 Static electricity   40
  4. 3 Current electricity and electron flow   41
  4. 4 Potential difference   42
  4. 5 Resistance   44
  4. 6 Power   48
  4. 7 Fuses   50
  4. 8 Wiring a plug   53
  4. 9 Potential hazards involved with electricity   54
Questions   55

CHAPTER 5 GENERAL PROPERTIES OF MATTER   57
  5. 1 Introduction   57
  5. 2 Physical and chemical changes   57
  5. 3 Elements   57
Questions   63

CHAPTER 6 ATOMIC THEORY   64
  6. 1 Introduction   64
  6. 2 Atoms as 'building blocks' of elements   64
  6. 3 Atomic structure   64
  6. 4 Valency   67
  6. 5 Crystal structure   72
  6. 6 Radioactivity   75
  6. 7 Molecular motion and kinetic theory   76
Questions   79

CHAPTER 7 CHEMICAL REACTIONS   80
  7. 1 Introduction   80
  7. 2 Factors affecting the rate of chemical reactions   81
  7. 3 Reactions involving oxidation and reduction   83
Questions   86

CHAPTER 8 ACIDS, BASES AND SALTS   87
  8. 1 Introduction   87
  8. 2 Acids   87
  8. 3 Bases   90
  8. 4 The pH scale   91
  8. 5 Neutralisation and salt production   94
Questions   96

CHAPTER 9 INTRODUCTION TO ORGANIC CHEMISTRY AND
            BIOCHEMISTRY   97
9. 1 Introduction   97
9. 2 The tetravalenet carbon atom   97
9. 3 Functional groups   101
9. 4 Alcohols   103
9. 5 Carboxylic acids   104
9. 6 Esters   104
9. 7 Flavouring agents   105
9. 8 Polymers   106
9. 9 Biochemistry and energy production   108
9.10 Enzymes   110
Questions   111

CHAPTER 10 THE BIOLOGICAL WORLD   112
10. 1 Introduction   112
10. 2 Characteristics of living things   114
10. 3 Conditions necessary for life   115
10. 4 Cell types   117
10. 5 Cellular differentiation   120
10. 6 Structure and function of the human skin   121
Questions   123

CHAPTER 11 MICRO-ORGANISMS   125
11. 1 Introduction   125
11. 2 The viruses   126
11. 3 The prokaryota   128
11. 4 The algae   133
11. 5 The protozoa   133
11. 6 The fungi   133
Questions   136

CHAPTER 12 THE PLANT KINGDOM   137
12. 1 Introduction   137
12. 2 The structure of a flowering plant   138
12. 3 Plants as foods   140
12. 4 Plants as the providers of raw materials   143
Questions   145

CHAPTER 13 THE ANIMAL KINGDOM   146
13. 1 Introduction   146
13. 2 The animal kingdom: helpful to the food industry   147
13. 3 The animal kingdom: harmful to the food industry   149
Questions   162

CHAPTER 14 GROWTH AND TRANSPORT 163
14. 1 Introduction 163
14. 2 Growth in an individual cell 163
14. 3 Growth in multicellular organisms 163
14. 4 Growth in populations of bacteria 165
14. 5 Transport in and out of the cell 169
Questions 173

CHAPTER 15 MODES OF NUTRITION 175
15. 1 Introduction 175
15. 2 Autotrophs 175
15. 3 Heterotrophs 176
15. 4 Types of nutritional association 177
15. 5 Chemical cycles 181
15. 6 Food chains and webs 182
Questions 184

CHAPTER 16 INTRODUCTION TO HUMAN NUTRITION 185
16. 1 Introduction 185
16. 2 Nutrients 185
16. 3 Water 186
16. 4 Carbohydrates 186
16. 5 Proteins 188
16. 6 Lipids 190
16. 7 Vitamins 191
16. 8 Minerals 192
16. 9 Effect of cooking on nutrients 192
Questions 193

CHAPTER 17 DIGESTION 194
17. 1 Introduction 194
17. 2 The digestive system 194
17. 3 The digestive process 196
17. 4 Absorption 199
17. 5 The role of the liver 200
Questions 201

CHAPTER 18 BASIC FOOD HYGIENE 202
18. 1 Introduction 202
18. 2 Causes of food poisoning 203
18. 3 Sources of food poisoning bacteria 203
18. 4 How food hygiene works 206
18. 5 Rules for personal hygiene 208
Questions 209

Experiment 1 Measurement of the density of solids   210
Experiment 2 Measurement of relative density   213
Experiment 3 Measurement of temperatures of foods using a
              probe thermometer   216
Experiment 4 To demonstrate Ohm's Law   217
Experiment 5 Electrical conductivity of materials   219
Experiment 6 To demonstrate the effect of temperature on
              solubility   220
Experiment 7 Measurement of the pH of liquids and solids   222
Experiment 8 Use of a compound microscope   223
Experiment 9 Examination of cells using microscopy   227
Experiment 10 To illustrate the effect of osmotic pressure on
              cells   229
Experiment 11 Identification of chemical groups in food   230
Experiment 12 To show the digestive effect of salivary
              amylase on starch   232

INDEX   235

ACKNOWLEDGEMENTS

The authors wish to thank Rentokil Ltd, and particularly Dr P. B. Cornwell, for their permission to reproduce the original photographs for Figs. 13.5, 13.6a, 13.6b, 13.6c, 13.6d, 13.7a, 13.7b, 13.7c, 13.7d, 13.8 which originally appeared in *Pest Control in Buildings* by P. B. Cornwell, published by Rentokil Ltd, 2nd Edition, 1979.

1

MEASUREMENT AND DENSITY

1.1 INTRODUCTION

Accurate measurement of mass, length, time, etc. is needed in many areas of catering, e.g. in the measurement of ingredients in food preparation, the estimating of lengths of curtaining or carpeting for hotels or in the gauging of cooking times or temperatures. Mass, length and time are examples of physical quantities, the measurement of which requires a set of standard units.

1.2 UNITS

At the present time there are two systems of units in operation:
1. The British or Imperial system based on length in feet, mass in pounds and time in seconds. This is the f.p.s. system.
2. The metric system based on length in metres, mass in grams or kilograms and time in seconds. The metric system was rationalised in 1960 to give one unit for each physical quantity for use in calculations, definitions and equations, e.g. mass is expressed in kilograms (kg). This system is known as the Système Internationale (SI).

The catering industry was originally committed to 'go metric' by 1975. A dual system still exists in many areas and a conversion table of SI units to British units and vice versa is shown in Table 1.1.

Since schools and colleges use SI units it is to be hoped that the entire catering industry will conform as far as possible in the near future. Problem areas include volume, where milk and beer are still sold in pints, with no immediate prospect of change, and temperature, where many measurements in catering are recorded in °F.

1.2.1 BASIC UNITS OF SI

By using a limited number of metric units, SI standardises measurements for all scientific disciplines. There are only seven basic units (see Table 1.2).

TABLE 1.1 Conversion factors between systems of units

Mass

1 oz	=	28.4 g
1 lb	=	454 g
	=	0.454 kg
1 kg	=	2.205 lb
1 ton	=	1,017 kg
metric tonne	=	1000 kg

'Two-and-a-quarter pounds of jam weigh about a kilogram'

Length

1 in	=	25.4 mm
1 ft	=	305 mm
	=	0.305 m
1 m	=	1.093 yd
1 yd	=	0.914 m

'A metre measures three foot three — it's longer than a yard you see'

Area

1 in^2	=	645 mm^2
1 ft^2	=	0.093 m^2
1 yd^2	=	0.84 m^2
1 m^2	=	1.19 yd^2

Volume

20 fluid oz	=	1 pint
	=	0.568 litre
1 gal	=	4.5 litre
1 litre	=	1.76 pint

'A litre of water's a pint and three-quarters'

TABLE 1.2 Basic units of SI

Physical quantity	SI unit	Symbol	Traditional unit
Length	metre	m	foot, yard
Mass	kilogram	kg	pound
Time	second	s	second
Electrical current	ampere	A	ampere
Temperature	Kelvin	K	°Fahrenheit or °Centigrade
Luminous intensity	candela	cd	candle
Amount of substance	mole	mol	equivalent in grams

1.2.2   DERIVED UNITS IN SI

All other physical quantities such as area, volume, energy, pressure, density, etc. are expressed in terms of the basic units, and are referred to as derived units (see Table 1.3).

TABLE 1.3 Derived units in SI

Quantity	Derivation			SI unit	Name	Symbol
Area	length × (m)	breadth (m)		m^2		
Volume	length × (m)	breadth × (m)	height (m)	m^3		
Force	mass × (kg)	acceleration $(m\ s^{-2})$		$kg\ m^{-1}\ s^{-2}$	**newton**	N
Energy or Work	force × (N)	distance (m)		N m	**joule**	J
Pressure	force × (N)	area^{-2} (m^{-2})		$N\ m^{-2}$	**pascal**	Pa

1.2.3   PREFIXES

In many instances we measure quantities far greater or smaller than the standard basic or derived unit, e.g. in small-scale food preparation only a fraction of a kilogram may be needed, whereas in bulk catering operations or food manufacture thousands of kilograms may be required. To describe a convenient unit size a system of multiples and sub-multiples is used which is achieved using a series of prefixes (see Table 1.4).

TABLE 1.4 Prefixes in SI

Factor	Name	Symbol
1 million, 1 000 000 or 10^6	Mega	M
1 thousand, 1000 or 10^3	kilo	k
1 tenth, 1/10, 0.1, 10^{-1}	deci	d
1 hundredth, 1/100, 0.01, 10^{-2}	centi	c
1 thousandth, 1/1000, 0.001, 10^{-3}	milli	m
1 millionth, 1/1 000 000, 0.000 001, 10^{-6}	micro	μ
1 thousand millionth, 1/1 000 000 000, 0.000 000 001, 10^{-9}	nano	n

1.2.4   PRACTICAL UNITS

Throughout this book SI units will be used. In certain instances it is more convenient to use practical metric units, e.g. small volumes are usually measured in litres (metric units) rather than cubic metres (m^3) (SI units). Bulk quantities, such as concrete for hotel floors, are measured in cubic metres.

1.3 DENSITY

If equal volumes (e.g. 1 litre) of two liquids, such as oil and water, are considered then:

1 litre of water has a mass of 1 kg
1 litre of oil has a mass of 0.89 kg

Oil has less mass for the same volume, i.e. oil is less dense. The same applies with equal volumes of baked goods, e.g. fruit cakes are more dense than sponge cakes. The relationship between mass and volume is expressed as the density of the substance, where density equals the mass per unit volume.

$$\text{Density } \rho = \frac{\text{mass}}{\text{volume}}$$

Using SI units, the mass is in kg and the volume is in m^3, so the unit of density is $kg\ m^{-3}$, although it is often expressed as $g\ cm^{-3}$, e.g.:

density of water = $1000\ kg\ m^{-3}$ or $1.00\ g\ cm^{-3}$;
density of oil   = $890\ kg\ m^{-3}$ or $0.89\ g\ cm^{-3}$.

   Density depends on volume which will vary with temperature. The variation is only slight for most liquids, although density values must be quoted for a particular temperature, e.g.:

density of water = $1.00\ g\ cm^{-3}$ only at 4 °C
                 = $0.99\ g\ cm^{-3}$ at 45 °C.

The change in density of air and water with temperature is responsible for convection currents. Hot air or water is less dense and rises, which causes circulation distributing heat through a room or hot water tank.

   The fact that the density of water is approximately equal to $1\ g\ cm^{-3}$ is of great importance because it means that densities can be compared relative to the unit value of water.

1.4 RELATIVE DENSITY (RD)

Calculation of the density of a substance requires accurate measurement of both mass and volume. Volume is less-accurately determined than mass and the concept of relative density overcomes this problem by comparing the density of a substance with that of water.

i.e. Relative density $= \dfrac{\text{Density of substance}}{\text{Density of water}}$

$= \dfrac{mv^{-1} \text{ for substance}}{mv^{-1} \text{ for water}}$

$= \dfrac{m \text{ of substance}}{m \text{ of same volume of water}}$

i.e. Relative density $= \dfrac{\text{Mass of any volume of substance}}{\text{Mass of equal volume of water at a given temperature.}}$

Relative density is a ratio which numerically equals density

e.g. density of milk $= 1.030 \text{ g cm}^{-1}$

relative density $= 1.030$

Solids with a relative density less than one, e.g. onions, will float on water, whereas those with a relative density greater than one, e.g. potatoes, will sink. Relative density can be measured using a relative density bottle which has an accurately calibrated volume (usually 50 cm^3) and can be used for both solids and liquids (see Appendix: Experiment 2).

1.5 HYDROMETRY

Hydrometers can be used to measure the relative density of liquids. If a weighted test tube is placed in a measuring cylinder of liquid, the depth to which it sinks depends on the density of the liquid. The lower the test tube sinks the lower is the density of the liquid and vice versa (see Appendix: Experiment 3). Hydrometry provides a very convenient, rapid and accurate method of measuring relative density. A typical hydrometer is illustrated in Fig. 1.1 and can be seen to consist of a hollow bulb with a weighted base and scale.

The hydrometer is allowed to float in the liquid. The scale reading corresponding to the liquid level is a direct reading of relative density. To measure the complete range of relative density (0.5–2.0) no single hydrometer could be used and hence a series of hydrometers are employed, each with its own narrow range, typically 0.1. The range of a hydrometer is determined by the weight in the base. Normal accuracy for readings is to three decimal places.

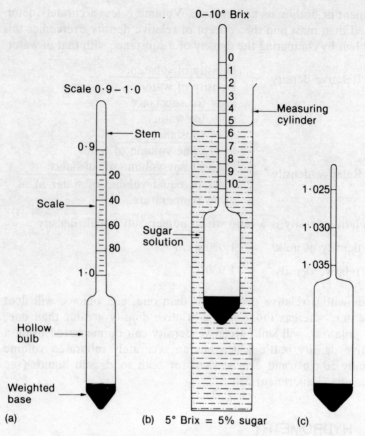

FIG. 1.1 Hydrometers (a) Hydrometer (b) Brix saccharometer (c) Lactometer

1.5.1 SPECIAL HYDROMETERS

These are adapted to measure either relative density or some other property, e.g. concentration, of particular liquids in the food industry. Hydrometers are compact, easy to use and extremely accurate and find considerable use in catering.

Lactometers

Used to measure the relative density of milk, a lactometer has a larger bulb and a narrower scale than the conventional hydrometer. The scale reads from 1.025–1.035, with a value of 1.030 as the expected value for a normal sample. With such an accurate scale any small discrepancies such as the presence of excess water or milk solids can be readily detected.

Saccharometers

These measure the concentration of sugar solutions. The scale on the stem is calibrated in °Brix where:

1 °Brix (approximately) = 1 per cent sugar by weight

A series of Brix hydrometers cover the range up to about 80 per cent sugar, although the most concentrated solutions are extremely viscous.

Sikes hydrometer

Used to determine the amount of alcohol in a solution in °proof spirit. The scale on the stem reads from 0° to 100° proof, where 100° proof equals 57.1 per cent alcohol by volume.

Gay-Lussac hydrometer

A hydrometer used to measure alcohol concentration directly in per cent volume. The scale on the stem reads from 0 to 100 per cent by volume.

QUESTIONS

1. State the SI units of:
   (a) length;
   (b) volume;
   (c) pressure;
   (d) energy;
   (e) power.
2. Calculate the volume of a container required to hold 500 kg of oil if the density of oil is 900 kg m^{-3}. Calculate the volume in litres if 1 litre = 1000 cm^3.
3. State the purpose of each of the following:
   (a) lactometer;
   (b) saccharometer.
   Draw a fully-labelled diagram of a lactometer.
4. How many carpet tiles 20 × 20 cm are required to carpet a hotel room with a floor area of 30 m^2?
5. Explain the term relative density and describe two methods of determing RD.

2

FORCE, WORK AND ENERGY

2.1 INTRODUCTION

Energy is a fundamental scientific concept, difficult to define, but can be regarded as the capacity to do work. Without energy no work can be done. Various forms of energy are involved in catering operations with probably the most important application being the addition or removal of heat energy from foods (see Ch. 3).

Energy cannot be destroyed but is converted to another form. The primary source of energy is the sun and is convertible to all other forms, e.g. chemical, electrical, etc. Food contains chemical energy which is used by the body to perform work.

Work and energy are both measured in the same SI unit, the joule.

2.2 FORCE

Force is a quantity which implies motion or attempted motion of some kind, such as pushing, pulling or turning. Figure 2.1 illustrates a waiter pushing a trolley and hence exerting a force on it.

Another common type of force is that used to change the shape of an object, such as rolling out a dough or stretching a spring. These tension/compression forces are combined in manipulation of a pizza base. A wine waiter exerts both pushing and turning forces while inserting a corkscrew into the cork of a wine bottle, and a pulling force to remove the cork from the neck of the bottle. In everyday terms a force can be considered as an 'action' which produces either motion or a change of shape.

There are many types of force apart from the ones described above including:
1. Force of gravity responsible for holding objects on the earth. This is the force which gives objects their weight.
2. Magnetic and electrical forces of attraction and repulsion, e.g. the like poles of magnets repel, unlike poles attract.

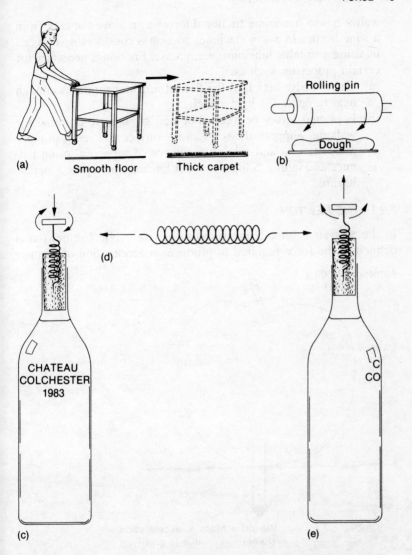

FIG. 2.1 Types of forces (a) Pushing forces (b) Force changing shape of dough (c) Pushing/turning forces (d) Force changing shape of spring (e) Pulling/turning forces

3. Frictional forces which oppose motion. Friction occurs where there is a relative motion between two surfaces. If a heavy object such as a fully laden sweets' trolley is moved across a smooth floor, it slides very easily provided enough force is applied. If the floor is uneven or thickly carpeted then there is greater resistance, i.e. more friction, and more effort is required. The wine

waiter has to overcome frictional forces to remove the cork from a wine bottle. In many machines friction is considerably reduced by using a suitable lubricant, e.g. grease. Friction is necessary for certain processes, such as:

(a) The abrasive action of the flint of a lighter produces enough heat to ignite the lighter fuel.

(b) Frictional forces between shoe and ground are essential for walking. Slippery shoes on an icy surface will result in minimum friction and maximum chance of a person losing balance and falling. Slippery or wet kitchen floors pose a similar hazard.

2.2.1   THE NEWTON

In the SI system force is measured in newtons (N). The newton is defined as the force required to produce an acceleration of 1 m per

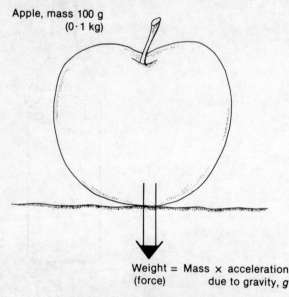

Apple, mass 100 g
(0·1 kg)

Weight = Mass × acceleration
(force)   due to gravity, g

g = acceleration due to gravity = 10 m s^{-2}

Weight
(force exerted
by apple)

$= 0 \cdot 1 \text{ kg} \times 10 \text{ m s}^{-2}$

$= 1 \text{ kg m s}^{-2}$

$= \underline{1 \text{ newton}}$

i.e. 1 newton = Gravitational force acting
on a mass of 0·1 kg

FIG. 2.2 The newton

second on an object with a mass of 1 kg, or $1\ N = 1\ kg\ m\ s^{-2}$. This can be illustrated by considering a medium-sized apple (see Fig. 2.2).

2.2.2 MASS AND WEIGHT

The terms mass and weight are frequently confused. Mass is the quantity of matter contained in an object. Weight is the force which that mass exerts on anything which supports it (due to gravitational attraction). A mass of 100 g placed on a table exerts a force or weight of 1 N.

2.3 WORK

In everyday language 'work' has many meanings ranging from physical to mental activities. In industry today 90 per cent of work is non-manual, compared to 10 per cent some years ago. It is often harder work to understand scientific concepts such as 'work' and 'energy' than it is to work in a busy kitchen!

In physics the word 'work' is interpreted as the 'result of an action by a force'. Work is done when an object moves in the direction of an applied force; the amount of work done depends on the magnitude of the force and the distance the object moves.

Work done = Force × Distance moved in direction of force

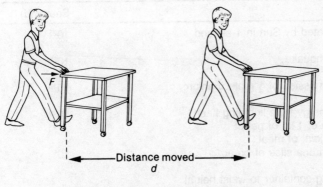

Work done = Force × Distance moved

= $F \times d$

= Newtons × metres

= Joules

FIG. 2.3 Work

If the force is measured in newtons (N) and the distance in metres (m), then work is measured in newtons × metres, or N m. The unit of work is the joule, J, where 1 J = 1 N m (see Fig. 2.3)

If the force is not sufficient to move an object then no work is done on the object although considerable energy may be expended, e.g. in attempting but failing to lift a large container.

2.4 ENERGY

Energy is a term which is often used but is difficult to define precisely. We readily accept that some people have much more energy, or are more energetic than others and as such are capable of greater achievement.

Energy is defined as the capacity to do work and a body loses energy when it does work. The unit of energy is therefore the same as the unit of work, i.e. the joule. All matter, including food, contains energy and any changes such as those involved in food preparation will change the energy content. An understanding of energy is important in catering. The relative amounts of energy involved in various processes are shown in Table 2.1.

There are various forms of energy – the most important are shown in the following sections.

TABLE 2.1 Energy of various processes

Process	Energy(J)
Energy radiated by Sun in 1 second	10^{25}
Severe earthquake	10^{20}
Energy from fission of 1 mole uranium	10^{15}
Electrical energy from lightning flash Combustion of 1 kg of petrol Roasting a joint of meat	10^{10}
Energy from one slice of bread	10^{5}
Lifting a 3 kg container to waist height Visible light from domestic light bulb in 1 second Lecturer shouting for 1 second	10^{0}
Lecturer talking normally for 1 second	10^{-5}

2.4.1 LIGHT ENERGY

The sun is the primary source of energy without which there would be no life (see sect. 15.6). Plants require sunlight for growth, converting light energy into chemical energy by a process called photosynthesis (see sect. 15.2). Chemical energy produced as a result of photosynthesis provides energy for the synthesis of complex organic molecules such as fat and protein (see Chapter 16) and the building of new cells etc. (see Sect. 10.2).

Light energy from the sun or other light sources, e.g. electric light bulb or gas lamp, is converted into chemical energy in the eye – enabling this page to be read. Light energy can be used to operate calculators and watches. Solar power may be used for heating although it is difficult to capture sufficient energy for large-scale use. The sun's rays must be concentrated to create temperatures high

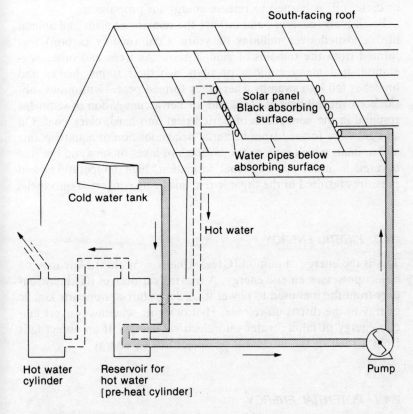

System basically provides sufficient energy for domestic hot water only

FIG. 2.4 Solar energy heating system for an individual house

enough to operate a generator and produce electricity. On a small scale, solar panels can be installed in the roofs of houses to provide hot water. The panel consists of a dark absorbent surface above pipes containing circulating water (see Fig. 2.4).

With the aid of a pump this can provide adequate domestic hot water. Direct conversion solar cells have been designed to convert solar energy directly into electricity.

2.4.2 CHEMICAL ENERGY

Food and fuels are 'stores' of chemical energy which is released in chemical reactions. Enzymes in the body allow the release of energy stored in food molecules in a process known as respiration (see sects. 9.9.2, 9.9.3). In the internal combustion engine a fuel, such as petrol or diesel oil, is burned to release energy for propulsion.

Fossil fuels (coal, gas and oil) are the remains of plant and animal life deposited over millions of years. Coal (mainly carbon) was formed from the remains of giant forests. As trees and other vegetation died many millions of years ago their stems, leaves and branches fell into swamps where they formed peat. Continuous subsidence over millions of years and further accumulation of sediment resulted in the conversion of buried peat into hard, black coal. Oil and gas were formed from bacterial decomposition of aquatic plants and animals which sank to the bottoms of lakes or seas and became covered in mud. As with coal formation, high temperatures and pressures resulted in the organic remains being converted into fuels.

2.4.3 KINETIC ENERGY

This is the energy of motion (Greek *kinesis* = motion). Any moving object possesses kinetic energy. A moving car derives its kinetic energy from the fuel used to power it. A discus thrower imparts kinetic energy to the discus on release. Hydroelectric schemes convert kinetic energy of falling water into electrical energy. If an object falls from a shelf in the kitchen it possesses kinetic energy.

2.4.4 POTENTIAL ENERGY

This is energy stored in a material which can be utilised by conversion to another form when required. Many examples of potential energy arise from either the position of an object or its shape. A heavy object balanced on a high shelf has potential energy by virtue of its position and if it were to fall considerable damage or work would result. A stretched spring has potential energy by virtue of its shape; on release, the spring reverts to its unstretched position. All forms of stored energy, e.g. chemical, magnetic, etc. are really types of potential energy.

2.4.5 HEAT ENERGY (see ch. 3)

Heat energy is usually derived from fuels and is a form of kinetic energy, since when a substance is heated the molecules within the substance move faster. Food energy provides body heat. Frictional forces can provide unwanted heat energy.

2.4.6 ELECTRICAL ENERGY (see ch. 4)

Electricity is derived from chemical reactions (cells and batteries) or electrical generators using steam turbines, hydroelectric schemes, wind power, etc. Electrical energy is used to provide motion, heat, light and sound.

2.4.7 MAGNETIC ENERGY

Magnetic energy is closely linked with electrical energy as in the operation of generators. Transformers and generators are based on the principle that a changing magnetic field results in an electrical current.

2.4.8 NUCLEAR (ATOMIC) ENERGY

Heat energy is released by the splitting (fission) of the nuclei of certain atoms.

2.4.9 SOUND ENERGY

Sound waves are produced by vibrating objects and can be detected by the ear. The amount of energy carried by a sound wave is the intensity and is measured in decibels (db). A whisper is about 20 db whereas the 'noise' from a rock concert is about 120 db. Very short wavelength sound waves, described as ultrasonic waves, cannot be heard by the human ear and are used in the cleaning of large vessels in catering.

2.5 CONVERSION OF ENERGY

Energy can be transformed from one form to another as illustrated in Fig. 2.5 and Table 2.2.

Many processes in which energy is converted from one form to another involve several intermediate forms of energy and are termed multistage processes. Many catering operations involve multistage energy conversions as illustrated in Fig. 2.6.

One specific example of a multistage process is the use of an elec-

TABLE 2.2 Different forms of energy

Energy form	Description	Applications/examples
Kinetic energy	Energy of motion	Any moving object possesses kinetic energy, e.g. hotel lift, objects falling from shelves
Potential energy	Energy stored by virtue of shape or position	Tray of drinks about to fall
Mechanical energy		Stirring, whipping, beating, grinding. Muscular energy
Heat energy	Associated with kinetic energy of molecules	Burning of fuels. Food energy provides body warmth. Cooking (addition), refrigeration (removal) of heat energy
Electrical energy	Derived from chemical reactions (cells/batteries) or generators	Power supply to operate cookers, mixers. Provides heat, light, sound
Chemical energy	Stored energy and is a form of potential energy	Fuels and foods are stores of chemical energy. Chemical reactions (cells) provide electricity
Magnetic energy	A form of potential energy	In generators to produce electricity. In food processing/conveyor systems. As electromagnets
Sound energy	Produced by vibrating objects	Ultrasonic waves used to clean large catering vessels. Loud speaker systems in hotels
Nuclear energy	Energy produced by splitting nuclei	Irradiation of foods for preservation. Disinfestation

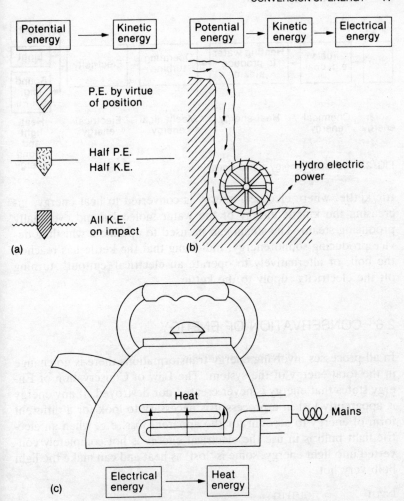

FIG. 2.5 Energy conversions (a) Pile-driver (b) Waterfall (c) Kettle

TABLE 2.3 The conversion of energy from one form to another

Process	Energy
Combustion of fuels	Chemical to heat
Hotel lift	Electrical to kinetic
Failure of lift system	Potential to kinetic (rapid fall)
Carving a joint	Chemical to mechanical
Radio set	Electrical to sound
Blending or mixing	Electrical to mechanical

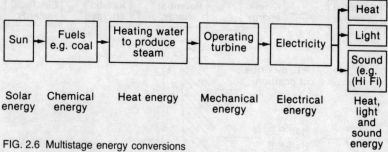

FIG. 2.6 Multistage energy conversions

tric kettle, where electrical energy is converted to heat energy, increasing the kinetic energy of the water molecules and eventually producing steam. The steam can be used to operate a whistling device producing sound energy, indicating that the kettle has reached the boil, or alternatively to operate an electrical 'cut-out', turning off the electricity supply to the kettle.

2.6   CONSERVATION OF ENERGY

In all processes involving energy transformations there is no change in the total energy of the system. The Law of Conservation of Energy states that energy is never created nor destroyed. If any energy is apparently lost in a process it is necessary to look for a different form of energy to account for the apparent loss, e.g. when an electric light bulb is in use the electrical energy is not completely converted into light energy, some is 'lost' as heat and can make the light bulb very hot.

INPUT   OUTPUT

$$\text{Electrical energy} = \text{Light energy} + \text{Heat ('lost')}$$

In any energy transformation some thermal energy is always produced since friction (see sect. 2.2(3)) is always present.

2.7   USEFUL AND NON-USEFUL WORK

It is convenient to define the terms useful and non-useful work by considering some examples:
1. Electric cookers or fires where electrical energy is converted, in the element, to heat, light and sound. Heat is useful work,

whereas light and sound, in this context, are both non-useful work (see Fig. 2.7).

2. In mixing processes where careful selection of the correct mixer blade reduces the non-useful work done in overcoming the frictional forces between the mixer blades and the substance being mixed.

3. Experience in 'waiting on' reduces the level of non-useful work. An inexperienced waiter will have to make many more trips between table and kitchen.

It is obvious that if a source supplies energy there must be a corresponding decrease in its own energy, e.g. in our tired inexperienced waiter the work involved results in a depletion of the chemical energy store of the body.

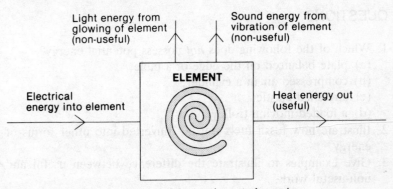

FIG. 2.7 Useful and non-useful work in the element of a cooker

2.8 POWER

Power is defined as the rate at which work is done or the rate at which energy is transformed (e.g. electrical energy to heat energy).

i.e. $\text{Power} = \dfrac{\text{amount of energy converted}}{\text{time taken to convert the energy in seconds}}$

The unit of power is the watt,

$$\text{Power} = \frac{\text{work}}{\text{time}}$$

$$= \frac{\text{joules}}{\text{second}}$$

$$= \text{watt (W)}$$

$$1000 \text{ Watts} = 1 \text{ kilowatt (1 kW)}$$

The difference between energy and power is illustrated when climbing stairs in a hotel. This can be achieved either by walking or running. In both cases the energy source is chemical energy produced by respiration (see sects. 9.9.2, 9.9.3). It is possible to ascend and descend many times by walking but to climb stairs by running is extremely tiring.

The speed of waiter service in a restaurant depends on the rate of energy expended by the waiter, which may depend on the rate of work done in the kitchen. Slow service could, of course, result in the customers expending energy by banging on the table with their cutlery. This last example serves as an illustration of the often complex interrelationships between work, energy and power!

QUESTIONS

1. Which of the following does *not* possess potential energy?:
   (a) plate balanced on the edge of a table;
   (b) compressed air in a cylinder;
   (c) stretched elastic;
   (d) a loaded moving trolley.
2. Illustrate how fossil fuels can be converted into other forms of energy.
3. Give examples to illustrate the difference between useful and non-useful work.
4. Define power. Explain the difference between energy and power.
5. Explain how friction is a force opposing motion. Calculate the work done by a force of 10 N moving an object a distance of 5 m.

3

HEAT

3.1 INTRODUCTION

Many catering operations involve heat energy, not just the obvious examples of adding heat energy, as in cooking and central heating, but also the removal of heat energy, as in freezing and refrigeration. Heating costs are a major overhead in running a hotel and minimisation of the wastage of heat energy is a major factor in the cost efficiency.

3.2 HEAT AND TEMPERATURE

Heat is a form of energy whereas temperature is a *relative* quantity and expresses the intensity of the heat energy present. Temperature is a measure of the 'hotness' or 'coldness' of an object and is related to the speed of the molecules within that object, i.e. their kinetic energy (see sect. 6.7.2). It indicates the direction of heat flow, i.e. whether heat will flow out of or into a body.

The difference between heat and temperature can be illustrated by placing two identical beakers which contain different amounts of water on the same heating source. The water in both boils at the same temperature (100 °C) but the one containing less water boils first since it requires less heat energy.

In the heating and cooling of foods the rate of temperature change is very important. If two pieces of meat of identical size and composition are heated to the same internal temperature their flavour, appearance and texture will differ widely if one is heated slowly and the other quickly, and one is more acceptable than the other. This illustrates the importance of the skill of the chef in determining the rate of cooking of particular cuts of meat. Rapid freezing of foods results in a more nutritious, palatable product.

3.3 MEASUREMENT OF TEMPERATURE – THERMOMETRY

The crudest measurement of temperature is by sense of touch, and can be misleading since the skin is more sensitive to heat flow than actual temperature. Various properties (e.g. expansion of liquids, change in electrical resistance, etc.) can be used to measure temperature provided that the property varies uniformly with change of temperature. A thermometer is a device which measures temperature changes quantitatively and the earliest type of thermometer consisted of a glass bulb with a narrow stem filled with a suitable liquid – the liquid-in-glass thermometer. The temperature range of this thermometer is limited and conventional liquid-in-glass thermometers use mercury or alcohol (see Fig. 3.1). Table 3.1 shows a list of different types of thermometers.

TABLE 3.1 Thermometers

Property	Type of thermometer	Range
Expansion of a liquid	Liquid in glass thermometer, e.g. mercury in glass or alcohol in glass	−39 to 360 °C
Expansion of two dissimilar metals	Bimetallic strip	−120 to 80 °C
Change in electrical resistance of a metal	Platinum resistance thermometer	−200 to 1500 °C
Thermoelectric effect of two metal wires with junctions at different temperatures	Thermocouple (probe)	up to 1500 °C
Intensity of light emitted matched against a filament of known temperature	Pyrometer	up to 3000 °C

The most common thermometers used in catering are mercury thermometers and thermocouples (often referred to as probe thermometers).

The scale used in thermometers is the Celsius scale (°C) which was defined by Celsius in 1742. This scale uses two fixed points, 0 °C the temperature of an ice-water mixture and 100 °C the temperature of steam from boiling water, and divides the interval between the fixed points into 100 parts. This scale is sometimes called the Centigrade scale but is more correctly named the Celsius scale. The SI unit of

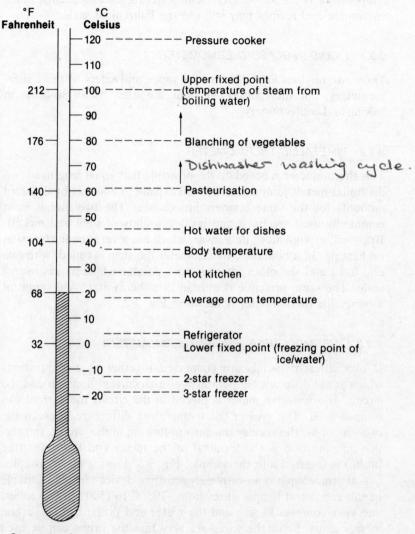

Conversion factors

$°C = \frac{5}{9}(°F - 32)$ e.g. $50°F$ $°C = \frac{5}{9}(50 - 32) = 10°C$

$°F = \frac{9}{5}°C + 32$ e.g. $45°C$ $°F = (\frac{9}{5} \times 45) + 32 = 113°F$

FIG. 3.1 Liquid-in-glass thermometer showing Celsius/Fahrenheit scales and some useful temperatures in catering

temperature is the kelvin (K). Some catering establishments, older equipment and recipes may still use the Fahrenheit scale.

3.3.1 LIQUID-IN-GLASS THERMOMETER

There are obvious limitations to the range and safety of these thermometers, but the 'pocket' versions are used by all students in baking and confectionery.

3.3.2 BIMETALLIC THERMOMETER

This thermometer is based on the principle that equal lengths of two dissimilar metals joined together will expand or contract by different amounts for the same temperature change. The two metals most commonly used are brass and invar (an alloy of steel and nickel). Brass will expand more than invar, which has a very small expansion on heating. In a bimetallic thermometer the strip is coiled, with one end fixed and the other attached to a pointer which moves over a scale. The same principle is utilised in a thermostat. A diagram of a bimetallic thermometer is shown in Fig. 3.2.

3.3.3 THERMOCOUPLE (PROBE THERMOMETER)

If two different metals are connected together by two junctions which are at different temperatures a small current flows around the circuit. If a sensitive meter is placed in the circuit the current can be measured. The greater the temperature difference between the two junctions, the greater the current flowing in the circuit. In practice one junction is the terminal of the meter and the other (the probe) is inserted into the sample. Fig. 3.3 shows a thermocouple.

A thermocouple is an extremely sensitive device and with suitable metals can detect temperatures from −200 °C to 1500 °C. It is robust and very compact in size and the meter and probe can be several metres apart. Since the wires are very thin the probe can be used inside an oven or a blast freezer, or even at different distances into a large piece of meat. Thermocouples can be easily incorporated into remote control and automated systems, and several different probes can be connected to one meter using a switching system to detect the temperature of each probe.

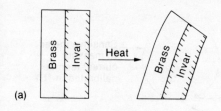

Brass expands far more than Invar

(a)

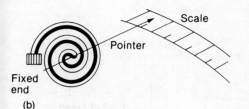

As bimetallic strip alters shape pointer registers temperature on scale

(b)

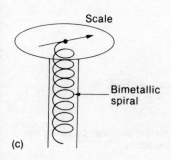

Coiled spiral enclosed in a cylindrical brass tube to provide practical instrument for temperature measurement

(c)

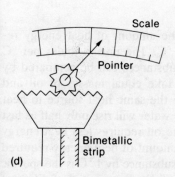

(d)

FIG. 3.2 Bimetallic strip, thermometer and applications (a) Bimetalic strip (b) Bimetallic thermometer (c) Coiled bimetallic spring (d) Ratchet-type bimetallic thermometer

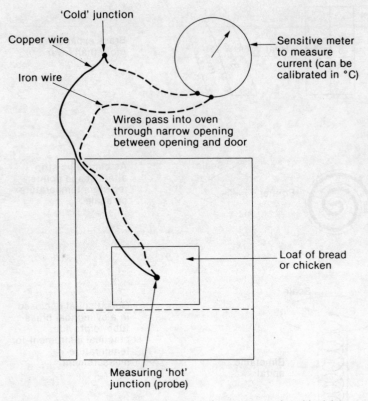

FIG. 3.3 A thermocouple which measures the current produced by joining two dissimilar metals with junctions at different temperatures

3.4 THERMAL CAPACITY

The thermal capacity of a body is the amount of heat energy required to raise its temperature by 1 °C. The unit is joules per °C (J °C⁻¹). The heating properties of substances can be compared by their specific heat capacities. If we take equal masses of oil and water in separate containers and use the same heat source to heat the two fluids, the temperature of the water will rise only half as fast as the temperature of the oil, i.e. the oil requires less heat energy or has a smaller heat capacity. The amount of heat energy required to raise the temperature of 1 kg of a substance by 1 °C is the specific heat capacity. The values for the specific heat capacities of different substances are shown in Table 3.2.

The amount of heat energy needed to raise the temperature of a substance can be calculated as follows:

TABLE 3.2 Specific heat capacities of some common substances

Substance	Specific heat capacity $(J\ kg^{-1}°C^{-1})$
Copper	400
Aluminium	900
Flour	2100
Oils (butter)	2100
Milk	3780
Water	4200

Heat energy required = mass × temperature difference × specific
heat capacity

If we compare the specific heat capacity for copper (410) with that
for water (4200) it can be seen that ten times more heat energy is
required to heat 1 kg of water. Oils require half the heat energy
required by water so that butter or cooking oils heat faster and cool
more quickly than substances with a high water content such as vegetables. Water has a higher specific heat capacity than most other
substances and is therefore a good coolant. Water can be used to
protect certain foods against too rapid an increase in temperature,
e.g. in the cooking of lemon curd and custard a double, water-filled
saucepan may be employed.

Example. *Calculate the heat energy required by 5 kg of cooking oil
when the temperature is raised from 20 °C to 160 °C (specific heat
capacity = 2100 J kg⁻¹ °C⁻¹).*

Heat energy required =   mass × temperature difference ×
                                  specific heat capacity
                         =   5 × (160 − 20) × 2100
                         =   1 472 000 J
Heat energy required =   1.47 MJ

From this we can calculate the cost of the process:

1 unit of electricity =   1 kW h
costing about 5 p =   3.6 MJ
Heat energy required = $\dfrac{1.47 \times 5}{3.6}$
                         =   2 p approximately.

3.5   CHANGE OF STATE AND LATENT HEAT

When heat energy is supplied to a solid the initial effect is to produce a rise in temperature. This heat energy is sometimes referred

to as 'sensible heat', i.e. detected by sense of touch. If heat is continuously supplied then a change of state will occur at the melting point of the solid and a liquid is formed. Further heating will produce another change of state resulting in the formation of a gas. If the change is from a solid to a gas without passing through the liquid state this is known as sublimation, which occurs in the change of solid carbon dioxide (dry ice) into gaseous carbon dioxide. The various changes of state are reversible as illustrated in Fig. 3.4.

During the melting of a solid the temperature remains constant even though heat energy is being supplied. Heat energy is needed to break down the forces of attraction between the solid particles and produce the mobility which is characteristic of the liquid state. The heat energy used for melting the solid is known as the latent (hidden) heat of fusion. Latent heat is also required at the boiling point of the liquid to separate the molecules completely and form

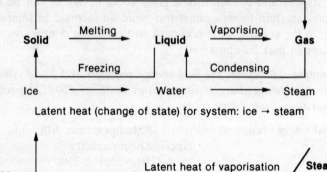

Latent heat (change of state) for system: ice → steam

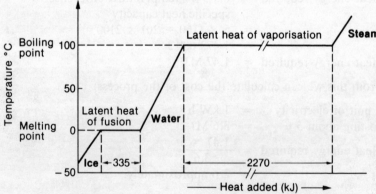

To convert 1 kg ice → water (at 0 °C), 335 kJ heat required
To convert 1 kg water → steam (at 100 °C), 2270 kJ heat required

FIG. 3.4 Change of state

a gas, and is known as the latent heat of vaporisation. The heat which is absorbed by a substance during melting or vaporising is given off in the reverse processes of freezing and condensation. Steam burns (scalds) are much more severe than boiling water burns although both are at the same temperature, since steam releases a large quantity of heat energy as it condenses. The condensation of 1 kg of steam at 100 °C to water at 100 °C releases 2270 kJ.

3.6 EFFECT OF PRESSURE ON THE BOILING POINT OF A LIQUID

As a liquid approaches its boiling point bubbles of gas are formed. The pressure of the gas inside the bubbles is called the vapour pressure. The bubbles collapse at first because the pressure due to the bulk of the liquid is greater than the vapour pressure inside the bubbles. Increased temperature means that more bubbles are formed with increased vapour pressure and these reach the surface of the liquid. At this stage when bubbles appear throughout the liquid and rise to the surface then the boiling point of the liquid has been reached, i.e. boiling occurs when the vapour pressure within the bubbles is greater than the pressure from the liquid plus the pressure from the atmosphere.

If the external pressure is increased then the molecules require more energy and hence a higher temperature is reached before they move fast enough to form bubbles which rise to the surface. This principle is utilised in the pressure cooker which is a device for reducing the cooking times of foods by increasing the pressure above the water and elevating the boiling point. Pressure cooking of vegetables has the advantage of retaining much more of the nutrients such as vitamin C which are destroyed by prolonged heating. Retorts, sterilisers and autoclaves which destroy micro-organisms also use the same principle.

Decreasing the pressure lowers the boiling point. At high altitudes where atmospheric pressure is lower, water boils at temperatures much lower than 100 °C, e.g. at about 3000 m above sea-level water boils at 90 °C. Cooking times are greatly extended at high altitudes and recipes have to be specially modified. Boiling at low pressures (using a vacuum) is extremely useful in processes such as sugar refining where too high a temperature could cause discoloration of the product. Low temperature boiling is used in the concentration of fruit juices and meat extracts.

3.7 EFFECT OF ADDITIVES

3.7.1 EFFECT OF ADDITIVES ON BOILING POINT

Non-volatile additives such as sugar and salt will produce an increase in the boiling point of water, i.e. more energy is needed for boiling. This is because the additive molecules occupy part of the surface area of the liquid and prevent the bubbles of gas reaching the surface.

3.7.2 EFFECT OF ADDITIVES ON FREEZING POINT

An additive or 'impurity' will lower the temperature at which a liquid freezes. The addition of a suitable quantity of salt to an ice water mixture can result in the lowering of the freezing point from 0 °C to −20 °C. Sugar and flavourings are added to an ice-water mixture in the preparation of sorbet; ice cream is a solution consisting of 40 per cent total solids (milk fat for flavour, milk solids for body and texture and sugar for sweetness). Sugar lowers the freezing point of water so that the mixtures do not freeze solid during storage.

3.8 ENERGY VALUE OF FOODSTUFFS

Food supplied to the body can be used for the production of energy in the process of respiration (see sects 9.3.1, 9.3.2). Different food-stuffs will supply different amounts of energy to the body. The energy values of foodstuffs can be compared by measuring the heat evolved when a sample of food is completely oxidised or burnt in an oxygen-rich atmosphere. Alternatively, provided the chemical composition of a food is known in terms of carbohydrate, fat and protein, the energy value can be calculated (see Ch. 16). Although the SI unit of energy is the joule the energy values are still widely expressed in large calories (capital C) or kilocalories, while the small (or 'fundamental') calorie, is used in physics and chemistry.

1 kilocalorie = 1 calorie = 4.2 kilojoules.

Typical values for the energy content of different foodstuffs are shown in Table 3.3.

3.9 METHODS OF HEAT TRANSFER

There are three methods of heat transfer:
1. Conduction – transfer of heat by contact, energy is transferred from molecule to molecule.

TABLE 3.3 Energy content of some foodstuffs

Sample	Energy value (kJ/100 g^{-1})
Butter	3012
Sugar	1680
Bread	1068
Milk	274
Lettuce	36
Potatoes	324
Beer	96

2. Convection   – transfer of heat by movement of a hot fluid (liquid or gas).
3. Radiation   – emission of heat in the form of infra-red waves from hot objects.

3.9.1 CONDUCTION

If a metal spoon is placed in a hot liquid the handle rapidly becomes warm. Heat flows from a high to a low temperature and the process of heat energy travelling through the metal along a temperature gradient is termed conduction. Two processes are involved in conduction. The first involves atomic vibration and is the passing on of increased vibrational energy from one atom to the next as they receive heat energy. This happens in all materials. A second mechanism operates in metals since they possess free loosely-bound electrons (see Fig. 6.4) which gain energy when heated and move to cooler parts of the metal. This is a very rapid process and explains why metals are good conductors, i.e. they have a high thermal conductivity.

The conductivity of metals is 1000 times greater than for non-metals and 10 000 times greater than for gases. Very poor conductors of heat, such as wood and rubber, are termed insulators. A list of conductors and insulators is shown in order of decreasing conductivity in Table 3.4.

The unit of conductivity is joules per second per metre per °C, i.e. watts per metre per °C (W m^{-1} °C^{-1}). Metals themselves differ widely in their conductivity; copper has a conductivity about twice that of aluminium, i.e. it is about twice as good a conductor of heat. Copper-bottomed saucepans transfer heat more efficiently than aluminium.

The rate of heat transfer by conduction depends on three factors:
1. The type of material;

TABLE 3.4 Conductors and insulators in order of decreasing conductivity

Conductors	Insulators	
1. Silver	6. Glass	10. Alcohol
2. Copper	7. Concrete	11. Wood
3. Aluminium	8. Brick	12. Cork
4. Iron	9. Water	13. Air
5. Lead		

2. The area of cross-section of material, which should be as large as possible;
3. The temperature gradient (change of temperature/thickness).

Handles of utensils are generally made of an insulating material such as wood or plastic. In large-scale food production, all-metal handles are used to avoid any fire risk.

Whatever method of cooking is initially used to transfer heat energy to the exterior of a foodstuff the final cooking process is by conduction. Since foods are poor conductors of heat it is essential to allow sufficient time to produce a properly cooked and microbiologically safe food, e.g. a tasty *Salmonella*-free cooked chicken (see Ch. 18). The rate of conduction through a food can be increased by the use of skewers or other metal objects, e.g. in the baking of potatoes. Bone conducts better than meat and boned-in meat cooks quicker than boned-out. Insulators such as oven gloves, cork table mats, etc. are used in the kitchen to prevent heat damage. Air is a very poor conductor and materials containing pockets of air can be used as insulators, e.g. the lining of a fridge is polystyrene which helps to keep heat out, glass fibre linings in ovens help to keep heat in. Glass is a very poor conductor and glasses washed in hot water sometimes crack since the heat causes localised expansion of the glass.

3.9.2 CONVECTION

Convection involves heat transfer where the heat is transferred by a hot fluid, e.g. air, oil or water. When a fluid is heated it expands and therefore its density (see sect. 1.3) is reduced. The hot, less-dense fluid rises and the colder, more-dense fluid falls to take its place (see Fig. 3.5).

Convection currents cook food more rapidly than conduction. Boiling, steaming, deep fat frying and oven baking depend mainly on convection. Convection and conduction are inevitably linked as in the example of pans on a gas burner. The heat reaches the pan by convection currents of burnt gas. Conduction of the heat through

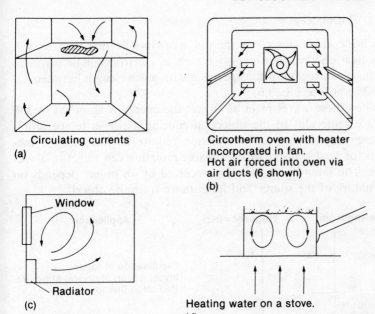

Circulating currents
(a)

Circotherm oven with heater incorporated in fan.
Hot air forced into oven via air ducts (6 shown)
(b)

Window

Radiator
(c)

Heating water on a stove.
(d)

FIG. 3.5 Convection currents (a) Conventional oven (b) Fan assisted oven (forced convection) (c) Room heating by natural convection of radiator (d) Heating water on a stove. Natural convection current

the pan heats the water. The pan should be constructed of a suitable material to give uniform, efficient heat transfer. If the pan contains vegetables in water then convection currents are set up in the water which heat the exterior of the vegetables which cook by conduction of heat from the water.

Convection currents are used in ovens and room heaters for the distribution of heat. In the human body blood acts as a convective fluid distributing the heat produced in biochemical reactions, especially in the liver, throughout the whole body.

Where natural convection is too slow then the fluid velocity can be increased by using a fan or pump. This is referred to as forced convection, and is utilised in fan ovens where circulation and heating efficiency are increased. Forced convection often allows equipment to be smaller than that required for natural convection, e.g. small-bore piping in central heating systems.

The effectiveness of convection depends on the viscosity of the fluid, thus soup can be allowed to simmer but thick custard or porridge will burn if not heated very slowly or stirred. In viscous fluids heated molecules find it more difficult to move and localised overheating and food decomposition may occur.

3.9.3 RADIATION

Any body which glows, e.g. the sun, a fire or a heating element, will emit heat energy. Heat energy travels as electromagnetic waves in the infra-red region of the spectrum with a wavelength between 2.5 and 25 μm (see Fig. 3.6).

When these waves meet an object the energy is absorbed by the surface molecules of the object, producing a rise in temperature. Whereas conduction and convection require an intermediate medium for heat transfer to take place, radiation can travel in a vacuum. The intensity of radiation received by an object depends on the nature of the source and its distance from the object.

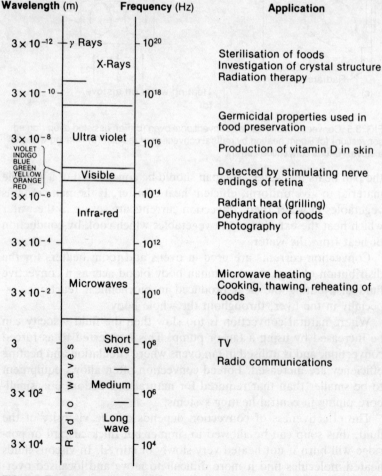

FIG. 3.6 Electromagnetic spectrum

Radiation is a very rapid method of heat transfer and radiant sources used in cooking include grill elements, toasters, glowing coils of electric appliances and gas flames. So-called household radiators emit almost 80 per cent of their heat by convection. In a gas oven about 23 per cent of the heating is due to radiation compared to about 42 per cent in an electric oven.

The nature of the surface affects the efficiency of radiation from an object. The darker and duller the surface of a hot object, the more efficiently it acts as a radiator. A matt, black surface is the best radiator and is said to possess a high emissivity. Shiny, metal surfaces are the poorest radiators. The most efficient radiators of heat are also the best absorbers. Emissivity is more important than conductivity, as illustrated by cooking cakes on a dull black steel tray and on a shiny copper tray in the same oven. Although copper is a much better conductor than steel the cakes on the dull black tray will require a much shorter cooking time. Choice of utensils in cooking must be governed by their radiant efficiency, e.g. thin pastry could brown excessively if baked on a dull baking tray. Highly polished silver coffee pots and teapots keep their contents hot longer. Light coloured clothing is much more comfortable than dark clothing in hot conditions.

3.10 MICROWAVE COOKING

In microwave cooking heat is generated in the food as a result of electromagnetic waves (energy) penetrating the food and making the water molecules in the food vibrate, producing internal heating. A microwave source generates electromagnetic radiation with a wavelength between 0.1 and 10 μm.

Foods with a high water content cook most rapidly. Various materials such as glass, paper, china and some plastics do not absorb or reflect the radiation and are suitable as cooking containers.

The advantage of microwave cooking is that cooking times are extremely short, so making efficient use of electrical energy. Microwave ovens are widely used in all types of catering establishment. One disadvantage of ordinary microwave cooking is that food does not turn brown or crispy since heat is not directed at the surface of the food. For this reason microwave ovens find great application for the reheating of precooked foods. In some microwave ovens a browning attachment using an additional form of heat transfer is employed.

3.11   EVAPORATION AND HUMIDITY

Evaporation occurs at the surface of a liquid and can occur at any temperature, involving the change of state from liquid to gas. Liquids with a low boiling point (such as alcohol or perfume) change from liquid to vapour easily at ordinary temperatures and are termed volatile liquids. If a small amount of a volatile liquid is placed on the hand it evaporates quickly, leaving the hand feeling cold. The heat required to produce the change from liquid to vapour is latent heat and is provided by the hand.

Evaporation always produces a cooling effect and this forms the basis of refrigeration (see sect. 3.12). Factors affecting evaporation are:

1. Temperature – increasing the temperature increases the rate of evaporation;
2. Surface area – the greater the surface area the greater is the rate of evaporation;
3. A current of air above the surface (a draught).

3.11.1   ATMOSPHERIC MOISTURE

The atmosphere always contains water vapour due to evaporation from seas, lakes, rivers and other water sources. In kitchens or buildings water is produced by evaporation in cooking processes, laundering, etc. This presence of water vapour in the air is termed humidity.

Absolute humidity
This is the actual amount of water vapour present in the atmosphere. If the humidity is high, i.e. the atmosphere is almost saturated, the rate of evaporation will be low and excess water vapour will condense out on cold surfaces, e.g. walls, windows, working surfaces, etc. High humidity reduces evaporation from the skin and results in tiredness, headaches and discomfort.

Relative humidity
The amount of evaporation which can occur is dependent on the amount of water vapour already present in the atmosphere, i.e. the degree of saturation. The critical factor therefore is how much more water the atmosphere can hold before it becomes saturated. This degree of saturation is expressed as the relative humidity.

Relative humidity = $\dfrac{\text{Mass of water vapour in a given volume of air}}{\text{Mass of water vapour required to saturate the same volume of air at that temperature}}$

The effect of temperature is critical; at 4 °C, 1 kg of air can hold up to 5 g of water vapour, whereas at 40 °C 1 kg of air can hold up to 50 g, i.e. 10 times as much. Relative humidity can be measured using a hygrometer (see below).

Equilibrium Relative Humidity (ERH)

ERH represents the equilibrium between the hygroscopic properties of a substance and the relative humidity of the atmosphere; the higher the ERH the more the product is able to withstand high humidities. Concentrated sugar solutions have to be protected from high humidities. In sugar confectionery glucose syrup is added to sucrose to increase the ERH of the product.

Applications of humidity and humidity control

Hygroscopic substances, e.g. flour and dried fruits, which absorb water from the atmosphere must be kept under conditions of carefully controlled humidity. Certain foodstuffs have humectants added to them to prevent them drying out. A substance with hygroscopic properties is called a humectant, e.g. glycerine which is used in confectionery, and sorbitol and glucose which are used in the preparation of jams and jellies.

Correct ventilation is important in kitchens to reduce relative humidity, with 20 volume changes per hour being recommended. Similarly control of humidity by air conditioning is very important.

Hygrometers

A hygrometer is an instrument which measures relative humidity. A wet and dry bulb hygrometer can be used in which the wet bulb records a lower temperature than the dry bulb due to evaporation producing a cooling effect. The difference in temperature between the two bulbs is proportional to the relative humidity of the air. An alternative to a wet and dry bulb hygrometer is a hair hygrometer in which the increase of length of a hair when it absorbs moisture can be used to measure relative humidity.

The normal relative humidity for body comfort is 60–70%.

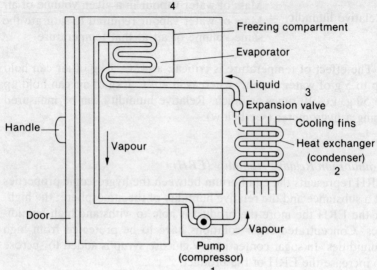

FIG. 3.7 A domestic refrigerator

3.12 REFRIGERATION

Refrigeration is a widely used method of food storage and preservation in catering. Storage of foods in a domestic refrigerator has only a limited effect in extending the shelf life of foods since some food spoilage organisms (psychrotrophic organisms) are capable of growth at low temperatures. Refrigeration (0–5 °C) is extremely important in food hygiene since most food poisoning organisms will not grow below 5 °C.

A typical refrigeration system is illustrated in Fig. 3.7.

It is a cyclic process and involves four stages as outlined below:

1. A suitable refrigerant gas (e.g. ammonia, Freon or methyl chloride) is compressed by a pump to increase pressure.
2. It is exhausted to a condenser where the gas condenses to a liquid.
3. The liquid is forced through an expansion valve which controls the amount of liquid entering the evaporator.
4. Liquid enters the evaporator where the pressure above the refrigerant is low enough for evaporation of the liquid to form a gas. This process extracts the latent heat of vaporisation of the refrigerant and produces cooling.

The vapour returns to the start of the cycle by the action of the pump.

QUESTIONS

1. Explain how the thermocouple and bimetallic strip both use a combination of different metals to measure temperature.
2. Define thermal capacity. Substance A has a specific heat capacity of 2000 J kg^{-1} °C^{-1} whilst that of substance B is only 400 J kg^{-1} °C^{-1}. If 1 kg of A takes 5 minutes to heat from 0 to 50 °C how long will 1 kg of B take? Suggest possible substances for A and B.
3. State the difference between conduction and convection. List the heat processes involved in:
   (a) roasting;
   (b) steaming;
   (c) boiling;
   (d) grilling.
4. State the factors affecting evaporation. Explain how humidity is related to evaporation and explain the importance of relative humidity in catering operations.
5. Illustrate the changes of state which occur when ice is converted to steam. How do each of the following affect the boiling point of water?
   (a) pressure;
   (b) additives.

4

ELECTRICITY

4.1 INTRODUCTION

Electricity has become an essential part of modern life, with electrical energy being the most common energy source in use today. As a form of energy electricity has two major advantages:

1. It is very easily conveyed from power stations to all parts of the country;
2. It can be readily converted to other forms of energy such as heat, light and sound.

There are two forms of electricity, static electricity and current electricity.

4.2 STATIC ELECTRICITY

If a plastic ruler or comb is rubbed with a clean, dry paper towel or on a sleeve and then held over the paper towel, the paper is attracted to the plastic. This effect is called static electricity and was discovered by the ancient Greeks who used amber (see sect. 12.4, gums and resins) instead of plastic. The Greek word for amber is elektron, hence the origin of the word electricity.

Atoms consist of negatively charged electrons orbiting around the positively charged nucleus (see Ch. 6). Electrons are relatively free to move and can be drawn from atoms making up the object (paper or sleeve) on to the plastic. The paper loses electrons and is left with a net positive charge, the plastic gains electrons and so becomes negatively charged (see Fig. 4.1). Opposite charges attract one another and the paper or sleeve is attracted to the plastic ruler.

The negatively charged plastic ruler will also pick up small pieces of previously uncharged paper because the negative charge on the ruler repels the electrons in the paper. This leaves a positive charge (called an induced charge) at the end of the paper nearer the ruler and causes attraction.

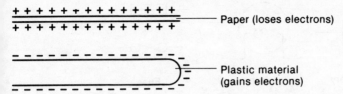

FIG. 4.1 Static electricity produced by rubbing (friction) between paper and plastic

Static electricity causes the cracking sound and tingling sensation on removal of clothing made from certain synthetic fabrics and the attraction of dust particles to polished surfaces. Where certain synthetic materials are used in buildings static electrical shocks can be quite pronounced, e.g. nylon carpets and synthetic fibre seat coverings. Build-up of static electricity can produce spectacular effects such as dust explosions in grain silos or lightning where electrons are drawn from air molecules resulting in the air becoming a conductor. Lightning streaks are the passage of electrons from highly negatively charged clouds to positively charged earth.

4.3   CURRENT ELECTRICITY AND ELECTRON FLOW

Current electricity involves the flow of electrons and will only occur in those substances where electrons are free to move and the structure of the material allows it to act as a kind of channel. Materials can be classified into groups according to how freely their electrons are able to move. Those substances with large numbers of free, mobile electrons are conductors and include all metals and carbon. Substances which do not conduct electricity are called non-conductors or insulators, and include wood, plastic, glass, rubber and air.

In conductors, free electrons move in a random manner at high speed throughout the material. Only when organised to drift in a given direction does this movement constitute an electric current. The unit of electricity is the ampere (A) which is a measure of the electrons flowing in one second, i.e. the rate of flow of charge. The electron itself is very small and a flow of 6.28×10^{18} electrons is required to produce a current of 1 A.

A driving force is required to organise the electron flow and a battery, cell or mains supply provides the energy for this process. The electrons flow from the negative terminal and return to the positive. The total number of electrons is a constant, indicating a closed system or circuit (see Fig. 4.3).

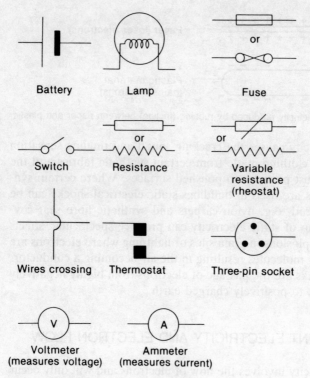

FIG. 4.2 Symbols for electrical components

The current used by a piece of equipment depends on its energy requirement, e.g. a household mixer requires 2 A whereas a fan-assisted oven requires 10 A and an industrial oven 30 A. Current is normally denoted by the symbol I.

4.4 POTENTIAL DIFFERENCE

The driving force or 'electrical pressure' is generated by the battery cell or mains supply and can be likened to the water pressure between one reservoir and a second, lower reservoir which are linked by a pipe. The difference in height between the two reservoirs determines the water pressure and hence the rate of water flow from one reservoir to the other. Water in the upper reservoir possesses greater potential energy than the water in the lower reservoir; the

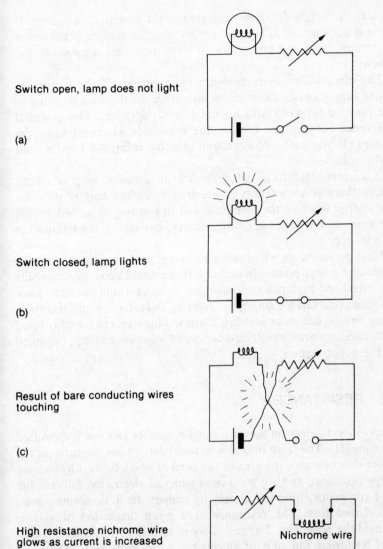

Switch open, lamp does not light

(a)

Switch closed, lamp lights

(b)

Result of bare conducting wires
touching

(c)

High resistance nichrome wire
glows as current is increased

Nichrome wire

(d)

FIG. 4.3 Circuits (a) Open (broken) circuit (b) Complete (closed) circuit (c) Short
circuit (d) Heating circuit

greater the height difference the greater the potential difference. If there is no potential difference, i.e. *no* height difference between the reservoirs, there will be no flow of water from one reservoir to the other.

The electrical pressure between the terminals of the battery or mains supply causes electrons to flow from the negative terminal to the positive terminal with no net loss of electrons. The potential difference between the ends of the conductor which produces the flow of electrons is usually referred to as the voltage (V) and its unit is the volt.

A current, therefore, will only flow in a closed loop or circuit where there is a continuity of electron flow. The battery provides the energy to drive the electrons and this energy is gained by the electrons at the expense of the battery, explaining the limited life of a battery.

Most premises are wired using a conventional ring-main circuit for lights and power points. In addition there would be separate circuits for ovens and high power appliances. A hotel would normally have additional circuits for emergency lighting and safety circuits incorporating smoke detectors and fire alarms. Many hotels are also fitted with burglar alarms to selected doors and windows and may be linked to the police station.

4.5   RESISTANCE

Opposition to electron flow is termed resistance (R) and is measured in ohms (Ω). The resistance of a material determines the current; the lower the resistance the greater the current which flows. Metals have a low resistance and are good conductors of electricity. Silver is the best conductor, followed closely by copper, then aluminium, zinc, nickel and iron. The resistance of a given dimension of wire is termed the resistivity. The resistivity of iron is six times that of copper. Nichrome (an alloy of nickel) has a resistivity 60 times that of copper and is therefore utilised in heating elements.

4.5.1   FACTORS AFFECTING ELECTRICAL RESISTANCE

Nature of material
The arrangement of the atoms in a substance determines the electrical resistance. Good conductors, such as metals, can be arranged in order but even the best conductors have some resistance as elec-

trons moving through the material collide with atoms. The collisions result in the atoms gaining energy, vibrating and producing a rise in temperature, i.e. conversion of electrical energy to heat energy. This factor is utilised in appliances such as kettles and grills where the element material has a high resistance. Undesirable heat production is a potential fire hazard and can cause problems in industry with overheating of electrical motors.

Physical dimensions

Thick copper wire has less resistance than thin copper wire. Doubling the length of a piece of wire doubles its resistance, since the electrons have twice as far to travel. Doubling the cross-sectional area halves the resistance because the electrons have greater opportunity for movement.

Temperature

In general for metallic conductors electrical resistance increases with rise in temperature. Conversely if the temperature falls the resistance decreases. Increase in resistance is directly proportional to the temperature increase, a fact which is utilised in the platinum resistance thermometer.

For carbon and certain semiconductors resistance actually decreases as the temperature rises. These materials are used in various electronic devices such as transistors. Because semiconductors are solids they are often referred to as 'solid state' components.

Arrangement of resistances (series and parallel)

Resistances can be connected together in series or parallel as illustrated in Fig. 4.4.

When the resistances are connected in series the values of the individual resistances are added together to give the total resistance (R_T) of the components.

$$R_T = R_1 + R_2 + R_3$$

When the resistances are connected in parallel the total resistance is given by the formula:

$$\frac{1}{R_T} = \frac{1}{R_1} + \frac{1}{R_2} + \frac{1}{R_3}$$

Example. *Three resistances of 3 Ωs, 4 Ωs and 12 Ωs are connected together in series and in parallel. Calculate the total resistance for each situation.*

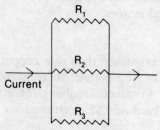

(a)   Total resistance = $R_T = R_1 + R_2 + R_3$

(b)   Total resistance, R_T given by:

$$\frac{1}{R_T} = \frac{1}{R_1} + \frac{1}{R_2} + \frac{1}{R_3}$$

FIG. 4.4 Resistances in series and parallel (a) Series (b) Parallel

In series:

$R_T = 3 + 4 + 12$
$ = 19\ \Omega$

In parallel:

$$\frac{1}{R_T} = \frac{1}{3} + \frac{1}{4} + \frac{1}{12}$$

$$\phantom{\frac{1}{R_T}} = \frac{4 + 3 + 1}{12}$$

$$\frac{1}{R_T} = \frac{8}{12}$$

$$R_T = \frac{12}{8}$$

$$ = 1.5\ \Omega$$

i.e. the total resistance when the resistances are connected in parallel is less than the value of a single resistance.

The obvious advantage of a parallel circuit is that if one resistance (component) fails the others are not affected since they are still in a complete circuit. Lights in houses and hotels are always wired in parallel for this reason.

A combination of resistances in series and parallel can be used to provide various heat settings for appliances such as electric fires, cooker ovens, hot plates and hair dryers. A heat selector switch is used to connect the appropriate resistances (heating coils) in the required manner.

4.5.2 OHM'S LAW

The relationship between current (I), voltage (V) and resistance (R) is known as Ohm's Law following experiments by Georg Ohm in 1827. Ohm found from experimental data that 'the current flowing in a wire is directly proportional to the voltage between its ends'.

current $\propto$ voltage   ('is proportional to' is written as $\propto$)

or $\dfrac{\text{voltage}}{\text{current}} = \text{constant}$

This constant is the resistance of the material and Ohm's Law is written:

$$\frac{\text{voltage}}{\text{current}} = \text{resistance}$$

$$\frac{V}{I} = R$$

Example *Calculate the current flowing in a wire if the resistance is 4 Ωs and the voltage across the wire is 12 V.*

$$\frac{\text{voltage}}{\text{current}} = \text{resistance}$$

$$\frac{12}{I} = 4$$

$$\text{or } I = \frac{12}{4}$$

$$= 3 \text{ A}$$

$$\text{Current} = 3 \text{ A}$$

4.5.3 HEATING EFFECT OF AN ELECTRIC CURRENT

As an electric current passes through a conductor heat is evolved due to collisions between electrons and the atoms making up the material of the conductor. The higher the resistance of the material the more heat will be produced. The amount of heat produced can be calculated from Joule's heating laws if the current flowing (I), the resistance of the conductor (R) and the time for which the current flows (t) are known:

Heat produced in joules = I^2Rt
    (work done)

4.5.4 APPLICATIONS OF RESISTANCE

1. Heater elements for cookers, etc. are made from nichrome which possesses a high resistance and produces a heating effect as electrons strike atoms.
2. Variable resistances are used for current control by effectively increasing or decreasing the length of the wire for applications such as dimmer switches, volume controls in radios, etc.
3. Tap water and the human body are conductors of electricity although they will not conduct at very low voltages. The effect of water on conduction by the human body is discussed in sect. 4.9(b).

4.6 POWER

Energy is measured in joules but the rates at which energy is delivered by an appliance, i.e. the power, is measured in watts (W) or kilowatts (kW), (1000 W = 1 kW).

Power = Rate of usage of energy

Every electrical appliance should have a plate stating its working voltage and its power consumption in watts.

The relationship between the power of an appliance when a current passes through it with a potential difference across its ends is given by:

Power = current × potential difference
or Watts = amperes × volts

This formula enables calculation of current or power required by an appliance operating at a particular voltage (the standard mains voltage in the United Kingdom is 240 V).

Example. *A typical food blender is rated at 480 W. Calculate the current taken if operated at a mains voltage of 240 V.*

$$\text{Watts} = \text{volts} \times \text{amperes}$$
$$480 = 240 \times A$$
$$A = 2$$
$$\text{Current} = 2 \ A$$

Example. *A fan convector oven takes a current of 10 A. If the mains voltage is 240 volts calculate the power delivered.*

$$\text{Watts} = \text{volts} \times \text{amperes}$$
$$= 240 \times 10$$
$$= 2400 \ W$$
$$= 2.4 \ kW$$
$$\text{Power} = 2.4 \ kW$$

4.6.1 COST OF ELECTRICITY

The cost of electricity is measured in kilowatt-hours (kWh) or units. One unit is consumed by using electrical energy at the rate of 1 kilowatt for 1 hour. The cost of one unit (the tariff) is determined by the establishment being supplied and the amount of electricity being used. A typical guide to running costs is shown in Table 4.1.

TABLE 4.1 Guide to running costs

Appliance	Use
100 W bulb	10 hours/unit
Hot tray	1.5 hours/unit
Kettle	12 pints of boiling water/unit
Extractor fan	24 hours/unit
Coffee percolator	75 cups/unit
Toaster	70 slices/unit
Food freezer	1.5 units per cubic foot per week (15–20 units for one week's meals for a family of 4)
Immersion heater	65 units per week for a family of 4

To calculate the cost of running appliances use the formula:

$$\text{Cost} = (\text{number of kW}) \times (\text{number of hours}) \times (\text{unit cost})$$

It is possible to calculate the quantity of heat required for a process such as the heating up of cooking oil (see sect. 3.4) and from this calculate the amount of electrical energy required using the following equation:

$$1 \ kWh = 3.6 \ MJ$$

From this the cost of the process and the time taken for the process if a particular heating element were used can be calculated, information which would be useful in the selection of a suitable heating element for a particular process in a catering establishment.

Example. *Calculate the cost of operating a 3 kW fan oven for two hours if the unit cost is 6p.*

Cost = $3 \times 2 \times 6$
   = 36p

Example. *Calculate the cost of using a 4 kW dish washer if it takes $\frac{3}{4}$ hour for a complete cycle, and the unit cost is 6p.*

Cost = $4 \times \frac{3}{4} \times 6$
   = 18p

Example. *Calculate the heat required to increase the temperature of 5 kg of cooking oil from 20 to 180 °C given that the specific heat capacity of oil is 2100 J kg^{-1} $°C^{-1}$.*

Heat   = mass × specific heat × rise in temperature
required = $5 \times 2100 \times 160$
       = 1 680 000 J
       = 1680 kJ
       = 1.68 MJ

i.e. approximately $\frac{1}{2}$ kWh

4.7   FUSES

A fuse is a safety device to protect appliances containing delicate electronic circuitry and wiring circuits from excessive current. For any type of wiring circuit there is a maximum safe current which if exceeded could cause the copper cable to become too hot, which may destroy the insulation and result in fire. The word fuse means 'to melt' and a fuse consists of a short length of tinned copper wire which melts and breaks when the current exceeds a certain value. The fuse is therefore the weakest link in the circuit and acts as a circuit breaker when overloading occurs.

Fuse links are either fitted as a rewirable type or a cartridge. In the rewirable type the fuse wire of correct thickness (ampere rating) is connected between the terminals of the fuse holder. Cartridge fuses are labelled with the size of current which they will allow to pass. Typical values of cartridge fuse size for plugs are 1 A (for calculators), 3 A, 5 A, and 13 A (see Table 4.2).

TABLE 4.2 Fuses

Appliance rating	Fuse size (A)
Up to 700 W	3
700 W to 3000 W	13
Mains fuses	
Lighting circuit	5
Immersion heater	15
Ring main circuit	30
Cooker	45

4.7.1 CALCULATION OF FUSE RATING

The formula used for calculation of the correct fuse rating for an appliance is the same as that given in sect. 4.6, i.e.:

Power = voltage × current

The fuse size should be equal to or slightly greater than the maximum working current. For example, for plug fuses in appliances up to 700 W operating at 240 V

$$\text{Current} = \frac{700}{240}$$
$$= 2.9 \text{ A}$$

A 3 A fuse would be fitted.

Some appliances although rated at less than 700 W still require a high starting current and, hence, manufacturers would recommend a 13 A fuse. The manufacturers' recommendations should always be followed. It is important to fit the correct fuse for a particular appliance. If a fuse is fitted with a higher rating than that actually required then parts of the appliance could be seriously damaged *before* the fuse wire melts and the fuse would have given no overload protection.

Example. *A domestic deep fat fryer has a typical output of 1600 W. If the mains voltage is 240 V calculate the required plug fuse size.*

$$\begin{aligned} \text{Power} &= \text{current} \times \text{voltage} \\ 1600 &= \text{current} \times 240 \\ \text{Current} &= \frac{1600}{240} \\ &= 6.3 \text{ A} \end{aligned}$$

Bearing in mind the availability of fuse sizes a 13 A fuse would be fitted.

A normal socket outlet is 13 A, i.e. this is the total available current and must not be exceeded. The use of an adaptor to connect several appliances to one socket outlet is only acceptable provided that the total current is less than 13 A. The use of a fused adaptor would overcome the need for calculations of the total current needed to operate various appliances from a single socket outlet.

Example. *The individual currents for the following appliances connected via an adaptor to a 13 A socket outlet are as follows:*

2 kW electric fire   Current = 2000/240 = 8.3 A
2 kW kettle   Current = 2000/240 = 8.3 A
500 W colour TV   Current = 500/240 = 2.1 A

If all three appliances were connected the total current would be 18.7 A and the system would be overloaded. No two appliances should be used if the total current required exceeds 13 A.

4.7.2   REPLACING A FUSE

In domestic and hotel circuits two types of fuse are used to protect against overloading:
1. A cartridge fuse fitted in each appliance or plug;
2. A main fuse for each circuit in the mains fusebox.

If the mains fuse blows then the mains supply must be switched off before the fuse is replaced. The cause of failure should be identified before replacement or the new fuse will also blow. Many fuseboxes have cartridge fuses for easy replacement. The fuse holder (carrier) should be checked for scorch marks before fitting the new fuse of the correct rating. To replace a fuse wire, all traces of the old wire must be removed before fitting the new wire taking care not to overtighten the new wire in the fitting as this weakens it.

Plug fuses are exclusively of the cartridge type. Switch off the supply to the appliance at the socket and remove the plug from the socket. Unscrew the cover of the plug and take out the blown fuse. When the new fuse is inserted the plug should be checked for any loose wires. If the appliance does not work after a new fuse has been fitted it should be checked by an electrician.

If you are in any doubt consult a qualified electrician

4.8   WIRING A PLUG

Electricity enters premises via an underground cable containing a
live wire (brown), passes through any switched-on appliance and
returns to the power station via a neutral (blue) wire to complete
the circuit. A third wire, the earth (green and yellow) acts as a safety
device but does not normally carry electricity. An incorrectly wired
circuit or plug is **Extremely Dangerous**.

A typical three-pin plug is shown in Fig. 4.5.

Modern plugs are of the flat-pin variety which are available in one
size only. They are designed for use with 13 A socket outlets. The
wiring procedure is as follows:

1. Unscrew the plug cover and remove the fuse.
2. Cut away approximately 5 cm (2 in) of outer insulation sheath
   (cord) to expose the brown, blue and green and yellow insulated
   wires.
3. Insert under the cord grip, clamp and cut the wires to reach approximately 1 cm beyond their respective terminals.
4. Strip the insulation of each wire to expose approximately 1 cm
   of copper wire. The strands are twisted together and either fitted
   into the hole in the terminal or looped clockwise around the ter-

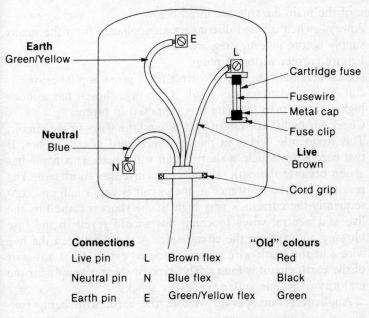

Connections			"Old" colours
Live pin	L	Brown flex	Red
Neutral pin	N	Blue flex	Black
Earth pin	E	Green/Yellow flex	Green

FIG. 4.5 The plug

minal. Tighten each terminal screw to ensure good contact. Check that there are no whiskers of bare wire which could cause a short circuit.
5. Fit the correct fuse and replace the plug cover.

4.8.1   EARTH AS A SAFETY DEVICE

If an appliance developed a fault in which the live wire came in contact with the metal frame of the appliance then touching the frame would result in electricity flowing to earth through the body of the person touching the frame giving a violent electric shock. The earth of every socket outlet is connected to 'earth' using either a connection to a metal water pipe (or copper plate buried in the ground) or to any earth connection in the supply cable. The earth connection of a plug is connected to the metal casing of the appliance and if the case becomes 'live' due to a fault the current will take the path of least resistance to earth, i.e. via the earth wire and not the human body.

4.9   POTENTIAL HAZARDS INVOLVED WITH ELECTRICITY

Some of the main hazards are listed below.
1. Always switch off and disconnect an appliance from the mains supply before investigating any fault.
2. Ensure correct wiring of plugs.
3. Check that the fuse size is correct for a given appliance or circuit. Serious damage can result if the fuse chosen has a much higher rating than the wire it is supposed to protect.
4. Check for badly worn insulation around the wires in the circuit. This frequently occurs in the appliance cord near the plug. If two bare wires touch, a short circuit will result. This name has arisen because the path taken by the current is shortened. The result is that the resistance of the circuit is very small and consequently the current is very high. If the short is caused by the live and neutral wires touching this should result in the fuse blowing and making the circuit safe. A short between the live wire and the earth wire is more serious, especially if any part of the earth circuit is faulty. This type of short accounts for the majority of people suffering electric shocks.

Appliances can operate without the earth wire being connected and outdoor appliances such as lawn mowers, hedge trimmers, etc. are a high risk. If the flex is cut when the person is standing directly on the ground, rather than on linoleum or carpet, then a serious electric shock will be produced. New regulations require that any socket outlet for outdoor appliances should be fitted with a residual current device.

5. Ensure that plugs are of a good quality (to British Standard) and are not damaged or cracked.
6. Never handle plugs, switches or any electrical appliance with wet hands. The human body is a poor conductor when the skin is dry. The bulk of the body's electrical resistance is in the epidermis (see sect. 10.6) and for a dry body the resistance between one hand and the other is about 10^5 Ω. As the skin becomes wet the resistance drops because water is a good conductor and more current will flow in the circuit and an electric shock could be fatal. Currents in excess of 20 mA can be dangerous.
7. Avoid long trailing flexes and do not lay flexes under carpets, since this practice creates a major fire hazard. Do not join flexes with tape, always use the approved connectors.
8. Never overload a socket outlet with too many appliances connected to an adaptor (the Christmas tree effect).
9. Ensure appliances such as fires are fitted with a permanent safety guard.
10. Never continue to use equipment which is giving intermittent electrical problems. Consult a qualified electrician.
11. Ensure that the earth wire is properly connected in those appliances where an earth is needed. Appliances made of an insulating material, such as plastic, are not usually fitted with an earth and should be labelled as double insulated (symbol ▣).
12. Hotel wiring should be thoroughly checked periodically (every five years).
13. Never plug appliances such as irons into lampholder sockets.
14. Never make any adjustment to electrical equipment, such as mixers, slicers, etc. while the machine is plugged in.
15. If extension leads are used these should be fully unwound.

Remember: If sudden death is your ambition
Be an amateur electrician!

QUESTIONS

1. State the units of:
   (a) current;

(b) potential difference;

(c) power.

Write an equation relating power, current and resistance.

2. If a three-way adaptor is fitted to a single socket outlet and a kettle (2 kW), a slow cooker (250 W) and an infra-red toasted sandwich maker (1500 W) were plugged in and used simultaneously, what would be the consequences?

3. Calculate the total resistance of three resistances, 3 Ω, 5 Ω and 15 Ω, when connected:

    (a) in series;

    (b) in parallel.

4. List some of the important electrical hazards which could arise in a hotel.

5

GENERAL PROPERTIES OF MATTER

5.1 INTRODUCTION

Food is a mixture of chemicals (see Ch. 16) and any study of the reactions which occur in foods, e.g. on heating, digestion or mixing with other substances, entails a study of the chemistry of food. The development of new or 'novel' food products and many aspects of quality control requires a chemical understanding of foods. Many other, more everyday, aspects of catering also involve chemistry, ranging from the use of cleaning materials to food preparation.

5.2 PHYSICAL AND CHEMICAL CHANGES

Substances undergo physical or chemical changes. If sugar is gradually added to water then the changes which occur can be investigated by measuring physical properties such as concentration, density, viscosity (resistance to flow), and appearance. If a concentrated sugar solution is heated then a series of changes occur leading to caramelisation (browning) and a product is formed which has different chemical properties to the original sugar. The effect of heat on two different substances, bread and water, illustrates the difference between physical and chemical changes.

Bread	Water
Strong heating produces toast; it is impossible to recover the original bread.	Strong heating produces steam, which can be condensed to recover the original water.

One change, the physical change is reversible, the other, the chemical change is not. The main differences between physical and chemical changes are listed in Table 5.1.

5.3 ELEMENTS

An examination of common foods containing lipids, proteins and

TABLE 5.1 Physical and chemical changes

Physical changes	Chemical changes
Reversible	Not easily reversible
No new substance formed	Always produces at least one kind of new substance
No appreciable energy (heat) change	Usually an energy (heat) change
No change in mass	Individual masses of products differ from those of reactants
Examples	*Examples*
Boiling of water	Digestion of food
Melting of fat	Heating and cooking of most foods
Dissolving sugar or salt in water	Fermentation of dough
	Explosion of dust and gases
	Rusting of cooking utensils

carbohydrates (see Ch. 16) would show that these substances could be broken down to give simpler substances called elements, e.g. carbohydrates can be broken down to give the elements carbon, hydrogen and oxygen. Elements themselves cannot, by any known chemical process, be broken down any further, e.g. carbon will only yield carbon. There are 105 known elements which can be solids, liquids or gases depending on the physical conditions, e.g. oxygen under normal conditions of temperature and pressure is a gas, at low temperatures and high pressures it can be liquified to give light blue liquid oxygen. Some of the most common elements are listed in Table 5.2.

TABLE 5.2 Some common elements

Gases	Liquids	Metallic solids	Non-metallic solids
Hydrogen	Mercury	Copper	Carbon
Nitrogen		Aluminium	Sulphur
Oxygen		Tin	Iodine
Chlorine		Iron	Phosphorus
Fluorine		Silver	
		Zinc	
		Calcium	

All substances are made up from elements, either physically or chemically combined. The human body, like the food we eat, predominantly contains the elements carbon, oxygen, hydrogen and nitrogen. Some other elements required by the human body are shown in Table 5.3.

TABLE 5.3 Some elements required by the human body

Element	Function	Source in food
Calcium	Bone/tooth structure	Cheese, milk, fish, eggs
Iron	Production of haemoglobin	Meat, especially liver and eggs
Zinc	Enzyme systems	Meat, whole grains and legumes. Oysters
Cobalt	In vitamin B_{12}	Liver and milk
Iodine	Thyroid function	Sea foods. Iodized salt

Elements are divided into two groups, metals and non-metals. Metallic elements because of their crystalline structure (see sect. 6.5 have characteristic properties of being good conductors of heat and electricity. Hence iron, aluminium and copper are used for cooking utensils, copper wire is used for electrical wiring.

5.3.1 COMPOUNDS

Apart from the elements themselves all other known pure substances consist of chemical combinations of two or more different elements known as compounds. Water (hydrogen and oxygen, H_2O), common salt (sodium and chlorine, NaCl) and sugar (carbon, hydrogen and oxygen, $C_{12}H_{22}O_{11}$) are examples of compounds. In contrast to the fixed number of elements there are millions of different possible compounds.

5.3.2 MIXTURES

Compounds involve chemical combination of elements whereas mixtures involve the physical mixing of substances. Two or more elements (e.g. air is a mixture of gases), two or more compounds (e.g. salt and water), or elements and compounds (e.g. oxygen dissolved in water) may form a mixture.

The main differences between compounds and mixtures are listed in Table 5.4.

Mixtures can be separated into their constituents by physical methods (see Table 5.5).

It is very difficult to obtain a pure element or compound and virtually all foodstuffs are mixtures. The levels of impurities can be extremely low, e.g. in salt and white sugar. Tap-water is really a dilute solution of dissolved solids and gases. The composition of mixtures of foodstuffs and changes occurring during processes such as heating are of great importance in catering.

TABLE 5.4 Differences between compounds and mixtures

Compounds	Mixtures
Fixed composition Different chemical behaviour from components e.g. sodium chloride (common salt) is formed from the elements sodium and chlorine, which individually are highly reactive dangerous elements; combined they give a harmless compound which acts as a flavouring and a preservative	*Variable composition* Properties are the sum of the properties of the components e.g. a mixture of dry coffee powder and dry sugar reflects the properties and appearance of its constituents
Homogeneous appearance which is different to the component elements	Appearance reflects amounts of individual components which can be easily identified
Can only be separated into components by chemical means	Separation can be achieved by physical means (see Table 5.5)
Heat change normally results on formation of compound	No heat change on mixing
Examples Salt Sugar	*Examples* Air Milk

TABLE 5.5 Physical methods of separation

Method	Separation	Examples
Sieving	Separation of solids by particle size	Separation of coffee powder and dry sugar
Solvent extraction	Separates solids where one is soluble and the other is not	Separation of salt and sand using water. Separation of fats using organic solvents
Evaporation	Separates dissolved solid from liquid	Salt or sugar from solution by evaporation
Filtration	Separates insoluble solid from liquid	Removal of calcium carbonate from water after treatment to remove hardness
Crystallisation	Used to separate solid in solution from impurities	Used to purify sucrose
Distillation	Separation of two miscible liquids	Alcohol from water in manufacture of spirits

5.3.3   SOLUTIONS

The simplest examples of solutions are salt in water or dissolving sugar in hot tea. The following terms are used:

Solute – the substance which dissolves, e.g. sugar.

Solvent – the (continuous) medium in which the solute is dissolved, e.g. water.

Solution – the mixture obtained by dissolving a solute in a solvent.

There are three types of solution: true solutions, suspensions and colloids, the differences between these are summarised in Table 5.6.

TABLE 5.6 Types of solution

True solution	Colloid	Suspension
Particle size less than 10^{-6} mm	Particle size between 10^{-4} and 10^{-6} mm	Larger than 10^{-4} mm
Particles not seen even with microscope	Particles only observed by Tyndall effect*	Particles easily seen with microscope or naked eye
Clear, transparent but not necessarily colourless, light passes through	Translucent	Opaque
Passes through ordinary filter paper, parchment and cellophane	Passes through even the finest filter paper, but not through parchment or cellophane	Cannot pass through filter papers of any size
Examples Sugar in water Salt in water	*Examples* Soap in water Starch solution Egg white	*Examples* Cocoa in water

* Tyndall effect. Light scattering by particles makes beam visible as it passes through the colloid.

In catering, the main solvent used is water but solvents need not be liquids and could be solids or gases. Solutes can also be solids, liquids or gases and there are therefore nine possible types of solution as shown in Table 5.7.

If a small amount of solute is added to a large amount of solvent the solution is said to be dilute; a large amount of solute produces a concentrated solution. In a dilute solution there is plenty of room for the solute molecules to be dispersed among the solvent mole-

TABLE 5.7 Examples of solutions

System	Example	Components	Solution type
Solid in solid	Alloys, e.g. bronze	Copper and tin	Colloid
Solid in liquid	Sugar solution	Sugar and water	True solution
Solid in gas	Smog	Dust in air	Colloid
Liquid in solid	Set jelly	Water in gelatine	Colloid (gel)
	Butter	Water in oil	Colloid (solid emulsion)
Liquid in liquid	Wines	Alcohol in water	True solution
	Milk	Oil in water	Colloid
Liquid in gas	Steam	Water in air	Colloid
Gas in solid	Meringue	Air in egg white	Colloid
	Bread	CO_2 in protein	Colloid
Gas in liquid	Aerated drinks	CO_2 in water	True solution
	Beaten egg white	Air in egg white	Colloid
Gas in gas	Air	Nitrogen, oxygen, etc.	True solution

cules, and it is described as unsaturated. Addition of more solute produces a more concentrated, viscous solution but one which is still unsaturated. The addition of still more solute results in a stage being reached where the solute will not dissolve but remains as crystals on the bottom of the container and even stirring the solution will not dissolve any more. The solution is now said to be saturated. If a saturated solution is heated then more solute can be dissolved and the solution is described as supersaturated. Although supersaturated solutions may remain unchanged for long periods of time they are unstable and special precautions need to be taken to prevent crystallisation of the excess solute on storage. In the manufacture of jams care is taken to prevent crystallisation of sugar on storage. In the preparation of fondant icing (used in confectionery) a large number of very small crystals are produced by rapidly cooling and agitating a supersaturated solution of sugar.

The extent to which a solute can be dissolved in a solvent is described as the solubility and is usually defined as the number of grams of solute which will saturate 100 g of solvent at a given temperature.

$$\text{Solubility } (s) = \frac{\text{Mass of solute}}{\text{100 g of solvent}} \quad \text{i.e. } \% \text{ by weight.}$$

Other methods of expressing solubility in catering include grams of solute per 100 millilitres (ml) of solution, % weight per volume (%w/v) and grams of solute per 100 g of solution (%w/w). For solutions of liquid in liquid, e.g. alcohol in water, the degree of solubility is often referred to as the miscibility, and the concentration of such solutions is expressed as % volume per volume (%v/v).

Factors affecting solubility include:

1. *Temperature* (see Appendix: Experiment 6). For solutions of solids in liquids an increase in temperature results in an *increase* in solubility. The solubility of gases in liquids *decreases* with rise in temperature. Champagne should be stored at low temperature to avoid the loss of gas from the liquid into the air space and the building up of pressure which could cause the bottle to explode.

2. *Pressure*. Pressure only affects the solubility of gases in liquids where increasing pressure increases the solubility. Carbonated drinks such as soda water, lemonade and lager if left in unstoppered containers lose gas and become flat.

3. *Particle size*. For solid solutes the smaller the particle size the more easily a solution will be formed, e.g. icing sugar will dissolve more easily than sugar lumps.

4. *Stirring and other forms of energy input*, e.g. light and sound, increase the rate of solution.

5. *Nature of solute*. Two forms of the same compound can have different solubilities, e.g. anhydrous lactose and hydrated lactose.

Other applications of solubility in catering include cleaning operations where the selected solvent removes the stain (solute) by dissolving it. The choice of solvent will depend on the nature of the stain. Although water acts as a solvent for many substances some stains are removed more easily with specialised cleaning fluids.

QUESTIONS

1. List two examples of physical and chemical changes in catering.
2. State whether each of the following are elements, compounds or mixtures:
   (a) ink;   (f) flour;
   (b) coffee;   (g) nitrogen;
   (c) oxygen;   (h) starch;
   (d) salt water;   (i) steam;
   (e) copper;   (j) tap water.
3. List five factors which could affect solubility and briefly explain any two.
4. Explain the main differences between true solutions, colloids and suspensions.
5. How would you distinguish between an unsaturated, saturated and supersaturated solution of sugar in water.

6
ATOMIC THEORY

6.1 INTRODUCTION

An understanding of the chemistry of foods requires a knowledge of the particles which make up elements and compounds, that is the structure of atoms and the interactions between atoms to form molecules. A knowledge of atomic structure (see sect. 6.3) enables caterers to appreciate the properties of the substances which they use.

6.2 ATOMS AS 'BUILDING BLOCKS' OF ELEMENTS

The Ancient Greeks first proposed the idea of elements being composed of very small particles called atoms (atom means indivisible) although it was not until the publication of Dalton's Atomic Theory in 1808 that this was accepted scientifically. Dalton defined the atom as 'the smallest part of an element which can take part in a chemical change'. There are four main points to Dalton's theory:
1. Matter is made up of minute, indivisible particles called atoms.
2. Atoms can neither be created nor destroyed.
3. Atoms of a particular element have identical properties, atoms of different elements have different properties.
4. When elements combine to form compounds, chemical combination occurs between small, whole numbers of atoms.

Modern chemistry has shown that Dalton's theory is not strictly true and needs modification. However, it is the foundation of modern chemistry and still provides a valuable simplified picture of a very complicated subject.

6.3 ATOMIC STRUCTURE

Atoms are extremely small, with an average diameter of 10^{-8} cm, and one gram of a substance contains many millions of atoms. Atoms are built up from three basic particles: protons which are positively charged; neutrons which are uncharged; and electrons which are negatively charged. The charges and masses of the three particles are shown in Table 6.1.

TABLE 6.1 Atomic particles

Particle	Charge	Mass
Proton	+1	1
Neutron	0 (neutral)	1
Electron	−1	negligible

The positive charge of the proton balances the negative charge of the electron and hence atoms, which have equal numbers of protons and electrons, have no overall charge.

The atom consists mostly of space with the nucleus, containing the protons and the neutrons, occupying a minute volume in the centre. The electrons are located in a series of orbits around the nucleus and are maintained there by electrostatic attraction between their negative charge and the positive nucleus. In a model of the hydrogen atom where the nucleus is represented by a tennis ball the electron would be 2.5 km away.

There are 105 elements, each with a different number of protons. The number of protons is the atomic number and defines the element. The number of neutrons can vary for different atoms of the same element and these are termed isotopes. Chlorine, which has 17 protons and 17 electrons can exist in two forms, one with 18 neutrons, the other with 20 neutrons. The sum of the number of protons and the number of neutrons is called the mass number and defines the isotope. The mass numbers of the two isotopes of chlorine are 35 and 37 respectively.

Atomic number is the number of protons.
Mass number is the number of protons plus the number of neutrons.
Number of neutrons = Mass number − Atomic number.

Symbols are used to represent atoms of elements and act as a 'chemical shorthand'. The symbols are derived from the names of the elements in several different languages and consist of an initial letter (as a capital) or the initial letter plus one letter from the name. The symbol is quantitative since it represents one atom of the element. Carbon is represented by the symbol C, chlorine by the symbol Cl, and copper by the symbol Cu.

The following notation is used to show the atomic number and mass number of a particular atom:

Mass number
Atomic number   Symbol for element

The two isotopes of chlorine would therefore be represented as:

$^{35}_{17}Cl$ $^{37}_{17}Cl$

6.3.1   ELECTRONIC CONFIGURATION

The electrons are arranged in a series of orbits or shells around the nucleus. These shells are numbered outwards from the nucleus 1,2,3, etc. Each shell can contain a maximum number of electrons which for the first two shells are two and eight respectively. Once a shell is full the electrons must go into the next shell. The way the electrons are arranged is called the electron configuration. Carbon has six electrons which would be arranged with two electrons in the first shell and four in the second; sodium has eleven electrons, two in the first shell, eight in the second and one in the third. Electron configurations are shown numerically as:

Carbon 2,4   Sodium 2,8,1

TABLE 6.2 The first twenty elements

Name	Symbol	Atomic number	Electron configuration
Hydrogen	H	1	1
Helium	He	2	2*
Lithium	Li	3	2,1
Beryllium	Be	4	2,2
Boron	B	5	2,3
Carbon	C	6	2,4
Nitrogen	N	7	2,5
Oxygen	O	8	2,6
Fluorine	F	9	2,7
Neon	Ne	10	2,8*
Sodium	Na	11	2,8,1
Magnesium	Mg	12	2,8,2
Aluminium	Al	13	2,8,3
Silicon	Si	14	2,8,4
Phosphorus	P	15	2,8,5
Sulphur	S	16	2,8,6
Chlorine	Cl	17	2,8,7
Argon	Ar	18	2,8,8*
Potassium	K	19	2,8,8,1
Calcium	Ca	20	2,8,8,2

*Full outer electron shell

The electron configuration for the first twenty elements is shown in Table 6.2 together with the names, symbols and atomic numbers.

Elements which have a full outer electron shell are stable and very unreactive. Elements take part in chemical reactions in an attempt to gain, lose or share electrons to achieve maximum stability with a full outer electron shell. Some gases, e.g. helium, neon and argon, have a full outer electron shell (see Table 6.2), are unreactive and have an inert gas structure. Elements with the same number of electrons in the outer shell, such as lithium, sodium and potassium (one electron) have similar chemical properties and underline the importance of the electron configuration in determining the chemical nature of and element (see Figs 6.1 and 6.2).

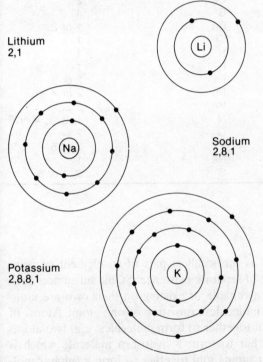

Lithium
2,1

Sodium
2,8,1

Potassium
2,8,8,1

FIG. 6.1 Electronic configurations of lithium (Li), sodium (Na) and potassium (K); all have one electron in outer electron shell

6.4 VALENCY

When atoms combine to form molecules the number of atoms which join together depends on their combining power or valency. This represents the number of electrons which need to be lost or gained to achieve a full outer electron shell. For example, oxygen has a valency of two and hydrogen a valency of one, two atoms of hydrogen will combine with one of oxygen, to form water. Sodium and chlorine both have a valency of one and one atom of sodium will combine with one atom of chlorine to form sodium chloride (common salt). The valencies of some common elements are shown in Table 6.3.

TABLE 6.3 Symbols and valencies of common elements

Element	Symbol	Valency
Aluminium	Al	3
Calcium	Ca	2
Carbon	C	4
Copper	Cu	1 or 2
Chlorine	Cl	1
Hydrogen	H	1
Iodine	I	1
Iron	Fe	2 or 3
Lead	Pb	2 or 4
Mercury	Hg	2
Nitrogen	N	1, 2, 3, 4 or 5
Oxygen	O	2
Phosphorus	P	3 or 5
Sodium	Na	1
Sulphur	S	2, 4 or 6

6.4.1 MOLECULES

A molecule is defined as the smallest part of an element or compound which is capable of separate existence. Stable substances such as inert gases which are capable of existing on their own are monatomic molecules, i.e. molecules consisting of one atom. Atoms of less stable elements join together to form molecules, e.g. two atoms of hydrogen join together to form a hydrogen molecule which is diatomic. Eight sulphur atoms join together to form a sulphur molecule. Some stable elements exist in a monatomic form but may join together to form complex structures, e.g. diamond which is formed from millions of carbon atoms (see Fig. 6.4).

Molecules of compounds are more complex since many different atoms can be involved. A simple example such as sodium chloride contains one atom of sodium and one atom of chlorine. Sodium hydrogen carbonate is a slightly more complex molecule containing one atom of sodium, one of hydrogen, one of carbon and three of oxygen.

Some atoms remain joined together and take part in chemical reactions as groups known as radicals. These cannot exist on their own and only occur in compounds. Examples include carbonate, sulphate and hydroxyl. Each radical has a fixed valency when it takes part in chemical reactions (see Table 6.4).

TABLE 6.4 Radicals

Radical	Group symbol	Valency
Ammonium	NH_4-	1
Carbonate	$-CO_3$	2
Hydrogen carbonate	$-HCO_3$	1
Hydroxyl	$-OH$	1
Nitrate	$-NO_3$	1
Sulphate	$-SO_4$	2

6.4.2 MOLECULAR FORMULAE

Molecules can be represented in symbolic form using the symbols of its constituent atoms. The number of atoms of each element is shown as a lower case suffix, i.e. as a small number below and to the right of the symbol for the element, e.g. the hydrogen molecule consists of two hydrogen atoms which would be represented as H_2. Similarly oxygen is written as O_2, water would be shown as H_2O. Where radicals are involved, brackets are placed around the symbols representing the radical and the appropriate number of radicals again shown as a lower case suffix. Calcium carbonate is shown as $CaCO_3$ whereas calcium hydrogen carbonate is shown as $Ca(HCO_3)_2$.

6.4.3 BONDING

Atoms react to attain the electronic configuration of an inert gas (full outer electron shell) and thus gain maximum stability. There are two different ways in which a full outer electron shell may be achieved:

1. By the transfer of electrons from one atom to another, i.e. ionic or electrovalent bonding; or
2. By the sharing of electrons between atoms, i.e. covalent bonding.

The type of bonding between the atoms affects the physical and chemical properties of the compound (see Table 6.5).

TABLE 6.5 Comparison of ionic and covalent compounds

Property	Ionic compounds	Covalent compounds
Bonding	Involves transfer of electrons, strong electrostatic bonds	Sharing of electrons. Weak intermolecular forces, molecules much easier to separate
State	Crystalline solids	Mainly liquids and gases. More complex compounds such as carbohydrates are solids
Melting point	Very high (NaCl — m. pt. 801 °C)	Low melting point
Boiling point	High (NaCl 1465 °C), non-volatile	Simple covalent compounds are volatile
Composition	Giant lattice of oppositely charged ions	Consist of molecules
Conductivity	They conduct electricity if melted or dissolved in water. Lattice breaks down to give mobile ions which carry current Electrolytes	No ions formed, hence they do not conduct electricity Non-electrolytes
Solubility	Usually soluble in water, rarely in organic solvents (e.g. benzene and toluene)	Usually *in*soluble in water unless they contain a hydroxyl group (–OH), e.g. alcohols. Soluble in organic solvents

Ionic or electrovalent bonding

When an atom loses or gains electrons it forms a charged particle called an ion. Ions are charged because the number of protons no longer equals the number of electrons. An atom which loses an electron will have more protons than electrons and become positively charged. Conversely, an atom which gains an electron becomes negatively charged. Sodium and chlorine react together to form sodium chloride. Sodium (2,8,1) needs to lose one electron to achieve the stable electron configuration 2,8. Chlorine (2, 8,7) needs to gain one electron to become 2,8,8. If the outer electron from the sodium atom is transferred to the chlorine atom then both achieve a stable full outer electron shell. Sodium (Na) loses one electron to form a positively charged ion (Na^+), chlorine (Cl) gains one electron to form a negatively charged chloride ion (Cl^-). The oppositely charged ions are electrostatically attracted to form the compound sodium chloride (common salt, Na^+Cl^-, more commonly written as NaCl). Compounds formed in this way are termed ionic or electrovalent compounds. The formation of sodium chloride is shown in Fig. 6.2.

Simple equation **Na + Cl → NaCl**

Electrical configuration

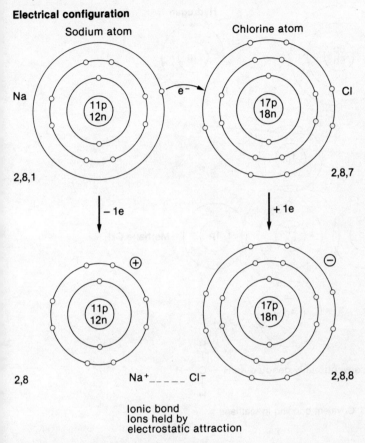

Na

2,8,1

Cl

2,8,7

2,8

Na⁺ _ _ _ _ _ Cl⁻

2,8,8

Ionic bond
Ions held by
electrostatic attraction

FIG. 6.2 Ionic bonding in sodium chloride

Covalent bonding
Atoms whose outer electron shells are about half full of electrons
would require a very large amount of energy to achieve a stable
structure by the loss or gain of electrons. Elements with a half-full
outer electron shell tend to form covalent compounds by sharing
electrons with other atoms. Carbon has four electrons in its outer
shell and achieves a stable structure by sharing electrons with other
elements. For example, in the formation of methane, CH_4, carbon
shares electrons with four atoms of hydrogen giving four covalent
bonds (see Fig. 6.3).

Covalent bonds are also formed between atoms of the same element in diatomic molecules such as O_2 and H_2.

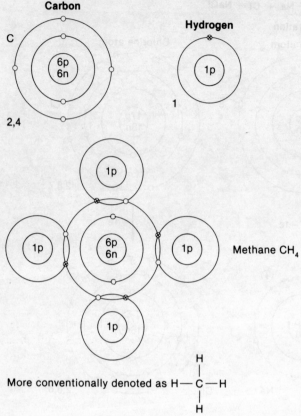

More conventionally denoted as

$$H - \underset{\underset{H}{|}}{\overset{\overset{H}{|}}{C}} - H$$

FIG. 6.3 Covalent bonding in methane

6.5 CRYSTAL STRUCTURE

If crystals of a substance are examined they are observed to possess a definite shape, e.g. cubic or needle shaped, etc. A crystalline solid is made up of a characteristic repeating three-dimensional pattern or network of ions, atoms or molecules held together in a lattice structure. Various types of structure exist as shown in Table 6.6 and Fig. 6.4.

In sodium chloride the sodium ions and the chloride ions are closely packed together in a cubic structure involving many millions of ions in a whole crystal to give a giant ionic lattice. There are such strong forces of electrostatic attraction between the ions in the lattice that considerable energy is required to disrupt the lattice. Hence ionic compounds have high melting and boiling points.

TABLE 6.6 Crystal structures

Crystal structure	Particles	Bonding	Examples
Monatomic	Single atoms	Weak	Inert gases
Non-polar Molecular Lattice	Non-polar Covalent Molecules	Covalent and weak intermolecular	Iodine, methane, carbon dioxide
Polar Molecular Lattice	Polar Covalent Compounds	Covalent and intermolecular and electrostatic	Ammonia
Giant Atomic Lattice	2/3-dimensional network of atoms	Covalent	Diamond, graphite, zeolites
Giant Ionic Lattice	Ions	Electrostatic	Sodium chloride
Metallic	Positive ions in a 'sea' of electrons	Metallic bonds	Metals, e.g. copper, iron, etc.

Covalently bonded molecules can be arranged in lattices similar to sodium chloride, with a molecule made up of several atoms at each corner of the structure, e.g. carbon dioxide. This molecular lattice formed has weak intermolecular forces between the nuclei in one molecule and the electrons in another. Molecular crystals have low melting and boiling points, e.g. carbon dioxide is a gas at normal temperatures and pressures.

Covalent bonding between atoms can result in the formation of a giant atomic lattice, e.g. carbon in its two forms diamond and graphite. Studies of these have shown that their vastly different properties are due to the different arrangement of the carbon atoms within the lattice. Carbon has a valency of four and in diamond the four bonds are arranged symmetrically to form a three-dimensional pyramid-type structure. In graphite, three of the four electrons form bonds in one plane only; the fourth electron gives a weak link between the layers, allowing them to slide over one another like a pack of cards, and also gives graphite the ability to conduct electricity, unlike diamond which will not.

The crystalline nature of metals is responsible for their properties of high thermal and electrical conductivity which are so important in catering. Metals have 'free' electrons which are not associated with any particular nucleus. These mobile electrons are able to move randomly through the structure, which can be visualised as nuclei

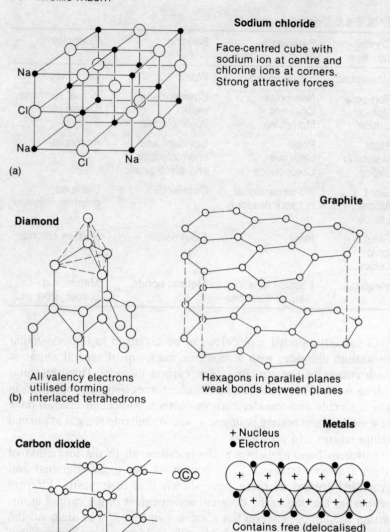

Sodium chloride

Face-centred cube with sodium ion at centre and chlorine ions at corners. Strong attractive forces

(a)

Diamond

All valency electrons utilised forming
(b) interlaced tetrahedrons

Graphite

Hexagons in parallel planes weak bonds between planes

Carbon dioxide

Infinite structure similar
(c) to that of sodium chloride

Metals

+ Nucleus
● Electron

Contains free (delocalised) electrons not attached to any particular nucleus. Ions arranged to take up minimum space giving
(d) maximum packing

FIG. 6.4 Crystal structures (a) Ionic lattice (b) Giant atomic lattice (covalent bonding) (c) Molecular lattice (carbon dioxide) (d) Metallic lattice

embedded in a sea of electrons. The metallic lattice is held together by attractive forces between the moving electrons and the nuclei and metals generally have high melting and boiling points.

6.6 RADIOACTIVITY

The ratio of protons to neutrons in the nucleus is critical to its stability. The nucleus is a mass of positive charge held together by neutrons which act as a stabilising force. The ratio of protons and neutrons in particular isotopes of elements may make the nucleus unstable and would result in the spontaneous splitting of the nucleus to achieve stability. Isotopes which are unstable are termed radioactive isotopes. There are three types of radioactive emission, depending on the particular isotope present. Radioactive emissions of high penetrating power find use in the food industry.

1. *Alpha* (α) *particles*. These are positively charged particles consisting of two protons and two neutrons, i.e. they are helium nuclei. Alpha particles have a low penetration (up to 0.01 mm of metal foil) and are easily absorbed by a few centimetres of air.
2. *Beta* (β) *particles*. β-particles are fast-moving electrons produced by the splitting of a neutron to yield a proton and an electron. The proton is retained, the electron is ejected. Beta particles can be stopped by about 3 mm of metal but since fast-moving electrons striking a metal can produce X-rays, plastic is used to absorb β-radiation.
3. *Gamma* (γ) *radiation*. This is high-energy radiation, able to penetrate up to 1 m of concrete or 2.5 m of steel.

All atoms with an atomic number greater than 83 are radioactive, while many of the lighter elements, e.g. carbon, also have radioactive isotopes. Disintegration of a radioactive isotope results in the formation of a new element with a different atomic number, e.g. uranium disintegrates to give an alpha particle and a new element thorium.

$$\begin{matrix} 238 \\ 92 \end{matrix} U \rightarrow \begin{matrix} 234 \\ 90 \end{matrix} Th + \begin{matrix} 4 \\ 2 \end{matrix} \alpha$$

6.6.1 HALF-LIFE

The half-life of an isotope is defined as the time taken for the isotope to lose half its mass by radioactive emission. The half-life can vary widely for different isotopes.

238_U	4500 million years
14_C	5700 years
$212_{Polonium}$	1 μs (microsecond)

6.6.2   USES OF ISOTOPES IN THE FOOD INDUSTRY

Radiation sources consist of two types:
1. Radioactive isotopes which emit γ-radiation, e.g. cobalt-60 (with a half-life of 5.3 years) or caesium-137 (with a half-life of 30 years).
2. Accelerated electrons from a linear accelerator or cyclotron which produce a high-energy beam.

The main use of radioactivity in the food industry is for irradiation in food preservation. Both the sources listed above are effective in killing micro-organisms although the γ-rays produced by cobalt-60 or caesium-137 have far greater penetration of foodstuffs than electrons. Electron bombardment has the advantage of controllability but is considerably more expensive than isotopes such as caesium-137 which are by-products of nuclear reactors.

Research is still being carried out regarding the safety and nutritional quality of irradiated foods for the consumer. Sale of such foods is not allowed in the U.K., although this policy is currently under Government review. In the U.S.A. irradiation can be used for sterilising bacon, for controlling infestations in cereal products and the inhibition of vegetable sprouting. Irradiated meat and bread were used by astronauts in the Apollo space flight. At the present time Japan is the only country irradiating foods on a large scale.

6.7   MOLECULAR MOTION AND KINETIC THEORY

6.7.1   EVIDENCE FOR MOLECULAR MOTION

Brownian motion

Robert Brown (1827) examined the behaviour of pollen grains in water and observed that they were in a constant state of random motion, although at the time he could not give a reason for this. This random motion is now known to be due to the continual bombardment of the pollen grains by the molecules of water. Similarly Brownian motion can be observed in milk (an emulsion containing millions of minute fat globules in water) and other food products.

Diffusion

Smells, pleasant or otherwise, are produced by the spreading of odorous molecules through the air. This process is called diffusion and again illustrates random motion of particles. It occurs in liquids and gases but not in solids (see sect. 14. 5.1). The addition of a sugar lump to a cup of tea will result in the dissolution of the sugar and

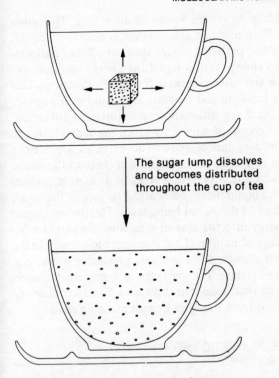

The sugar lump dissolves
and becomes distributed
throughout the cup of tea

FIG. 6.5 Diffusion of sugar molecules in tea

distribution of the sugar throughout the cup, making the tea taste
sweet (see Fig. 6.5).

Removal of stains by soaking the stained article in a suitable solvent is another example of diffusion in liquids. Diffusion in gases
can be illustrated by an air freshener which once sprayed in one part
of a room will diffuse throughout the room. Diffusion occurs much
more rapidly in gases than in liquids (see sect. 14.5.1).

Diffusion in solids can be very slow indeed. The time taken for
meat curing is related to the rate of diffusion of brine (saturated salt
solution) through the product. Diffusion of salt through lean meat is
twenty times faster than through fatty meat. Mechanical agitation can
be employed to increase the rate of diffusion of the brine through the
meat.

6.7.2   KINETIC THEORY AND STATES OF MATTER

The effect of heating a substance and the resultant changes of state
are shown in Fig. 3.4. In a solid the particles are closely packed to-

gether and held in place by strong forces of attraction. This gives a solid rigidity and a definite shape and volume. If a solid is heated, the energy gained by the particles causes them to vibrate more violently. For a solid to change into a liquid the energy must be sufficient to break down the intermolecular forces of attraction. This gives the particles the freedom and mobility associated with a liquid.

In the liquid state there are still considerable forces of attraction. This is analogous to a crowd of people in which the individuals are continually moving in a confined space. The particles are further apart in a liquid than in a solid and a liquid can take up the shape of any container in which it is placed. Forces of attraction exerted in the main body of the liquid on particles at the surface of the liquid will result in the surface of the liquid being level. Heating the liquid and putting more energy into the system results in the particles acquiring sufficient energy of motion (kinetic energy) to overcome the attractive forces and a change of state occurs producing a gas, e.g. boiling water produces steam. The particles in a gas are far apart and moving rapidly, so that a gas can diffuse to fill any container. The word gas is derived from the Greek word meaning chaos.

6.7.3   APPLICATIONS OF KINETIC THEORY

Effect of temperature
The effect of changes in temperature on a gas can be interpreted in terms of kinetic theory. Input of heat increases the kinetic energy of the molecules and enhances their tendency to move even further apart from one another, resulting in expansion of the gas at constant pressure.

If, however, the volume of a gas must remain constant or cannot increase, then increased pressure will result as the molecules of the gas strike the sides of the container more violently. Pressure equals force per unit area.

Effect of pressure
Gas pressure is produced by molecular bombardment of the gas with the walls of the vessel in which the gas is contained. Gas pressure can be increased by increasing the temperature of a fixed volume of gas or by increasing the number of molecules present.

For gas appliances to operate efficiently they must be supplied with gas at the correct pressure. Normal gas pressure is 20×10^2 Pa. There is a safe minimum pressure of 15×10^2 Pa; equally excessive pressures can affect combustion and may present a hazard. Natural gas is fed through a series of compressors in the National Grid to maintain pressure and keep the gas flowing.

Evaporation (see sect. 3.11)

Evaporation is the change in state from a liquid to a gas and occurs at the surface of the liquid when molecules moving faster than average are able to overcome intermolecular forces of attraction and 'escape' into the atmosphere. Some of these molecules collide with other molecules above the surface of the liquid and return to the liquid. Loss of water from foods, e.g. those left out on display, is due to evaporation. Liquids with a low boiling point evaporate readily and are termed volatile liquids, e.g. dry cleaning fluids, petrol and perfumes. The heat energy required for evaporation (latent heat) is obtained by the liquid from its surroundings.

Sublimation (see Fig. 3.4)

Sublimation is the change of state directly from a solid to a gas without passing through the liquid state. Applications of sublimation include the use of solid carbon dioxide (dry ice) as a refrigerant and accelerated freeze drying. Accelerated freeze drying (AFD) is used during the preparation of such products as coffee and sugar minimising loss in quality due to enzymatic action and oxidative rancidity. Under reduced pressure water can be removed very quickly from the frozen product by sublimation. One disadvantage of sublimation is freezer burn, where rapid dehydration of foods (ice → water vapour) results in the loss of taste, appearance and palatability.

QUESTIONS

1. Explain the difference between an atom, a molecule and an ion. List the three particles which constitute the atom, and show the charge and mass of each particle.
2. Illustrate the bonding in tetrachloromethane, CCl_4; carbon, $^{12}_{6}C$, and chlorine, $^{35}_{17}Cl$.
   Name the type of bond formed.
3. Illustrate a crystalline, metallic lattice and show how this explains the high thermal conductivity of metals.
4. List any three properties which illustrate the main differences between electrovalent and covalent compounds. Name two examples of each type of compound which are used in catering.
5. Describe how evaporation and diffusion can be explained using the kinetic theory.
   List two examples of diffusion in catering.

7

CHEMICAL REACTIONS

7.1 INTRODUCTION

Changes occurring in foods can be of a physical or a chemical nature (see Sect. 5.2). Chemical changes produce new substances as a result of rearrangements of the atoms taking part in the reactions, and can be represented by elemental symbols and molecular formulae. Representation of chemical reactions in this way is termed a chemical equation. These not only show the atoms or molecules taking part in a chemical reaction but are quantitative in that it is possible to calculate the amount of product from a given amount of reactant. Ideally, chemical equations should always indicate whether the reactants and products are solid (s), liquid (l), or gaseous (g). + is used to mean 'reacts with' and $\rightarrow$ means 'to produce'.

For example, when carbon is burnt in oxygen carbon dioxide is produced.

carbon + oxygen $\longrightarrow$ carbon dioxide
$C_{(s)}$ + $O_{2(g)}$ $\longrightarrow$ $CO_{2(g)}$

This is an equation since there are equal numbers of each type of atom on the left-hand side and the right-hand side of the equation. Equations must be adjusted or balanced so that the numbers of atoms on each side of the equation are the same (see Sect. 6.2).

For example, hydrogen and oxygen react to form water.

hydrogen + oxygen $\longrightarrow$ water
H_2 + O_2 $\longrightarrow$ H_2O Not balanced

This is not a proper equation as the numbers of atoms on each side of the equation do not balance. Since the formulae for the individual molecules cannot be altered we must balance the equation by multiplying the number of molecules.

i.e. $2H_2 + O_2 \longrightarrow 2H_2O$ Balanced

More examples of the balancing of equations are shown in Table 7.1.

TABLE 7.1 Balancing equations

1. Analysis of baking powder using sulphuric acid (Chittick experiment). sulphuric acid plus sodium bicarbonate produce sodium sulphate and carbon dioxide and water

   $H_2SO_4 + NaHCO_3 \quad \rightarrow \quad Na_2SO_4 + CO_2 + H_2O$ Not balanced

   $3H_2SO_4 + 6NaHCO_3 \quad \rightarrow \quad 3Na_2SO_4 + 6CO_2 + 6H_2O$ Balanced

2. In curing solutions, potassium nitrate is reduced to potassium nitrite by the action of micro-organisms. The same reaction can be achieved in the laboratory using carbon.

   $KNO_3 + C \quad \rightarrow \quad KNO_2 + CO_2$ Not balanced

   $2KNO_3 + C \quad \rightarrow \quad 2KNO_2 + CO_2$ Balanced

3. Ammonia can be oxidised to nitrogen oxide using a platinum catalyst.

   $NH_3 + O_2 \quad \rightarrow \quad NO + H_2O$ Not balanced

   $4NH_3 + SO_2 \quad \rightarrow \quad 4NO + 6H_2O$ Balanced

4. The removal of temporary hardness of water ($Ca(HCO_3)_2$) by the addition of calcium hydroxide (slaked lime, $Ca(OH)_2$).

   $Ca(HCO_3)_2 + Ca(OH)_2 \rightarrow \quad CaCO_3 + H_2O$ Not balanced

   $Ca(HCO_3)_2 + Ca(OH)_2 \rightarrow \quad 2CaCO_3 + 2H_2O$ Balanced

5. Removal of silver tarnishing from silver involves the formation of silver from black silver sulphide

   $Ag_2S + H_2 \quad \rightarrow \quad Ag + H_2S$ Not balanced

   $Ag_2S + H_2 \quad \rightarrow \quad 2Ag + H_2S$ Balanced

7.2 FACTORS AFFECTING THE RATE OF CHEMICAL REACTIONS

Some chemical reactions require a much shorter time to reach completion than others; e.g. reactions between ionic compounds in solution, such as neutralisation (see Sect. 8.5) and precipitation reactions, are extremely rapid.

The main factors which influence the rate of a chemical reaction are: the physical state of the reactants; the concentration of reactants (or the pressure for reactions involving gases); the temperature of the reaction mixture; the presence of catalysts. These factors are summarised in Table 7.2 which shows the hydrogenation of vegetable oil in the production of margarine.

7.2.1 EFFECT OF PHYSICAL STATE

This affects the ability of the reactants to come into contact with one another. Molecules of gases move quickly and therefore reactions involving gases occur rapidly, molecules of liquids move less rapidly thus these reactions occur more slowly, while reactions between sol-

TABLE 7.2 Factors affecting reaction rate in the production of margarine by the hydrogenation of an unsaturated fat, e.g. oleic acid, using a nickel catalyst

oleic acid plus hydrogen produce stearic acid
$C_{17}H_{33}COOH + H_2 \rightarrow C_{17}H_{35}COOH$

Factor	Notes
Physical state	The nickel catalyst must be finely divided to maximise the surface area on which the hydrogen and vegetable oil react
Concentration/pressure	The reaction takes place at high pressure, 400 kPa (4 atmospheres)
Temperature	The temperature is maintained at 170 °C
Catalyst	Finely divided nickel (0.05 %) is required to increase reaction rate

ids tend to be very slow indeed. For solids, the smaller the particle size the greater the exposed surface area and the more rapidly the reaction will occur. All solid (and liquid) foods possess surfaces and these surfaces have energy. Grinding a solid (comminution) or making an emulsion (emulsification) in a liquid increases surface area and increases the energy content of the system.

A finely divided or powdered crystalline solid dissolves more rapidly than large crystals because the increased surface area of particles gives them more surface energy. A solid cube of side 1 cm has a surface area of 6 cm^2; divided into 1000 cubes of side 0.1 cm, the surface area becomes 60 cm^2. This means more atoms are available at the surface of the solid for reaction.

Icing sugar will dissolve more rapidly than granulated sugar due to its finer particle size.

7.2.2 EFFECT OF CONCENTRATION OF REACTANTS

As would be expected, an increase in the concentration of the reactants will lead to an increased rate of reaction. Since any chemical reaction depends on contact between the molecules of the reactants, the increasing of the number of molecules increases the possibility of contact between the reactants and speeds up the reaction. Impurities reduce the concentration of the reactants present and so reduce the rate of reaction. Doubling the concentration of the reactants, in general, halves the reaction time.

Change of pressure has little effect on the volume of solids or liquids. An increase of pressure in a gas brings the molecules closer together and produces the same effect as an increase of concentration in reactions between solids and liquids.

7.2.3   EFFECT OF TEMPERATURE

In general the rate of a chemical reaction is increased if the temperature is increased; an increase of 10 °C in reaction temperature approximately doubles the reaction rate. A rise in temperature results in the molecules moving faster; this increases the likelihood of collisions between molecules. Many reactions will only take place above a certain temperature, at which molecules possess sufficient energy for the reaction to take place. This energy is called the activation energy. Use of low temperatures in food preservation slows down the rate of chemical reactions and delays food spoilage (see Sect. 3.12).

7.2.4   EFFECT OF CATALYSTS

A catalyst modifies the rate of a chemical reaction and is defined as a substance which alters the rate of a chemical reaction but itself remains chemically unchanged. Only a small amount of catalyst is required to produce a large change in the reaction rate. Titanium chloride is used to convert ethene (ethylene) to polyethene (polyethylene, polythene), a plastic used in food packaging. Enzymes are biological catalysts (see Sect. 9.10).

A substance which prevents a chemical reaction taking place is called an inhibitor. Impurities can act as inhibitors by poisoning the catalyst. Catalysts, as well as modifying the rate of desirable reactions, can also speed up undesirable reactions, e.g. the presence of minute traces of metallic ions such as copper or iron in fats can increase the rate of development of rancidity (spoilage of fats).

7.3   REACTIONS INVOLVING OXIDATION AND REDUCTION

In catering, the presence and effect of oxygen on food substances is of considerable importance. Oxygen is a component of air, the composition of which is shown in Table 7.3, and is a colourless, odourless gas at room temperature.

Oxygen is essential for combustion (burning) which will not take place in its absence. A chip pan fire can be extinguished by covering the burning pan with a damp tea towel, thus depriving the fire of its oxygen supply. The fat burns in oxygen to produce carbon dioxide and water.

Fatty material plus oxygen produces carbon dioxide and water
$$2C_{18}H_{37}COOH + 57O_2 \longrightarrow 19 CO_2 + 19H_2O$$

TABLE 7.3 The composition of air

Component	% volume	Property
Nitrogen	78.1	Colourless, odourless gas, will not support life
Oxygen	20.9	Colourless, odourless, tasteless gas. Will ignite glowing splint. Essential for combustion and life
Carbon dioxide	0.03	Fundamental in carbon cycle (see 15.5.1)
Other gases	0.7	Includes inert gases (helium, neon, argon)
Impurities such as sulphur dioxide	Minute traces	Compounds of sulphur blacken silver utensils

In addition to combustion, other examples of oxidation include bleaching, rusting and aerobic respiration. Oxidation is the chemical addition of oxygen to an element or compound or the removal of hydrogen from a compound. Reduction is the opposite of oxidation and involves the removal of oxygen from a compound or the addition of hydrogen to an element or compound. Some of the more important applications of oxidation and reduction in catering are shown in Table 7.4.

One disadvantage of oxidation is corrosion, which can badly damage building installations such as central heating systems, cooking utensils and other kitchen equipment made of iron. Iron undergoes corrosion due to the effect of atmospheric oxygen and water to form rust, a complex iron oxide. Painting, electroplating and plastic coatings are used to protect metals from corrosion:

iron plus oxygen produce iron oxide
$$4Fe + 3O_2 \longrightarrow 2Fe_2O_3$$

Aluminium is widely used today in place of iron as it forms a protective coating of aluminium oxide which protects the metal from further attack:

aluminium plus oxygen produce aluminium oxide
$$4Al + 3O_2 \longrightarrow 2Al_2O_3$$

Anodised aluminium, used for the construction of windows, does not corrode and can reduce the long-term costs of building maintenance.

In the absorption of oxygen by foods, such as fats (giving oxidative rancidity), one obvious solution of the problem is to exclude oxygen by suitable packaging or the use of inert gases. Excluding

TABLE 7.4 Examples of oxidation and reduction in catering

Example	Process	Explanation
Spoilage (rancidity) of fats and oils	Oxidation resulting in off flavours	Prevented by the use of phenolic anti-oxidants, such as butylated hydroxytoluene or propyl gallate (approx. 0.01%)
Hydrogenation of fats	Reduction	Addition of hydrogen to carbon-carbon double bonds (see 9.2.5)
Improving flour quality	Oxidation	Oxidising agents (improvers) act as bleaching agents to remove the slight yellow tinge of milled flour and improve quality of finished loaf, e.g. potassium bromate
	Reduction	Reducing agents have a dough-weakening effect giving inelastic dough as found in brown flour
Browning of fruit and vegetables	Oxidation	Atmospheric oxidation results in brown colours developing in crushed, peeled or cut products
Food preservation	Reduction	Addition of substances such as sulphur dioxide to food produces sulphurous acid in solution which acts as a reducing agent which helps to preserve nutrients, e.g. ascorbic acid
Energy from food	Oxidation	Body obtains energy from foods by oxidation during respiration (see 9.9.2)
Bleaching	Oxidation	Household bleach (sodium hypochlorite) is used as an oxidising agent and will remove colour and destroy bacteria
Cleaning of silver	Reduction	Removal of sulphide tarnishing from silver

light is also important, since light serves as an energy source to initiate oxidation.

In all reactions, oxidation of one substance is accompanied by reduction of another. These oxidation-reduction reactions are known as REDOX reactions. One example of a redox reaction is in the oxidation of ethanol to ethanoic (acetic) acid by oxygen as in the production of vinegar (5 per cent acetic acid in water) by the souring of wine. In this reaction oxygen is reduced to water:

ethanol plus oxygen produce ethanoic acid plus water

$$C_2H_5OH + O_2 \longrightarrow CH_3COOH + H_2O$$

QUESTIONS

1. Balance the following:
   (a) The combustion of butane to form carbon dioxide and water.
   $$C_4H_{10} + O_2 \longrightarrow CO_2 + H_2O$$
   (b) The heating of sodium hydrogen carbonate to form sodium carbonate, carbon dioxide and water.
   $$NaHCO_3 \longrightarrow Na_2CO_3 + CO_2 + H_2O$$
2. State whether each of the following normally increases or decreases the rate of a chemical reaction.
   (a) increasing concentration;
   (b) increasing pressure;
   (c) addition of catalyst;
   (d) decreasing temperature;
   (e) increasing particle size (for solids).
3. Define oxidation and reduction and list two examples of oxidation important in catering.
4. Briefly explain any two processes in catering involving reduction.
5. Describe how the frequency of molecular collisions can explain the effects of concentration, pressure and temperature on the rate of reaction.

8

ACIDS, BASES AND SALTS

8.1 INTRODUCTION

The most common characteristic of acids encountered in catering is their sour taste, as experienced in the consumption of fruits, certain vegetables and vinegar. However, control of acidity is of greater importance in catering than flavour alone, for instance in the addition of acids in jam manufacture, the preparation of sauces, or in the control of enzyme activity (see Sect. 9.10).

Acids can be neutralised by bases to form salts. The cure for some upset stomachs is to take an antacid, or base, to neutralise excess acid. Salts find a wide range of uses in catering. Common salt (sodium chloride) is very widely used for flavouring and as a preservative. Acid salts are used as aerating agents in baking powders and self-raising flours.

8.2 ACIDS

Most acids are solids and have certain characteristic features such as sour taste, corrosivity and their effect on litmus (a vegetable dye which is red in acid conditions). In the event of acid spillage the simplest and quickest remedy is to add copious amounts of water to dilute the acid. Acid spillage on the skin should be treated by holding the affected part under a running tap. Safety spectacles should be worn when hazardous chemicals are being handled. In the event of acid entering the eye, wash with running water, holding the head so that acid is not washed into the unaffected eye. Medical attention should be sought after washing acid from the eye. The general properties of acids are listed in Table 8.1, and some common acids used in catering are shown in Table 8.2.

8.2.1 ACIDITY AND HYDROGEN ION CONCENTRATION

An acid is a substance which breaks down (dissociates) in aqueous solution to release hydrogen ions, H^+.

TABLE 8.1 General properties of acids

Acid property	Effect/examples
Effect on litmus	Will turn blue litmus red
Sour taste	Citrus fruits/fruit juices have a sour taste due to the presence of citric acid
Solubility	Most dilute acids are soluble in water
Conductivity	Acids will conduct electricity due to the presence of ions
Corrosive effect	Strong acids will corrode metals and dissolve cottons, linens and flesh
Reactions with metals	Common metals, such as magnesium, zinc and iron are attacked by dilute acids. Aluminium is only attacked by dilute hydrochloric acid. Gold and silver are not attacked Acids react with metals to produce hydrogen, e.g. zinc and sulphuric acid react to produce hydrogen gas and zinc sulphate $Zn + H_2SO_4 \rightarrow ZnSO_4 + H_2$
Reaction with carbonates	Most acids react with carbonates and hydrogen carbonates to produce carbon dioxide. This is the basis of gas production (aeration) in baking powder
Neutralisation	Acids can be neutralised by the addition of a base or alkali to form a salt and water only Acid + base → Salt + water
Acid strength	Due to degree of dissociation (see 8.2.1)

TABLE 8.2 Common acids in catering

Acid	Common name	Applications/uses
Ascorbic	Vitamin C	Used in bread making and as an antioxidant
Benzoic		Effective preservative at pH = 5. Permitted in fruit juices and squashes
Boric	Boracic	Mild antiseptic
Carbonic		Soda water, aerated drinks
Ethanedioic	Oxalic	Found in rhubarb leaves. Poisonous. Used for stain removal and cleaning brass
Ethanoic	Acetic	Vinegar. Solution used to brighten coloured fabrics

TABLE 8.2 Contd.

Acid	Common name	Applications/uses
Hydrochloric		Strong mineral acid. 1% in gastric juice
2-Hydroxybutanedioic	Malic	Found in apples, prunes, cherries. Used in jams and jellies
2,3-Dihydroxybutanedioic	Tartaric	Found in grapes. Used as acid salt in certain baking powders, leaves unpleasant taste. Flavouring for jams and jellies
Hydroxypropanetricarboxylic acid	Citric	Principal acid of citrus fruits, also in pineapples, tomatoes, etc. Prevents browning of apples and potatoes. Used to flavour jams/jellies
2-Hydroxypropanoic	Lactic	Produced in sour milk by bacterial action. Used for flavouring sauces, etc
Phosphoric		Used to flavour jams/jellies. Acid salts, e.g. calcium dihydrogen phosphate $(Ca(H_2PO_4)_2)$ (ACP), used in baking
Propanoic	Propionic	Permitted only in bread and flour to prevent mould growth and 'rope'
2,4-Hexadienoic acid	Sorbic	Important preservative in cheese and confectionery to prevent growth of yeasts and moulds
Sulphuric acid		Strong acid used in the determination of CO_2 in baking powders. Used in the manufacture of fertilisers
Sulphurous		Formed by dissolving sulphur dioxide in water. Used as a preservative and a reducing agent. Used in a wider range of foods than any other permitted preservative, e.g. in dried fruit, fruit juices, jams, alcoholic beverages, soft drinks. Sulphur dioxide is added directly to fermenting grape juice

e.g. hydrochloric acid ⟶ hydrogen ion and
chloride ion

HCl ⟶ $H^+ + Cl^-$

In hydrochloric acid *all* the molecules ionise, i.e. there is 100 per cent dissociation and hydrochloric acid is a strong acid. Weak acids, such as citric or acetic, only partially dissociate to release hydrogen ions. Weak acids find wide use in catering as preservatives, flavourings and setting agents.

8.3 BASES

A base is defined as a substance which reacts with an acid, accepting the hydrogen ion to form a salt and water only (see Sect. 8.5). Bases are usually metallic oxides or hydroxides. An alkali is a base which is soluble in water. There are only a few alkalis, the common ones being sodium hydroxide (caustic soda), potassium hydroxide (caustic potash) and ammonium hydroxide (ammonia solution). The general properties of bases are listed in Table 8.3 and examples of some common bases used in the catering industry in Table 8.4.

Strong alkalis are just as dangerous as strong acids and should be treated with extreme caution.

TABLE 8.3 General properties of bases

Basic property	Examples
Effect on litmus	Turns red litmus blue
Corrosive effect	Strong alkalis are corrosive and dissolve wool, silk, hair, etc. They can be used to clear sinks which have become blocked
Saponification	Bases react with oils and fats to form soaps, and hence are soapy to touch because they react with natural oils of the skin
Neutralisation	Reaction between a salt and a base to form a salt and water only Salt + base = salt + water Alkalis are frequently used to neutralise acidic residues after bleaches
Reaction with metals	Reactions between metals and bases are not violent and alkalis are used — often in aerosol form — for the cleaning of ovens and other catering equipment

TABLE 8.4 Common bases used in catering

Base	Common name	Application/uses
Sodium hydroxide	Caustic soda	Grease remover. Aerosol cleaners. Manufacture of household soaps
Potassium hydroxide	Caustic potash	Used in manufacture of toilet soaps
Calcium oxide	Quicklime	Preparation of gelatine. Water softener
Calcium hydroxide	Slaked lime	Treatment of skin and bones for gelatine extraction. When dissolved in water forms lime water which reacts with carbon dioxide to form a cloudy precipitate
Calcium hypochlorite		Bleaching powder. Releases chlorine and cannot be used with wool, silk or nylon
Sodium hypochlorite		Liquid household bleach
Ammonia		Used as a refrigerant in large scale (industrial) refrigeration units
Ammonium hydroxide		Used to remove temporary hardness from water. Used in a variety of household cleaning agents, e.g. non-scratch cream cleaners, baths, etc. Used to clean copper and brass

8.4 THE pH SCALE

The acidity or alkalinity of aqueous solutions is measured on the pH scale. The scale ranges from 0 to 14 and is a measure of the number of hydrogen ions present in solution. Strong acids have a pH of 1, strong alkalis a pH of 14, and pure water which is neutral a pH of 7. Pure water dissociates to produce equal numbers of hydrogen and hydroxyl ions:

water $\rightleftharpoons$ hydrogen ion plus hydroxyl ion
$H_2O \rightleftharpoons H^+ + OH^-$

Acids in water 'pump in' hydrogen ion by dissociation; the stronger the acid, the more H^+ and the lower the pH. Bases, e.g. sodium hydroxide, dissociate to release large numbers of hydroxyl ions which react with (mop up) H^+ to form water molecules, leaving a surfeit of OH⁻ ions or a deficit of H⁺, i.e. a high pH. The pH values of some common substances used in catering are shown in Fig. 8.1.

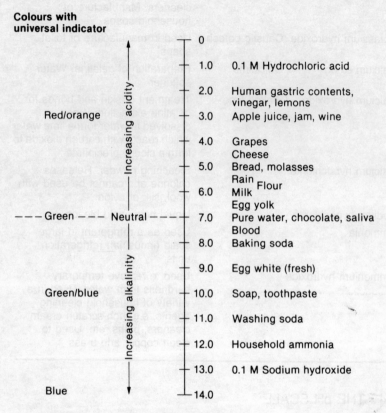

Colours with universal indicator

Colour		pH	Substance
	Increasing acidity	0	
		1.0	0.1 M Hydrochloric acid
		2.0	Human gastric contents, vinegar, lemons
Red/orange		3.0	Apple juice, jam, wine
		4.0	Grapes / Cheese
		5.0	Bread, molasses
		6.0	Rain / Flour / Milk / Egg yolk
– – – Green – – –	Neutral – – –	7.0	Pure water, chocolate, saliva / Blood
		8.0	Baking soda
		9.0	Egg white (fresh)
Green/blue		10.0	Soap, toothpaste
		11.0	Washing soda
	Increasing alkalinity	12.0	Household ammonia
		13.0	0.1 M Sodium hydroxide
Blue		14.0	

FIG. 8.1 pH values for some common substances

8.4.1 MEASUREMENT OF pH

1. *Using universal indicator paper or solution.* Universal indicator is a mixture of indicators and is able to indicate the pH of a solution by a progressive change of colour through the pH range (see Fig. 8.1).
2. *Using a pH meter.* A pH meter is a sophisticated electronic instrument which is able to indicate the pH of a solution by detecting the small electrical charge carried by H⁺ ions in solution. An electrode is dipped into the sample and the resulting pH is indicated on a pre-calibrated scale. Portable pH meters are inexpensive, convenient and are widely used in the food industry.

8.4.2   APPLICATIONS OF pH IN CATERING

Some of the applications of pH in catering are shown in Table 8.5.

TABLE 8.5 Applications of pH in catering

Application	Explanation
Detergents	Soaps are prepared by adding alkalis to fats. The pH of these mildly alkaline soaps is 8 to 10, causing them to sting the eye. Soapless detergents (e.g. triethanolamine lauryl sulphate) have a pH of 7. The pH is of great importance in laundering, with cottons requiring a pH of 10 to 11 and protein materials, such as wools and silk, requiring a pH of 7 to 8
Cooking	Meat, fish and other proteins are denatured by cooking at low pH. Protein in meat becomes tender
Vegetables	Sodium bicarbonate is sometimes added to cooking water of vegetables. This raises the pH and retains the green colour of chlorophyll, but destroys the vitamins B and C
Cake texture	Cakes of fine texture (fruit cakes) are produced at low pHs (pH 5) whereas those with a coarser texture (sponges) are produced at higher pH numbers (pH 7). Lower pH slows down the rate of staling
Jam production	Jam sets at a pH of 3.5. Fruits, such as strawberries, which do not set (gel) readily must have the pH lowered by the addition of small amounts of acid, e.g. citric or tartaric
Pigments	The coloration of foods such as blackcurrants and red cabbage is caused by natural pigments which often act as indicators and change colour according to the pH. Red cabbage is red in acidic solutions but green in alkaline solutions
Meat	Meat is allowed to hang after slaughter for lactic acid to accumulate, improving keeping quality and texture
Food spoilage	Acid foods, e.g. fruits, are more likely to be spoiled by moulds than by bacteria, which prefer less acidic conditions

8.4.3   BUFFERS

Buffers are solutions whose pH remains constant even on addition of small amounts of strong acids or alkalis. They are extremely important in biological systems, e.g. the blood stream is buffered at a pH of 7.4. Buffers are also important in the food industry, e.g. in the fermentation of dough the pH is kept constant, allowing the functioning of yeast and flour enzymes.

Buffers are usually a mixture of weak acids or bases and their salts, and a particular buffer is only effective over a limited range of pH.

8.5   NEUTRALISATION AND SALT PRODUCTION

A salt is produced as a result of the neutralisation of an acid by a base, e.g. the neutralisation of hydrochloric acid by potassium hydroxide yields potassium chloride and water.

hydrochloric acid	plus	potassium hydroxide	produce	potassium chloride	plus	water
HCl	+	KOH	$\longrightarrow$	KCl	+	H_2O .
Cl^-	+	K^+	$\longrightarrow$	K^+Cl^-		
acidic ion	plus	metallic ion	produce	neutral salt		

Similarly nitric acid reacts with sodium hydroxide to form sodium nitrate and water.

nitric acid	plus	sodium hydroxide	produce	sodium nitrate	plus	water
HNO_3	+	NaOH	$\longrightarrow$	$NaNO_3$	+	H_2O
NO_3^-	+	Na^+	$\longrightarrow$	$Na^+NO_3^-$		

Tartaric acid reacts with potassium hydroxide to give potassium hydrogen tartrate (Cream of Tartar) and water.

tartaric acid	plus	potassium hydroxide	produce	potassium hydrogen tartrate	plus	water
$H_2C_4H_4O_6$	+	KOH	$\longrightarrow$	$KHC_4H_4O_6$	+	H_2O
$HC_4H_4O_6^-$	+	K^+	$\longrightarrow$	$KHC_4H_4O_6$		

A salt consists of a positive metallic ion (from the base) and a negative ion (from the acid). These charges balance and the resulting salt is electrically neutral. When the salt is dissolved in water it ionises, i.e. breaks down into ions, and hence will conduct electricity. Salts are named according to:
(a) the name of the metallic ion;
(b) the name of the acidic ion (see Table 8.6)

TABLE 8.6 Acidic ions

Name	Formula	Acid source
Sulphate	SO_4^{2-}	Sulphuric acid
Carbonate	CO_3^{2-}	Carbonic acid
Hydrogen carbonate	HCO_3^-	Carbonic acid
Chloride	Cl^-	Hydrochloric acid
Phosphate	PO_4^{3-}	Phosphoric acid

TABLE 8.7 Salts

Salt	Common name	Formula	Type
Aerating agents			
Ammonium hydrogen carbonate	Bakers vol	NH_4HCO_3	Acid salt
Sodium hydrogen carbonate	Sodium bicarbonate (baking soda)	$NaHCO_3$	Acid salt
Calcium hydrogen phosphate	ACP	$Ca(H_2PO_4)_2$	Acid salt
Potassium hydrogen tartrate	Cream of tartar	$KHC_4H_4O_6$	Acid salt
Anti-caking additives (keeps product dry)			
Calcium phosphate		$CaPO_4$	Normal salt
Humectants (keeps product moist)			
Magnesium oxide		MgO	Normal salt
Sodium lactate			Normal salt
Anti-oxidants			
Calcium ascorbate			Normal salt
Sodium ascorbate			Normal salt
Bread additives			
Ammonium persulphate		$(NH_4)_2S_2O_8$	Normal salt
Calcium carbonate	Chalk	$CaCO_3$	Normal salt
Ferric ammonium citrate			Normal salt
Potassium bromate		$KBrO_3$	
Dietary additives			
Calcium lactate (for milk protein-free diets)			Normal salt
Potassium chloride (for salt-free diets)		KCl	
Preservatives and flavourings			
Aluminium sulphate		$Al_2(SO_4)_3$	Normal salt
Calcium sulphate		$CaSO_4$	Normal salt
Sodium sulphite		Na_2SO_3	Normal salt
Potassium nitrate Saltpetre		KNO_3	Normal salt
Sodium nitrate		$NaNO_3$	Normal salt
Sodium nitrite		$NaNO_2$	Normal salt
Sodium chloride	Common salt	$NaCl$	Normal salt
Sodium polyphosphate			Normal salt
Monosodium glutamate			Acid salt
Detergents (water treatments)			
Sodium fluoride		NaF	Normal salt
Sodium metasilicate			Normal salt
Sodium carbonate	Washing soda	Na_2CO_3	Normal salt
Sodium hexametaphosphate			Normal salt

8.5.1   NORMAL AND ACID SALTS

If an acid dissociates to give more than one hydrogen ion then it is possible for one or more of the hydrogen ions to react. If only one of the hydrogen ions of the acid is replaced then an acid salt is formed, which can further dissociate to release the remaining hydrogen ions resulting in a normal salt. Carbonic acid contains two hydrogen ions; replacement of one yields a hydrogen carbonate, an acid salt; replacement of both results in the formation of a carbonate, a normal salt.

carbonic acid	plus	sodium hydroxide	form	sodium hydrogen carbonate	plus	water
H_2CO_3	+	$NaOH$	$\longrightarrow$	$NaHCO_3$	+	H_2O
HCO_3^-	+	Na^+	$\longrightarrow$	$Na^+HCO_3^-$		

sodium hydrogen carbonate	plus	sodium hydroxide	form	sodium carbonate	plus	water
$NaHCO_3$	+	$NaOH$	$\longrightarrow$	Na_2CO_3	+	H_2O
$Na^+CO_3^=$	+	Na^+	$\longrightarrow$	$(Na^+)_2CO_3^=$		

Some of the important salts used in catering are listed in Table 8.7.

QUESTIONS

1. Name and state the use of two important acids used in catering. What is meant by the strength of an acid.
2. Explain the terms 'pH' and the 'pH scale'. List two substances used in catering which have a high pH and three which have a low pH.
3. Explain the difference between a normal salt and an acid salt, giving two examples of each.
4. List three examples of applications of pH in catering.
5. List four properties of bases and two examples of bases used in catering.

9

INTRODUCTION TO ORGANIC CHEMISTRY AND BIOCHEMISTRY

9.1 INTRODUCTION

Initially organic chemistry was defined as the chemistry of living things because many organic chemicals were of natural origin and could be extracted from living organisms. Today organic chemicals used by Man play an important role in life but the majority, e.g. plastics, dyes and drugs, are not of natural origin. Thus a better definition of organic chemistry is the study of carbon-containing compounds, although for historical reasons a few, e.g. carbonates (CO_3^{2-}) and hydrogen carbonates (HCO_3^-), are not included as organic chemicals. With the exception of salt and water all foods contain organic compounds, therefore a study of foods requires a knowledge of organic chemistry. Biochemistry is the study of the organic chemicals making up living things and examines their structure and metabolism.

9.2. THE TETRAVALENT CARBON ATOM

A carbon atom has six electrons, two in the first electron shell and four in the second (outer) shell. On combination with other atoms carbon requires to share four electrons to make a stable outer shell of eight electrons (see Sect. 6.3.1), i.e. carbon is tetravalent, forming four covalent bonds (see Fig. 9.1). Carbon compounds in which each carbon atom is joined to four other atoms are termed 'saturated'. A carbon atom can form more than one covalent bond with another carbon atom, such carbon compounds contain double or triple bonds and are termed 'unsaturated' (see Sect. 9.2.4).

9.2.1 FORMATION OF CARBON CHAINS

Carbon is the only element which can combine with itself to form *stable* chains, rings or more complex structures. Carbon can also combine with other elements giving rise to an extremely diverse range of chemicals on which life on Earth is based. Carbon is nearly

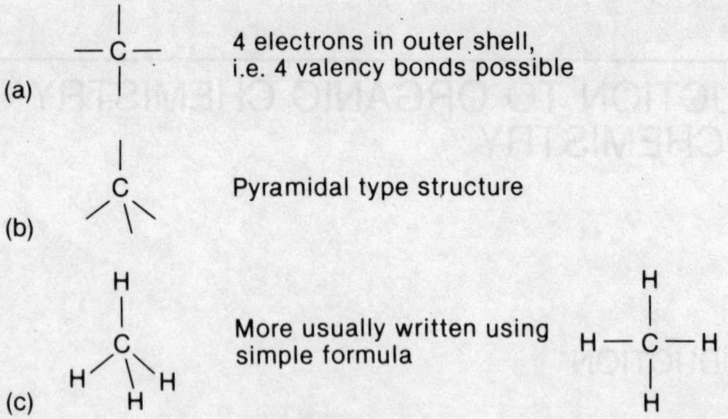

(a)
$$-\overset{|}{\underset{|}{C}}-$$
4 electrons in outer shell,
i.e. 4 valency bonds possible

(b)
$$\overset{|}{C}$$
Pyramidal type structure

(c)

More usually written using
simple formula

FIG. 9.1 Tetravalent carbon atom (a) Simple representation (b) Actual structure – Tetrahedral (c) Bonding in methane

always associated with other elements, particularly hydrogen as in the hydrocarbons, the exceptions being graphite and diamond (see Sect. 6.5).

9.2.2 HYDROCARBONS

Compounds consisting of carbon and hydrogen only are termed hydrocarbons, the simplest example being methane (a major component of natural gas) which consists of one carbon atom and four hydrogen atoms, CH_4 (see Fig. 9.1). Ethane consists of two carbon atoms and six hydrogen atoms, C_2H_6. By increasing the length of the carbon chain by the addition of one carbon atom and two hydrogen atoms each time a series of compounds is produced. This is an example of a homologous series, each member of the series differs from the next by CH_2 and can be expressed by a general formula. Members of the series possess similar chemical properties and graded increases in such physical properties as melting point and boiling point as the molecular weight increases (see Fig. 9.2).

Methane and ethane are the first two members of a homologous series called the alkanes (see Table 9.1) which has the general formula C_nH_{2n+2}. Short-chain alkanes are gases at room temperatures; as the number of carbon atoms (chain length) increases first liquids and then solids are formed.

Both propane and butane can be stored in cylinders and used as 'non-mains' gas supplies.

9.2.3 ISOMERISM

Isomers are compounds with the same molecular formula but a dif-

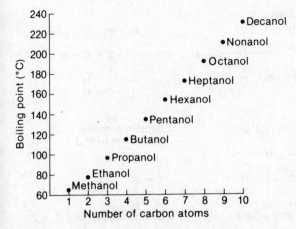

FIG. 9.2 The alcohols ($C_nH_{2n+1}OH$), a homologous series, show a gradation of physical properties, e.g. boiling point

TABLE 9.1 Naming of organic compounds and homologous series

Number of carbon atoms	Stem	Alkane	Alcohol	Carboxylic acid
1	meth-	meth**ane**	meth**anol**	meth**anoic acid**
2	eth-	ethane	ethanol	ethanoic acid
3	prop-	propane	propanol	propanoic acid
4	but-	butane	butanol	butanoic acid
5	pent-	pentane	pentanol	pentanoic acid
6	hex-	hexane	hexanol	hexanoic acid
7	hept	heptane	heptanol	heptanoic acid
8	oct-	octane	octanol	octanoic acid
9	non-	nonane	nonanol	nonanoic acid
10	dec-	decane	decanol	decanoic acid

ferent arrangement of atoms within the molecule, e.g. C_4H_{10}, in which the atoms can be arranged in two different ways, i.e. as two isomers (see Fig. 9.3). As the number of carbon atoms in the compound increases the number of possible isomers increases.

Where atoms of different elements are included in the formula isomerism can give rise to compounds with vastly different characteristics, e.g. the formula C_2H_6O can represent ethanol or dimethyl ether, one a liquid the other a gas with completely different chemical properties.

9.2.4 SATURATION

In the alkanes each carbon atom is linked by a single bond and such

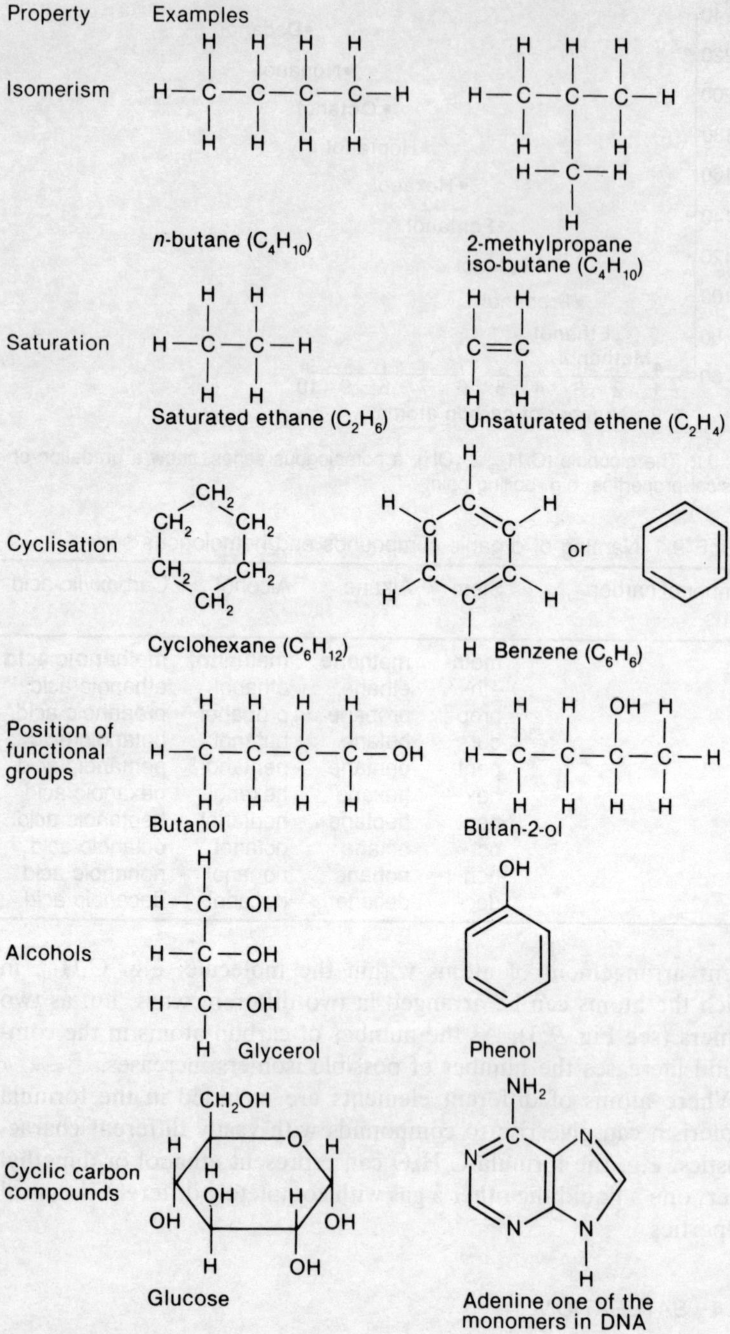

FIG. 9.3 Carbon compounds

compounds are described as being saturated. Unsaturated compounds have double or triple carbon–carbon bonds and therefore less hydrogen is joined to the carbon backbone (see Fig. 9.3). Unsaturated compounds can be saturated by the addition of hydrogen, usually in the presence of a catalyst. Vegetable oils are unsaturated and are converted to saturated fats in the manufacture of margarine. Saturated fats in the diet are implicated in heart disease and it is thought that increasing the ratio of unsaturated fats to saturated fats in the diet may be beneficial to health. The alkenes are a homologous series with the general formula C_nH_{2n} which contain one double carbon–carbon bond and are very important in the manufacture of plastics, e.g. ethene (formerly called ethylene) is the starting material in the manufacture of polythene (see Sect. 9.8). Alkynes, e.g. ethyne (acetylene) are compounds which contain triple carbon–carbon bonds.

9.2.5 CYCLIC CARBON COMPOUNDS

Cyclic hydrocarbons contain rings of carbon atoms. The most common rings contain five or six carbon atoms and can be saturated or unsaturated, e.g. cyclohexane C_6H_{12} and benzene C_6H_6 (see Fig. 9.3). Benzene occurs in fuels derived from petroleum and forms the basis of aromatic compounds including drugs and dyes.

Other atoms, such as oxygen and nitrogen, can be included in the ring structure, e.g. glucose and adenine (see Fig. 9.3). Compounds of this type are much more common in foods than cyclic hydrocarbons.

9.3 FUNCTIONAL GROUPS

Carbon–carbon single bonds and carbon-hydrogen bonds are very stable and therefore saturated alkanes are not very reactive. The introduction of other atoms or groups of atoms greatly increases the reactivity of organic compounds. The atom or group of atoms which replaces a hydrogen atom in the carbon backbone of a hydrocarbon is called a functional group (see Table 9.2). Functional groups dictate the reactions of the compound in which they are contained.

The name of the compound formed by replacement of the hydrogen atom is derived from the number of carbon atoms in the longest carbon chain in the molecule (see Fig. 9.4). A systematic name is obtained by numbering the carbon atoms in the chain and indicating the position of any functional groups. Older, common or trivial

TABLE 9.2 Functional groups

Functional group	Formula	Prefix or suffix	Example
Alcohol	-OH	-ol	Ethanol (ethyl alcohol) in wines, beers, etc.
Aldehyde	-CHO	-al	Methanal (formaldehyde) disinfecting agent and preservative
Amine	-NH$_2$	amino or -amine	Aminoacetic acid (glycine) in proteins
Carboxylic Acid	-COOH	-oic acid	Ethanoic acid in vinegar
Chlorine	-Cl	chloro-	Tetrachloromethane (carbon tetrachloride) dry cleaning solvent
Ketone	-C=O	-one	Propanone (acetone) industrial solvent

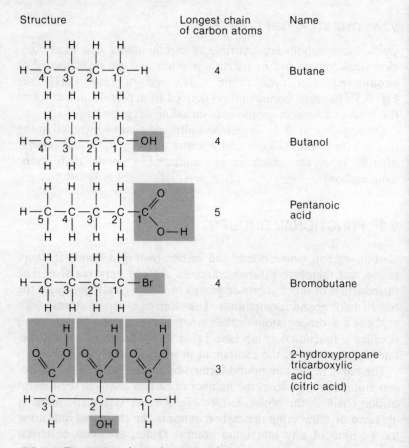

Structure	Longest chain of carbon atoms	Name
	4	Butane
	4	Butanol
	5	Pentanoic acid
	4	Bromobutane
	3	2-hydroxypropane tricarboxylic acid (citric acid)

FIG. 9.4 The naming of organic compounds

names are still widely used, e.g. ethyl alcohol is the older name for ethanol. Where two names are used in this book for the same compound the first name is the systematic name with the common name shown in brackets after.

Since the functional groups can be inserted into hydrocarbon backbones of any length. homologous series of compounds (see Sect. 9.2.2) can be formed (see Table 9.1).

Alcohols, which have a hydrogen atom replaced by an –OH group, can be represented by the general formula $C_nH_{2n+1}OH$; carboxylic acids, in which a hydrogen atom is replaced by a –COOH group, have the general formula $C_nH_{2n+1}COOH$. Many organic compounds have functional groups at positions other than at the ends of the carbon backbone. There can also be more than one functional group in the molecule, thus giving rise to a diverse range of compounds. One important example of a group of organic molecules which contains more than one functional group are the amino acids which contain a carboxylic acid group and an amino group attached to the same carbon atom (see Sect. 16.5), e.g. aminoacetic acid (glycine), $NH_2.CH_2.COOH$.

9.4 ALCOHOLS

Alcohols are organic compounds which contain a hydroxyl group (–OH) as their functional group (see Table 9.1). The lower members of the series are liquids with low melting and boiling points, distinctive smells and tastes, and are extremely soluble in water. As the molecular weight increases the melting point and boiling point (see Fig. 9.2) increase and the solubility in water decreases.

Alcohols are used as solvents for paints, varnishes and for general stain removal and for the manufacture of dyes and perfumes. They are also used as preservatives and humectants (see Sect. 3.11.1).

The most common alcohols are methanol and ethanol. Methanol (methyl alcohol or wood alcohol) is poisonous and is produced by the distillation of wood. The methanol content of wines is very low, but is higher in red wines than in white wines. Ethanol is manufactured industrially from ethene and increasingly by fermentation (see Sect. 9.9.3). Ethanol is the main alcohol of beers, wines and spirits in which it is produced by the fermentation of glucose. The ethanol content of light beers is about 3 per cent; of strong ales, 4–6 per cent; of wines, 9–12 per cent; sherries, 16–20 per cent; spirits, 40 per cent.

Some alcohols contain more than one –OH group, e.g. glycerol which contains three –OH groups and is termed a trihydric alcohol. Glycerol is an important constituent of fats and oils (see Sect. 16.5) and is used as a softening agent in confectionery (see Fig. 9.3). Hydroxybenzenes (phenols) are aromatic alcohols and are used in many disinfectants.

Higher alcohols (mainly butanol and pentanol) are formed at low concentrations during fermentation. These not only contribute directly to the bouquet of wines but also indirectly by the slow formation of pungent aromatic esters during storage. Higher alcohols are termed fusel oils and are more toxic than ethanol. Beverages of grain origin, e.g. from barley, have a higher fusel oil content than those of fruit origin, e.g. from grapes.

9.5 CARBOXYLIC ACIDS

Carboxylic acids are organic compounds which contain the functional group –COOH and are sometimes called organic acids or fatty acids. Carboxylic acids are found in many foods, especially fruits and vegetables and give most foods their acidic pH (see Fig. 8.1). The acid strength of a carboxylic acid is related to the length of the carbon atom chain; the shorter the chain of carbon atoms the more acidic is the carboxylic acid. Many naturally occurring carboxylic acids contain more than one functional group, e.g. 2-hydroxypropanoic acid (lactic acid) which contains a hydroxyl group as well as an acidic group; most contain more than one –COOH group, e.g. 2-hydroxypropane tricarboxylic acid (citric acid) and 2-hydroxybutanedioic acid (malic acid).

Carboxylic acids can be used as preservatives in foods to increase their shelf life (e.g. benzoic acid, 2,4-hexadienoic (sorbic) acid and propanoic acid) and as flavouring agents (see Sect. 9.7).

9.6 ESTERS

Esters are formed by reaction between a carboxylic acid and an alcohol in a process called esterification (see Fig. 9.5). Depending on the particular alcohol and acid selected a wide range of esters can be produced (see Table 9.3), many of these have a characteristic fruity odour.

An ester can be prepared in the laboratory by mixing ethanol (10 cm^3) with ethanoic (acetic) acid (6 cm^3) and a few drops of concentrated sulphuric acid as a catalyst. After warming for approximately five minutes if the mixture is poured into a large beaker of cold water the fruity aroma of ethyl ethanoate can be detected.

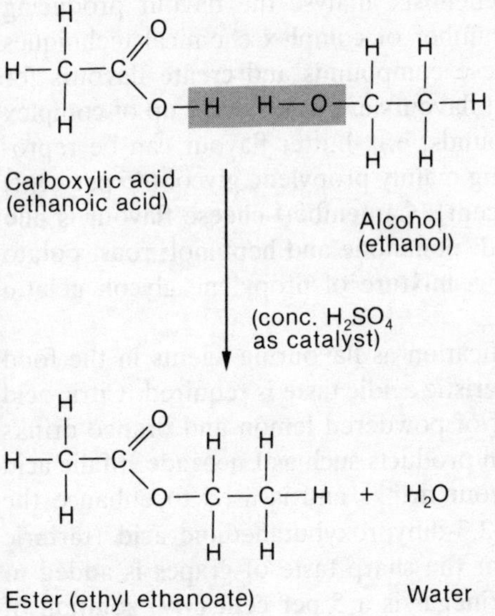

Carboxylic acid
(ethanoic acid)

Alcohol
(ethanol)

(conc. H_2SO_4
as catalyst)

Ester (ethyl ethanoate)   Water

FIG. 9.5 Esterification

TABLE 9.3 Esters

Alcohol	Acid	Ester	Flavour
Ethanol	Ethanoic acid	Ethyl ethanoate	Rum
Ethanol	Hexanoic acid	Ethyl hexanoate	Banana
Ethanol	2-hydroxypropanoic (lactic)	Ethyl hydroxypropanoate (Ethyl lactate)	Grape
Propanol	Ethanoic acid	Propyl ethanoate	Pear
Pentanol	Ethanoic acid	Pentyl ethanoate	Pear
Pentanol	Butanoic acid	Pentyl butanoate	Peach

Fats and oils are esters formed by reaction between glycerol and three long-chain carboxylic acids (see Sect. 16.6) and are often termed triglycerides. Glycerol monostearate (G.M.S.) is an ester formed by reaction between glycerol and one molecule of stearic acid and is widely used as an emulsifying and texturising food additive in cake and biscuit-making, ice-cream manufacture and margarine production.

9.7 FLAVOURING AGENTS

Flavour and foods are inseparable. Our senses of taste and smell enable us to enjoy food and drink and we associate likeable odours with 'good' food. Flavour chemists analyse the flavour producing compounds in foods by a number of complex chemical techniques in an attempt to imitate these compounds and create flavours for specific applications. Natural flavours are often made up of complex mixtures of aromatic compounds, e.g. butter flavour can be reproduced by a mixture containing mainly propylene glycol (85 per cent) and ethyl butanoate (4 per cent); Camembert cheese flavour is due to a mixture of butanoic acid, nonanone and heptanol; roast potato flavour can be produced by a mixture of propylene glycol, gelatin and certain ketones.

Carboxylic acids find application as flavouring agents in the food industry where their characteristic acidic taste is required. Citric acid is the main flavouring agent of powdered lemon and orange drinks and is used with lactic acid in products such as Lucozade. Malic acid is often added to apple-flavour drinks and is used to enhance the flavour of apple products. 2,3-dihydroxybutanedioic acid (tartaric acid) which is responsible for the sharp taste of grapes is added to drinks and boiled sweets. Vinegar is a 5 per cent (v/v) solution of ethanoic (acetic) acid. Butanoic (butyric), hexanoic (caproic) and octanoic (caprylic) acids are responsible for the flavour of sour milk and mild cheeses.

Esters are a group of odiferous molecules which make an important contribution to the flavour and aroma of foods and the aroma and bouquet of wines. There is a distinction between the terms 'aroma' and 'bouquet' in wines. Aroma is generally used to designate the odiferous components of young wines and depends on the primary aroma from the grape plus a secondary aroma from alcoholic fermentation. Bouquet is used to refer to the transformation of aroma during ageing giving rise to two sorts of bouquet; one is caused by oxidation and found in sherry or port type wines, the other is caused by reduction and found in mature table wines.

9.8 POLYMERS

Polymers are giant molecules made up of long chains of many repeating subunits called monomers. *Poly* is a prefix meaning many; *mer* is from the Greek word meros meaning part; *mono* means one. A polymer can be thought of as a string of pearls in which each pearl is a monomer. In chemistry to represent a large number of molecules the symbol n is used, n molecules of a monomer combine to form a polymer consisting of n subunits. The process of forming a polymer from monomers is called polymerisation.

There are many examples of naturally occurring polymers. The most important polymer to life on this planet is deoxyribosenucleic acid (DNA) (see Sect. 10.2) and is composed of nucleic acid monomers, e.g. adenine (see Fig. 9.3). Polysaccharides are long chains of sugar units, e.g. starch, cellulose and glycogen are long chains of glucose units (see Sect. 16.4). Proteins (see Sect. 16.5) are large molecules made up of amino acid monomers in which the amino group of one is linked to the acid group of the next by a peptide linkage. There are about twenty different naturally-occuring amino acids. The particular protein formed is determined by the type, number and the order of the amino acids. Rubber is a natural polymer produced as latex by the rubber tree and consists of long chains of isoprene monomers.

Many important man-made materials are examples of synthetic polymers, with probably the simplest example being polythene (polyethene) a polymer manufactured by the polymerisation of the monomer ethene (C_2H_4). Ethene is an unsaturated molecule (see Fig. 9.3) and can react with other ethene molecules to form a long saturated chain. A range of important monomers and their resultant polymers is shown in Table 9.4.

Synthetic polymers find important applications in the food industry in the production of a range of packaging materials and textile fibres. Fibres are solids with a high length-to-width ratio and most are elastic. Spinning together of fibres produces a yarn. Spinning of protein fibres is used in the food industry to produce simulated meat products from plant and bacterial proteins, e.g. texturised vegetable proteins.

Fibres can be classified into three groups:

1. *Natural fibres*. These include those fibres of mineral origin (e.g. asbestos, rockwool and glass), of plant origin (e.g. cotton, linen, jute and hemp, all of which are composed of cellulose, see Ch. 12) and of animal origin (hair, wool and silk). Dietary fibre is mainly cellulose and is important in the diet (see Sect. 16.4).

2. *Regenerated fibres*. Fibres can be made by the regeneration (chemical treatment) of natural polymers such as cellulose, which is used in the manufacture of rayon.

3. *Synthetic fibres*. A number of synthetic polymers, e.g. polyamides (Nylon), polyesters, polypropylene, polythene and polyurethanes, are used in the fibre production for fabrics, carpets, etc.

TABLE 9.4 Polymers

Monomer	Polymer	Use
Chloroethene (vinyl chloride)	Polychloroethene (polyvinylchloride, PVC)	Waterproof clothing, floor tiles, electrical insulation.
Ethene (ethylene)	Polyethene (polythene)	Sheets, pipes, and containers.
Phenylethene (styrene)	Polyphenylethene (polystyrene)	Trays, dishes and in expanded form (with gas blown through it) for ceiling tiles and thermal insulation
Propene (propylene)	Polypropene (polypropylene)	WC cisterns, sheets, pipes and containers
Tetrafluoroethene (CF_2CF_2)	Polytetrafluoroethene (PTFE, Fluon)	Non-stick linings for cooking utensils
Melamine-methanal (melamine-formaldehyde)	Melamine-methanal resin ('Melamine')	Switch covers, plugs, working surfaces
Phenol-methanal (phenol formaldehyde)	Phenol-methanal resin (phenol-formaldehyde resin, 'Bakelite')	Electrical switches, toilet seats
Methyl methacrylate	Polymethyl methacrylate ('Perspex')	Glass substitute

9.9 BIOCHEMISTRY AND ENERGY PRODUCTION

9.9.1 INTRODUCTION

The wide range of living things (see Ch. 10) have fundamental similarities in their biochemical makeup and metabolism. Chemical compounds important in living things include carbohydrates, lipids and proteins (see Ch. 16). Metabolism involves a series of complex, inter-related biochemical reactions requiring energy. All living things, with the exception of some micro-organisms normally require oxygen for energy production.

9.9.2 AEROBIC RESPIRATION

Respiration means the release of energy from organic compounds and is often wrongly applied only to describe inspiration (breathing in) and expiration (breathing out) with no mention of the biochemical processes involved. Aerobic respiration can be summarised as:

$$C_6H_{12}O_6 + 6O_2 \longrightarrow 6CO_2 + 6H_2O + \text{ENERGY}$$

carbohydrate + oxygen → carbon dioxide + water + energy

The equation above shows the oxidation of one molecule of a carbohydrate, glucose, the most common substance used for energy production and derived from food. The complete breakdown of 1 mole (180 g) of glucose to carbon dioxide and water is a very efficient method of energy production and yields 2880 kJ. In reality the chemical changes involved in respiration are very complex and involve a series of small steps rather than one large step, each step being controlled by biological catalysts or enzymes (see Sect. 9.10).

Man breathes in air which passes into the lungs resulting in the diffusion of oxygen into the blood. Oxygenated blood passes to the heart and is pumped around the body. Oxygen diffuses into the respiring tissues where it is used for the release of energy as shown above. As a result of aerobic respiration carbon dioxide is formed and diffuses back into the blood to be carried to the lungs for removal from the body in expiration.

9.9.3 ANAEROBIC RESPIRATION

Some organisms prefer to live in the absence of oxygen and are termed anaerobic while others can live with or without oxygen and are facultative anaerobes. Such organisms utilise methods for the release energy which do not require oxygen – anaerobic respiration.

Animals, although dependent on atmospheric oxygen, are also able to obtain energy in the absence of oxygen to help overcome a very short term demand for energy, e.g. playing squash or other strenuous exercise.

In animals anaerobic respiration involves the incomplete breakdown of glucose to form lactic acid a process which does not require oxygen and results in the release of only 150 kJ per mole of glucose, since chemical energy remains locked up in the lactic acid. An exercising athlete will produce lactic acid in his muscles if oxygen cannot be supplied quickly enough for aerobic respiration to continue. Lactic acid builds up in the muscles and being slightly toxic causes them to ache and may result in cramp. Yeast is a facultative anaerobe and use is made of this in the food industry. In bread-making yeast respires predominantly aerobically resulting in the production of carbon dioxide which aerates the dough. In the manufacture of alcoholic beverages fermentation of glucose to produce alcohol and some carbon dioxide is required as shown below:

$$C_6H_{12}O_6 \longrightarrow 2C_2H_5OH + 2CO_2 + \text{ENERGY}$$

glucose   ethanol   carbon   energy
                                            dioxide

In wine- and beer-making the main product is alcohol with the carbon dioxide a useful by-product helping to carbonate beer and sparkling wines. Surplus carbon dioxide can also be used in the manufacture of soft drinks. In the preparation of champagne a secondary fermentation of wine which has been stored for six months takes place in special bottles. Retention of the carbon dioxide produced gives the characteristic, sparkling appearance.

9.10   ENZYMES

Enzymes are proteins (see Sect. 16.5) which are biological catalysts, i.e. they modify the rate of biochemical reactions although they themselves remain unchanged in the reaction and can be used time and again. Since biochemical reactions occur slowly, if at all in the absence of an appropriate enzyme, most enzymes speed up biochemical reactions. Enzymes are specific to particular reactions, e.g. amylase breaks down starch to maltose.

The efficiency of an enzyme reaction is dependent on temperature and pH:

1. The rate of an enzymic reaction increases with temperature although at temperatures above 45 °C enzymes begin to be denatured (broken down) slowly by heat. The temperature at which an enzyme works best is called its optimum temperature and is 37 °C for most enzymes. Some enzymes can operate slowly at very low temperatures and frozen foods even if stored at −18 °C will deteriorate slowly thus some foods are given heat treatment (blanching) before freezing. Enzyme deterioration is significant in foods stored at −6 °C in a 1-star freezer.

2. The optimum pH for many enzymes is seven, the same as the pH of the body's tissues although some can function at extremes of pH, e.g. pepsin, the enzyme which breaks down protein in the stomach, operates at a pH of two.

Some enzymes are helped by the presence of particular vitamins or minerals which are described as coenzymes or cofactors, respectively. Many vitamins function as coenzymes, e.g. the B vitamins (see Ch. 16) are important in the functioning of respiratory enzymes. Other substances can poison enzymes and are known as inhibitors, e.g. cyanide inhibits respiratory enzymes resulting in death.

QUESTIONS

1. Explain the term 'homologous series' using the hydrocarbons as an example.
2. Illustrate the three isomeric forms of the molecular formula C_5H_{10}.
3. Distinguish between aerobic and anaerobic respiration. Write an equation for aerobic respiration.
4. Discuss one application of anaerobiosis in the food industry.
5. Define the term 'enzyme' and explain the importance of two factors affecting the activity of enzymes in catering.

10

THE BIOLOGICAL WORLD

10.1 INTRODUCTION

Biology is the study of living things (Greek: *bios* = life) and early biologists realised the need for a system of classification of living organisms. Taxonomy is the study of classification or the placing of related organisms into groups. This orderly arrangement is essential when it is realised that there are in excess of two million different types of living thing. Organisms that are so similar that they are capable of interbreeding and producing fertile offspring are said to belong to the same species. Similar species belong to the same genus. Every organism has two names, one for the genus and one for the species, e.g. *Homo sapiens* = Man; genus – *Homo*, species – *sapiens*. Similar genera belong to the same family, and similar families to the same order. Similar orders are grouped together into classes, classes into phyla and phyla into kingdoms.

The kingdom is the largest taxonomic unit, e.g. all plants belong to the plant kingdom (see Ch. 12), all animals belong to the animal kingdom (see Ch. 13). At the species level organisms are very similar and as they are placed into larger taxonomic groups the members of that group get more dissimilar. The phrase 'Kenneth Peter Cried Off From Going Swimming' (K = kingdom, P = phylum, C = class, O = order, F = family, G = genus, S = species) may help you to remember the order of the different levels of taxonomic grouping. The classification of the cow is shown in Table 10.1.

Identification is the placing of an unknown organism into one of these taxonomic groups. Man does this automatically, e.g. a large, moving living thing caught in a fishing net he describes as animal, probably fish (although this may not be correct) and if he is more knowledgeable he may identify it as a cod, plaice, haddock or even a whale (which is not a fish) if his fishing net was large enough.

For years biologists split the living world into two groups – plants and animals. It is now realised that this simple division is inadequate. Many living things, mainly small in size, cannot be easily categorised and the study of these small organisms is called micro-

TABLE 10.1 Classification of the cow (*Bos taurus*)

Level of classification	Group	Examples of excluded groups
Kingdom	**Animal**	Plant, Micro-organisms
Phylum	**Chordates (vertebrates)**	Invertebrates
Class	**Mammals**	Fish, Amphibians, Reptiles, Birds
Order	**Even-toed ungulates**	Rodents, Carnivores, Cetacea (whales and dolphins), Odd-toed ungulates
Family	**Bovidae**	Suidae (pigs), Camelidae (camels)
Genus	***Bos***	
Species	***taurus***	

biology. These micro-organisms can however differ quite considerably, one from another, and it is now considered that some of them should be allocated separate kingdom status, giving a total of five kingdoms (see Fig. 10.1).

The plant and animal kingdoms are retained, and in addition there are the kingdoms Protista (which includes the algae, protozoa and the fungi), Prokaryota (bacteria and blue-green algae) and the viruses. Viruses pose a problem to biologists as it can be argued that they are not living and lack many of the attributes of living things (see Sect. 10.2). For the sake of convenience they will be considered here as living things and given kingdom status.

As will be seen in the following chapters all five kingdoms are of importance to the caterer: the plants and animals because they include the food we eat; the animal kingdom because some of its members are pests, either spoiling food or causing damage to catering premises; the Protista because some of its members are edible and may become our major food supplies of the future, while others spoil foods or cause illnesses associated with food; the Prokaryota since some bacteria help in food production while others cause food spoilage or food poisoning. Although more information is needed it seems that viruses are also responsible for a number of illnesses spread via food.

10.2 CHARACTERISTICS OF LIVING THINGS

In order to be described as living, living things have certain properties or characteristics which distinguish them from non-living

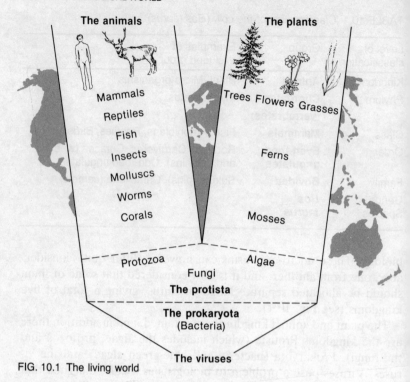

FIG. 10.1 The living world

things. Although it is difficult, if not impossible, to define life, biologists have observed that living things have the following common properties.

10.2.1 REPRODUCTION

All living things are able to reproduce themselves. Scientists discovered that the chemical *d*eoxyribose*n*ucleic *a*cid (DNA), found in the nucleus of the cell (see Sect. 10.4), contains the important genetic or hereditary information. This statement is not true for some viruses. Reproduction involves duplication of the genetic material. Without reproduction the number of living things in the world would decrease and eventually die out. This ability to reproduce is one of the few characteristics of living things possessed by viruses.

10.2.2 GROWTH AND NUTRITION

All living things grow and feed. The term growth can be applied to individual organisms and to populations of organisms (see Ch. 14). In individual organisms growth is usually taken to mean a permanent increase in size, usually involving cytoplasm (see Sect. 10.4), hence volume and mass also increase. Young start off small and may after a period of growth reach a maximum size. Populations of individuals also grow, i.e. after reproduction the number of individuals increases.

For growth of an individual cell or populations of cells the correct nutrients must be provided (see Ch. 15).

10.2.3 SENSITIVITY AND MOVEMENT

Living things are able to sense changes in their environment and respond to them. A man after detecting a fierce lion would run away from it, the lion after detecting the man might run after him. Similarly plants and micro-organisms (except viruses) detect stimuli in varying degrees and respond to them, e.g. plants grow towards light.

10.2.4 EXCRETION

As a result of the complex chemical reactions taking place in living organisms toxic waste products are formed and living things (except viruses) must be able to excrete and remove them.

10.2.5 RESPIRATION

All the properties of living things so far mentioned require energy (especially the man running away from the lion). Sunlight is the primary source of energy for life. Plants trap and store this energy in the form of complex chemical compounds such as sugars, starch and fats (see Ch. 16). When required, this energy can be released by respiration. This is a complex biochemical process, usually requiring oxygen, and involves the breakdown of sugars (see Sect. 9.9).

10.3 CONDITIONS NECESSARY FOR LIFE

For life to exist within a particular habitat the environment must be capable of allowing the characteristics of life to take place. Not all environments can support all forms of life: e.g. fish can live underwater, Man cannot; polar bears live in the Arctic, monkeys cannot; conifers live in temperate climates only. Factors important in deciding whether life can proceed within a particular environment include:

temperature   water
level of oxygen   sunlight
food

10.3.1 TEMPERATURE

The temperature range for life forms as we know them is relatively restricted, due to the restricted range in which biochemical reactions can take place. Water, the universal solvent, freezes at 0 °C and this prevents chemical reactions taking place. Use is made of this in the freezing of food for preservation. As temperatures rise above 45 °C most enzymes in the cell become denatured (see Sect. 9.10) preventing biochemical reactions taking place, thus heat is also used as a method of food preservation. Different life forms have adapted to particular temperature ranges, e.g. some animals have fur coats and layers of fat to survive cold climates. Bacteria generally show the greatest versatility with respect to temperature; some can grow at temperatures as low as −20 °C while others can grow at temperatures as high as 80 °C.

10.3.2 OXYGEN

Oxygen is required by many living things for energy production in respiration although some organisms are able to produce energy in the absence of oxygen (see Sect. 9.9.3). Organisms requiring oxygen are termed aerobic; e.g. Man would not survive more than about five minutes without oxygen. Some micro-organisms can survive with or without oxygen and are called facultative anaerobes; others not only cease to grow but may be killed rapidly by exposure to oxygen and are obligate anaerobes.

10.3.3 FOOD

For growth and reproduction organisms need a supply of nutrients or food which may be inorganic, or inorganic and organic in nature (see Ch. 16). Carbon dioxide is of prime importance as an inorganic nutrient for plants which produce organic carbon compounds during photosynthesis (see Sect. 15.2).

10.3.4 WATER

A large proportion of any living thing is composed of water (approximately 70 per cent in Man). Living things are continually taking in and losing water (see Sect. 16.3). Use can be made of this water requirement in the preservation of food. Dehydration of the food product to a sufficiently low level prevents the growth of food spoilage organisms. It is important that sufficient water is removed as some spoilage micro-organisms have adapted to growth under conditions of very low moisture.

10.3.5 SUNLIGHT

Sunlight is essential for plants to carry out photosynthesis (see Sect. 15.2) and as plants form the ultimate source of food for all animals they too are dependent indirectly on sunlight. It is only possible for a few forms of bacteria to exist without light or chemicals derived directly or indirectly from light.

10.4 CELL TYPES

Close examination of living things shows that they are composed of smaller units called cells. The plant and animal kingdoms contain organisms made up of many cells – multicellular. Multicellular organisms can consist of colonies of single, identical cells showing no differentiation, e.g. sponges. Alternatively there can be an interrelationship between constituent cells which become adapted to varying degrees to perform different functions (see Sect. 10.5). The Protista contains both multicellular and unicellular (single-celled) organisms. The Prokaryota are unicellular while the viruses are acellular being below the level of cellular organisation. Scientists studying cells found that not all cells had the same structure. Plant cells were found to differ slightly from animal cells. Protista have basically an animal or plant type of cell but the Prokaryotes (bacteria being the most important group) have a much simpler type of cell structure.

10.4.1 THE ANIMAL TYPE OF CELL (see Fig. 10.2)

A typical animal cell is composed of a cell membrane (or plasmalemma) on the outside, which is responsible for controlling the chemicals which pass in or out of the cell. The cell membrane is very thin (7–8 nm) and is made of two layers of protein separated by a layer of lipid (fatty substances, see Sect. 16.5) and contains pores. Inside the cell membrane is the cytoplasm which is a fluid, jelly-like complex containing organelles and inclusions, often appearing granular. Most of the chemical reactions take place in the cytoplasm and the organelles are important in many of these. Organelles are structures found permanently in the cytoplasm, e.g. mitochondria are important in respiration. Many inclusions are food storage substances, e.g. glycogen, starch and fat deposits, and become depleted in times of need. In the centre of the cytoplasm, surrounded by the nuclear membrane, is the nucleus which occupies approximately 10 per cent of the cell volume. The nucleus contains the DNA, the genetic information necessary for building the structures in the cell and manufacturing enzymes. Animal cells have a true nucleus and are thus eukaryotic (Greek: *eu* = true; *karyon* = nucleus).

10.4.2 THE PLANT TYPE OF CELL (see Fig. 10.2)

Although plant cells show some differences from animal cells (see Table 10.2) they are essentially similar in that they are both eukaryotic.

Plant cells have on their outside a cell wall which is lacking in animal cells. The plant cell wall is important to the human diet as it is made up of cellulose, a major component of roughage or dietary fibre (see Sect. 16.4). The cell wall gives shape, strength and support to the cell. Underneath the cell wall is a cell membrane (similar to that found in animal cells) surrounding the cytoplasm. Plant cell cytoplasm differs slightly from animal cytoplasm in having one or more quite large vacuoles – spaces filled with solutions of sugars, salts and often pigments, collectively known as cell sap. Vacuoles are important in maintaining the shape and form of the cell. Plant cytoplasm generally has fewer mitochondria than animal cells but contains additional organelles called chloroplasts which contain chlorophyll, a green pigment which traps light energy during photosynthesis (see Sect. 15.2).

10.4.3 THE CELLS OF PROTISTA

A number of different eukaryotic cell types are found among the Protista. Algae have cells similar to a typical plant cell while protozoa have an animal-type cell. Fungi have a basic plant type cell but their cell walls often differ chemically and their cytoplasm, although definitely eukaryotic, is slightly less complex and lacking in chloroplasts. Hence fungi cannot make their own food. Fungi may be unicellular, multicellular or coenocytic (nucleii distributed in cytoplasm without separation by cell walls).

10.4.4 THE PROKARYOTIC CELL

The main group of organisms in the Prokaryota – the bacteria, have

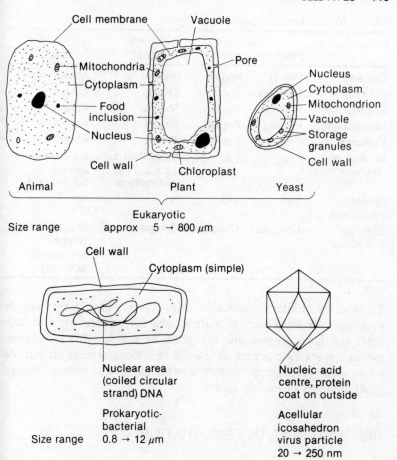

FIG. 10.2 Comparative diagrams of various cell types

cells that can neither be described as plant-like nor animal-like. Bacteria possess a cell wall but this is very different to either a plant or fungal cell wall. Bacterial cytoplasm is much simpler than that found in a eukaryotic cell and lacks mitochondria and chloroplasts. The main difference, however, is that they lack a true nucleus surrounded by a nuclear membrane. Instead, bacteria possess a much simpler nuclear area hence the term prokaryotic meaning 'before nucleus'. In summary bacterial cells are much simpler than eukaryotic cells.

10.4.5 VIRUSES

Viruses are acellular or akaryotic (without a nucleus) and are below

TABLE 10.2 Differences between cell types

| Properties | Eukaryotic | | Prokaryotic (bacteria) | Non-cellular (viruses) |
	Plant	Animal		
Cell wall	Present	Absent	Present	Absent
Cytoplasm	Complex	Complex	Simple	Absent
Chloroplasts	Present	Absent	Absent	Absent
Mitochondria	Present	Present	Absent	Absent
Vacuoles	Present	Absent	Absent	Absent
Nucleus and chromosomes	Yes	Yes	No nuclear area, equivalent to 1 chromosome	No – small amount of nucleic acid
Nuclear membrane	Yes	Yes	No	No
Chemical composition	Complex	Complex	Complex	Simple – protein and nucleic acid only

the level of cellular organisation. Most viruses have a very simple structure consisting only of nucleic acid surrounded by a protein coat, and have no nucleus, cytoplasm or cell membrane. Larger, more complex viruses may have a lipid envelope around the outside while some very simple viruses, known as viroids, consist only of small amounts of nucleic acid.

10.5 CELLULAR DIFFERENTIATION

Within multicellular organisms the exact shape and composition of the cell varies according to the function of the cell. Although all the cells within a particular organism contain exactly the same genetic information, in any one cell not all the genetic information is being used and different cells use different parts of the DNA. A nerve cell is elongated into a long, thread-like structure capable of conducting electrical impulses. Red blood cells are biconcave discs filled with haemoglobin for the carriage of oxygen.

10.5.1 TISSUES

In a multicellular organism cells with the same function are grouped together to form a tissue. In the human body there are a number of different tissues:

skeletal –   to support and protect the soft parts of the body and to provide an attachment for muscles

muscular –	to contract and relax, allowing movement
blood –	to carry oxygen, food, hormones and waste products around the body, and to fight infection
nervous –	to conduct nerve impulses and coordinate responses to stimuli
connective –	holds the other tissues together
epithelial –	form the skin and lining of the respiratory, digestive and reproductive organs.

10.5.2 ORGANS

Organs consist of different tissues grouped together to carry out a particular function or functions. The small intestine is an aggregation of muscular, nervous, blood, connective and epithelial tissues which together allow it to fulfil its role in the digestion and absorption of food (see Ch. 17).

10.5.3 SYSTEMS

Different organs and tissues may be linked by a common function to give a larger structure or system, e.g. the digestive system (Ch. 17).

10.6 STRUCTURE AND FUNCTION OF THE HUMAN SKIN (see Fig. 10.3)

One example of an organ is the human skin which is an aggregation of epithelial, connective, nervous and blood tissues. The skin consists of two main layers; an outer layer called the epidermis and an inner layer called the dermis, or true skin.

The epidermis consists of five distinct layers of cells and varies in thickness from 0.1 to 2 mm in different parts of the body, being thickest on the soles of the feet. The lowest layer consists of dividing cells which give rise to the four other layers. Cells move outwards from the lowest layer and die as they move away. The outer layer consists of flattened dead cells that act as a barrier against invading micro-organisms and are rubbed off during movements of the body. House dust is largely derived from dead human skin cells!

The dermis is about 3 mm thick and consists of a dense network of connective tissue which is well supplied with blood vessels and nerves. Hairs grow from deep narrow pits in the skin called follicles. A small muscle, the arrector-pili muscle (arrectores pilorum or

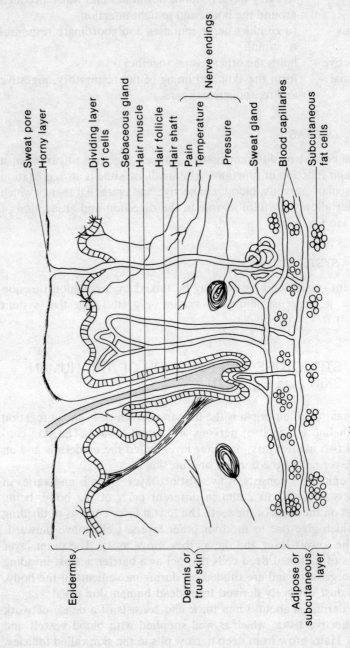

FIG. 10.3 The structure of the human skin

pilomotor muscle), can contract to make the hair stand on end when people become frightened or cold, in areas of skin without hair a goose pimple forms. Sebaceous glands are found at the side of the hair follicle and produce a fatty substance called sebum which helps to lubricate and waterproof the skin and hair shaft. Catering staff who have to wash their hands frequently for hygiene reasons (see Table 18.1) may need to replace natural oils with hand creams to prevent excessive drying out of skin. Barrier creams may be used to avoid this problem. An excess intake of fatty foods can result in over-production of sebum, leading to greasy hair.

The dermis is well supplied with small capillaries which carry oxygen and nutrients to the dividing cells. The capillaries can dilate (get wider) or constrict (get narrower) allowing more or less blood to flow to the skin. A chef working in a hot kitchen becomes red-faced due to increased blood flow to the skin and will also produce sweat, a watery fluid containing about 2 per cent salt and other dissolved substances. Sweating is important for controlling body temperature and cools the skin by evaporation (see Sect. 3.4). Most of the nerve endings lie in the dermis and allow the detection of temperature, pain and pressure although a few branched nerve endings enter the epidermis.

Beneath the dermis is a layer of fatty tissue which loosely connects the dermis with the underlying muscle. The amount of fat stored in this layer can vary (women tend to have more than men) and helps to insulate the body.

The functions of the human skin can be summarised as follows:
1. The human skin protects the underlying tissues from mechanical injury, ultraviolet radiation (from sunlight), bacterial infection and desiccation.
2. The presence of nerves in the skin allow it to be sensitive to the external environment.
3. Maintenance of body temperature by sweating and increasing and decreasing the blood flow to the skin.
4. Production of vitamin D by the action of ultraviolet light (see Sect. 16.6).

QUESTIONS

1. List and describe the five conditions necessary for life, relating these where possible to the principles of food preservation.
2. Construct a diagram to show the structure of a generalised animal cell. Briefly state the functions of each component.

3. Explain the term 'cellular differentiation'.
4. Draw a fully labelled diagram of the human skin. Explain why this is an example of an organ. Explain how the skin attempts to control the body temperature of a caterer working in a hot kitchen.
5. Compare a eukaryotic cell and a prokaryotic cell. Name the important group of prokaryotic organisms encountered in catering.

11

MICRO-ORGANISMS

11.1 INTRODUCTION

The microbial world includes the kingdoms Protista (protozoa, algae and fungi), Prokaryota (bacteria), and the viruses, all of which have a relevance to catering. These three groups although being very different in many respects have two main properties in common – their relatively small size and similar methods of study. Microbiology is the study of these micro-organisms (Greek *mikros* = small, *bios* = life). Within microbiology, bacteriology is the study of bacteria, virology is the study of viruses and mycology the study of fungi.

Microbiology really began after the development of the microscope. Certain bacteria and some of the protista were first described by Antonie van Leeuwenhoek in about 1674. Van Leeuwenhoek was probably not the first to see these micro-organisms but he was the first to publish his observations with accurate drawings and descriptions. He named these small life forms animalicules. Although the early studies were important it is only in the last 130 years that techniques of cultivation and microscopy have advanced sufficiently to make the science so important. Louis Pasteur, a brilliant chemist, surprised the wine industry in France by showing that spoilage of wine was often caused by specific micro-organisms. Heating the grape juice used in wine making prevented spoilage. The same technique forms the basis of the present pasteurisation process to preserve foods. In addition to his work on food, Pasteur made a considerable contribution to medical microbiology.

Viruses, due to their even smaller size and ultraparasitic mode of existence, have proved more difficult to study. Although their existence was demonstrated nearly 100 years ago and considerable knowledge has been gained in the last 40 years, more information about them is required. Their role in causing food-transmitted diseases is one area needing further study.

11.2   THE VIRUSES

Viruses are acellular particles ranging from 20 to 300 nm in size. Although viruses vary in shape most are either rod-shaped or icosahedrons (20-sided) (see Fig. 10.2 and Fig. 11.1).

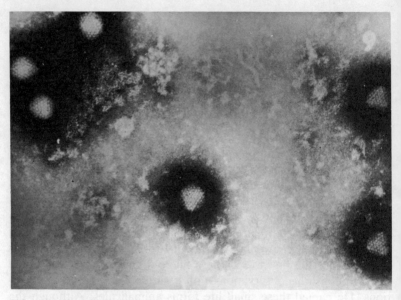

FIG. 11.1a   Electron micrograph of icosahedral virus particles

Viruses are very simple chemically, lacking many of the properties of living things (see Sect. 10.2) although they do possess the property of reproduction. Unlike bacteria or fungi which can grow in or on food, e.g. milk and bread, viruses are only capable of reproduction inside other living cells and are obligate intracellular parasites. The growth of a virus inside a cell results in the death of that cell. Viruses are specific in their choice of host cell. Plant viruses can only reproduce in certain plant cells, bacterial viruses called bacteriophages can only reproduce in particular bacterial cells. Similarly animal viruses are highly specific, e.g. the common cold virus only grows in cells of the human respiratory tract. Bacteriophages may be responsible for the killing of dairy starter cultures used in cheese making.

Viruses are widely distributed and although not actively growing can be isolated from soil, water, sewage, air, food, clothing, etc. It is known that a large number of enteric (gut) viruses can be trans-

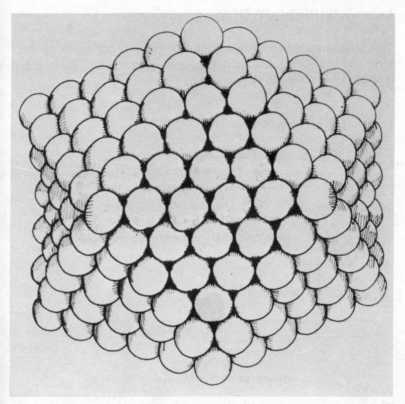

FIG. 11.1b Model of an icosahedral virus particle

mitted in food although it is not known how often the consumption of virus-infected food actually results in illness. This lack of information is due largely to the fact that viruses are much more difficult to isolate and cultivate from food samples than are bacteria. The illnesses caused by these enteric viruses range from simple stomach upsets (diarrhoea and vomiting) to more serious infections including polio and infectious hepatitis. Fortunately polio is now largely controlled by immunisation. This is not so for infectious hepatitis which is a problem where foods are produced or prepared in an unhygienic manner. Recent evidence has pin-pointed the consumption of virus-infected cockles in the contraction of infectious hepatitis which could lead to a revision of shellfish cooking methods. Careful breeding of shellfish is necessary to avoid contamination by sewage and the enteric viruses this would contain. Personal hygiene of food handlers is important so that they also do not contaminate the food with potentially harmful virus particles.

11.3 THE PROKARYOTA

This kingdom consists of two groups of micro-organisms – the bacteria and the blue-green algae (the cyanophytes). This latter group is of no importance to the caterer.

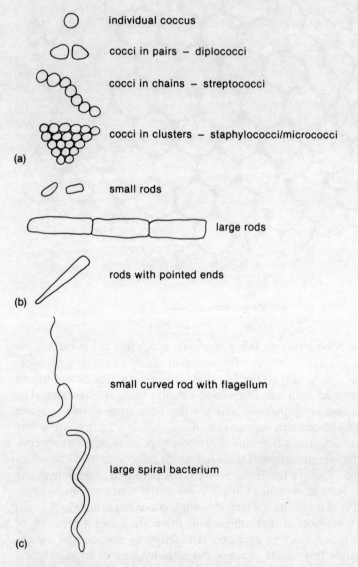

FIG. 11.2 Main shapes and groupings of bacteria (a) Round coccus (plural cocci) (b) Rod shaped (c) Spiral/curved rods

Bacteria are unicellular organisms mostly measuring between 0.5 μm and 12 μm in size, the exact size depending on the shape. If examined under the microscope three main shapes of bacteria are found (see Fig. 11.2):

(a) oval/spherical;
(b) rod-shaped (see Fig. 11.3);
(c) spiral/curved.

The cells of some species of bacteria grow together in a characteristic manner, e.g. chains or clusters. Under the microscope, after staining, some of the properties of the bacteria can be seen. Some of the bacteria are found to have flagellae (hair-like structures), either singly or all the way round. Flagellae are made up of contractile protein and enable bacteria to be motile (move).

Two groups of bacteria, *Bacillus* and *Clostridium*, can produce spores and these are extremely important to the food industry. Spores are dormant, resistant structures capable of surviving very long periods (tens of years) of adverse or unfavourable conditions (see Table 11.1).

Spores, being resistant, are difficult to remove from food and could germinate giving rise to bacteria so causing food spoilage and food poisoning.

Some other bacteria have, in addition to the typical bacterial cell wall, a jelly-like layer called a capsule around them. Capsule-forming

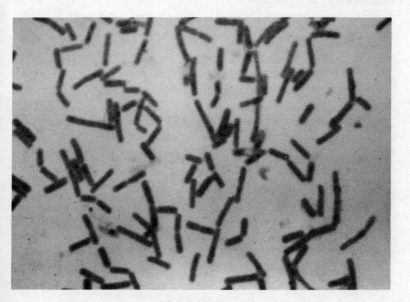

FIG. 11.3 Micrograph of rod-shaped bacteria

TABLE 11.1 Resistance of bacterial spores

Resistance to	Implications
Heat	Can survive cooking and inadequate food processing
Cold	Survive freezing easily
Chemicals	Resistant to disinfectants
Lack of food and water	Can survive years in soil and dust
Radiation	Resistant to ultraviolet radiation

bacteria growing in food may cause a type of spoilage known as 'rope', so called because of the sticky/slimy strands of bacterial growth. Rope can be found spoiling beer, raw milk, home baked bread and sometimes commercially baked bread.

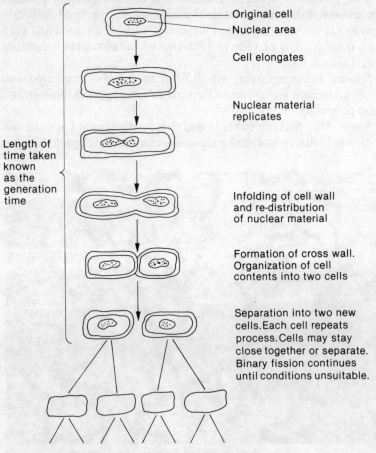

FIG. 11.4 Binary fission in a rod-shaped bacterium

When bacteria are reproducing they do so by a simple process of splitting into two – called binary fission (see Fig. 11.4).

Before growth (see Ch. 14) takes place bacteria must have an adequate nutrient supply. Some bacteria are autotrophic (literally 'self-feeding') (see Sect. 15.2) but it is the heterotrophic ones (literally 'fed by others') that are important to the food industry. These heterotrophic bacteria can be:

(a) saprophytes and spoil foods, e.g. souring of milk;
(b) parasites and cause diseases, e.g. typhoid, cholera and brucellosis;
(c) facultatively parasitic and cause food poisoning, e.g. *Salmonella*.

So far it is the harmful aspects of bacteria which have been mentioned but of all the very large number of bacteria it is a very small number that cause problems to humans and it must be remembered that some bacteria are extremely useful to Man (see Table 11.2 and Fig. 11.5). The uses range from soil fertility, sewage disposal, production of vinegar, butter, cheese and yoghurt, to the natural fer-

TABLE 11.2 Importance of micro-organisms to the food industry

Micro-organism	Helpful aspects	Harmful aspects
Virus		Food-borne diseases Killing of bacterial starter cultures, e.g. in cheese making
Bacteria	Dairy industry, cheese, butter, etc. Manufacture of vinegar Food fermentation Soil fertility in agriculture	Food poisoning Food-borne diseases Animal/plant diseases Food spoilage Blocking pipes/holding up industrial processes
Algae	Source of food	Unpleasant tastes in drinking water
Protozoa Fungi	Produce cellulase	Food-borne diseases
1. Yeasts	Source of protein and vitamins Breadmaking Alcoholic beverages	Food spoilage
2. Moulds	Mould ripened cheeses Food fermentations Food (e.g. mushrooms) Soil fertility	Food spoilage Certain types of food poisoning Plant diseases

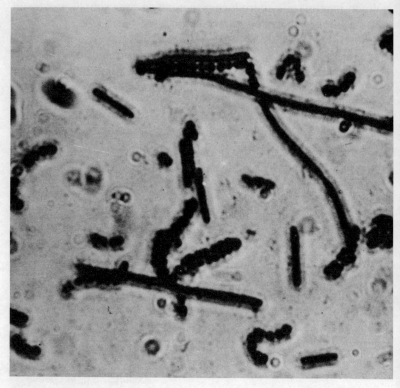

FIG. 11.5 Micrograph of bacteria – rods and chains of cocci growing in yoghurt

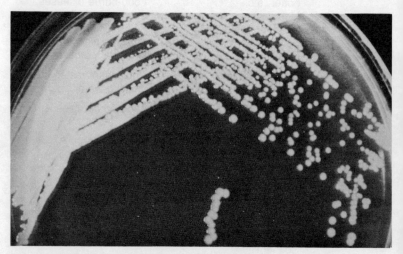

FIG. 11.6 Bacterial colonies growing on nutrient agar

mentation important in making cocoa and coffee beans. Bacteria are also used for the commercial production of enzymes.

Individual bacteria can be studied by microscopy but, in addition, microbiologists can cultivate bacteria using nutrient media. If grown on solid media containing agar, bacteria appear as colonies, each colony consisting of millions of more or less identical cells (see Fig. 11.6).

11.4 THE ALGAE

These are plant-like organisms which range in size from being microscopic and unicellular to being very large and multicellular (e.g. seaweeds). Algae are not very important to the food industry at the moment although in the future they may become more useful as a relatively cheap source of protein.

11.5 THE PROTOZOA

The protozoa is a diverse group containing unicellular animal-like organisms. They range in size from approximately 10 to 500 μm. Protozoa are widely distributed in soil and water and while most are harmless, some are capable of causing disease. Human diseases caused by protozoa include malaria and sleeping sickness which affect millions of people world-wide. Diseases caused by protozoa transmitted in contaminated food include amoebic dysentery (*Entamoeba histolytica*) which is not common in the UK but is endemic in certain parts of the world, and it has been estimated that 60 per cent of people in the Tropics harbour the parasite in their intestines. *Giardia lamblia* causes giardiasis, a disease spread in food and drink and is more common in the UK. Both *Entamoeba* and *Giardia* may be suspected in people returning from abroad with stomach upsets. *Toxoplasma gondii* is a parasitic protozoan which may be contracted from contaminated food or directly from infected dogs and cats.

11.6 FUNGI

The fungi are a plant-like group of organisms which lack chlorophyll and hence cannot make their own food, thus they live as parasites or saprophytes (see Sect. 15.4.3). Approximately 100 000 different types of fungi have so far been identified and are widely distributed in Nature, being found in air, water, soil, skin or the outside of plants, etc. Fungi vary in size from the unicellular organisms, e.g. yeasts which are approximately 10 μm in size, to the large multicellular fungi, e.g. giant mushrooms, puff balls, bracket fungi, etc. Fungi can be conveniently split into two groups, the moulds and the yeasts.

Moulds are multicellular and can often be seen growing with a cotton wool appearance made up of many long strands or filaments known as hyphae. A collection of these hyphae is known as a mycelium, i.e. a visible mould growth. The hyphae produce spores which may be coloured and make the mycelium appear coloured, e.g. some *Penicillium* appear green. Mould spores are important for reproduction and enable the mould to spread.

There are different types of mould spores but none are as resistant as bacterial spores (see Table 11.1). Some are formed in large numbers and being light can drift about on air currents inside or outside buildings. When spores find a suitable place to grow, which can range from a loaf of bread to damp wallpaper or leather, they ger-

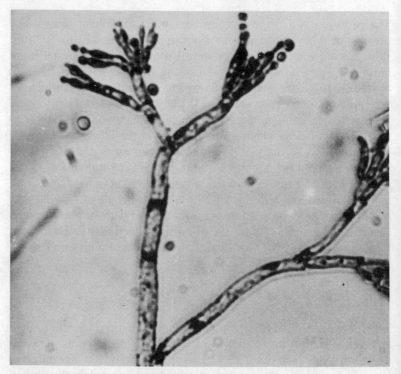

FIG. 11.7 Hyphae of *Penicillium* producing spores

minate and a new mycelium is formed. In turn the mycelium produces more spores and the whole cycle is repeated. The growth of moulds on food causes spoilage which is of considerable economic importance, costing the baking industry alone millions of pounds a year. Moulds can also grow on cakes, fruits, vegetables and meats. High levels of mould spores in the atmosphere increase the chances of mould spoilage. Some species of mould are capable of producing harmful toxins, known as mycotoxins, when growing on food, e.g. *Aspergillus flavus* when growing on nuts produces aflatoxin.

In other cases the growth of mould on food is actively encouraged, e.g. *Penicillium roqueforti* is essential for the ripening and flavouring of blue-veined cheeses. Moulds can also be useful in enzyme, vitamin and antibiotic production, as well as in fermentations leading to the production of exotic foods, e.g. *Aspergillus oryzae* in the production of soy sauce.

Yeasts typically grow as single cells, being oval or spherical in shape with a vacuole taking up approximately one-third of the cytoplasm. Although some yeasts can form spores, the main method of reproduction of all yeasts is a process known as budding (see Fig. 11.8).

In budding a swelling or bud grows out from the mother cell; when it is approximately equal in size, a cross wall then forms between the two and they separate. Yeasts are well known for their

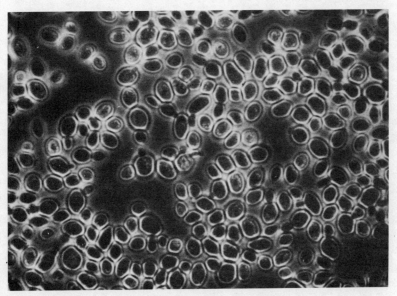

FIG. 11.8 Cells of yeast *Saccharomyces*. Some are budding

beneficial uses and have helped Man for centuries in leavening bread and in making alcoholic drinks. Their importance is even greater today, being used not only as a source of protein and vitamins but also in the production of vinegar and industrial alcohol. Unfortunately yeasts may also be undesirable causing plant and animal diseases and food spoilage, e.g. of jams, beers and wines.

QUESTIONS

1. What two properties do most micro-organisms have in common? List three major groups of micro-organisms and explain their importance to the food industry.
2. Illustrate and describe the three main shapes of bacteria. Which two shapes may be encountered in a smear of yoghurt?
3. Discuss the properties of bacterial spores and describe their importance to the food industry.
4. What are hyphae and what are a collection of hyphae known as? Name two organisms capable of producing hyphae, one which is of advantage to the food industry and one which is of disadvantage to the food industry.
5. What shape are yeasts? How do yeasts normally reproduce? List two reasons why yeasts may be desirable to the food industry and one reason why they may be undesirable.

THE PLANT KINGDOM

12.1 INTRODUCTION

The plant kingdom includes relatively simple organisms, such as the Bryophytes (liverworts and mosses), the Pteridophytes (ferns and bracken) which are more complex and the Spermatophytes (coniferous trees and the flowering plants) which show the greatest degree of complexity (see Table 12.1).

Plants differ from animals in a number of ways, the most important being that they are autotrophic and can produce organic nutrients from inorganic substances (see Table 12.2).

Animals, including Man, are completely dependent on plants as

TABLE 12.1 Classification of the plant kingdom

Phylum bryophyta	Liverworts
No vascular tissue	Not differentiated
	Mosses
	Stems and leaves, no true roots
Phylum pteridophyta	
Green plants with stems, leaves, true roots, etc. but no flowers, e.g. ferns, bracken, horsetails. etc.	
Phylum spermatophyta	*Gymnosperms*
Produce seeds	Naked seeds, not enclosed in a fruit, e.g. conifers have cones instead of flowers
	Angiosperms
	Flowering plants, seeds enclosed in some sort of fruit
	Dicotyledons 2 seed leaves, e.g. buttercup, rose, oak.
	Monocotyledons 1 seed leaf, e.g. grasses, lily

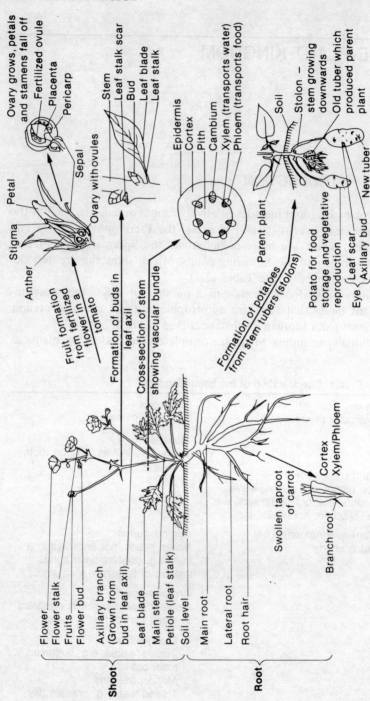

FIG. 12.1 A generalized dicotyledenous flowering plant

TABLE 12.2 Differences between plants and animals

Plants	Animals
Autotrophic	Heterotrophic
Can carry out photosynthesis	Cannot carry out photosynthesis
Generally remain in one place	Move about in search of food
Can produce lignin to give rigidity to tissues	Lignin is never found in animals
Growth is often restricted to certain regions, e.g. the tips of roots and shoots, and may continue for a long time	Growth occurs throughout the body and for a limited period only
Plant cells are generally larger with a more distinct shape	Animal cells are generally smaller with a less distinct shape
Cells have a cellulose cell wall	Cells lack a cell wall
Cells usually have a large central vacuole	Vacuoles are rarely present in cells, if they are present they are usually small.
Cells contain chloroplasts	Cells lack chloroplasts
Store carbohydrate in the form of starch	Store carbohydrate in the form of glycogen

producers of nutrients (see Sect. 15.6). In addition Man uses plants as a source of many raw materials which he needs for his day-to-day existence.

The kingdom Plantae is sub-classified into phyla, classes, orders, etc. in the same way as animals. Most of the plants on which Man relies for his food come from one section of the plant kingdom, the Angiosperms or flowering plants (see Table 12.1). Caterers rather than use the scientific classification divide plant foods into the three categories of fruit, vegetable and cereal, depending on their use. Fruits are sweet and are used as desserts, whereas vegetables are savoury. Rhubarb is a fruit in culinary terms although botanically it is a vegetable. Tomatoes are fruits although they are used as vegetables in the kitchen. Thus culinary classification may bear relationship to a botanical one, although there is little disparity between the culinary and botanical application of the term cereal.

12.2   THE STRUCTURE OF A FLOWERING PLANT

A flowering plant can be divided simply into two parts, a part above the ground, the shoot, and a part below the ground, the root (see Fig. 12.1).

This simple division is not completely true as not all underground structures are derived from the root system. Much of the shoot is modified into leaves, structures which have a large surface area relative to their thickness, thus adapting them for their role in photosynthesis (see Sect. 15.2). The stem contains vascular tissue, xylem and phloem, which enables the transport of water and food materials, respectively, around the plant. The root is concerned with the uptake of water and dissolved salts from the soil and helps to form a firm anchorage for the plant. The water is required for photosynthesis and to maintain cell turgidity (see Sect. 14.5.2).

Surplus food produced in the leaves which is not required for the immediate metabolism of the plant is stored in the vegetative parts of the plant as starch. The exact location of starch storage varies between different species but is used the following spring for rapid growth. The potato plant, for example, stores its starch in tubers (potatoes) which are modified stem structures. Carrots store their starch in the root (see Fig. 12.1). Man utilises food stores as vegetable food commodities.

The plant reproduces by production of flowers which, when fertilised, can give rise to fruits and seeds, all of which may be used as food sources, depending on the particular species.

12.3 PLANTS AS FOODS

12.3.1 VEGETATIVE PARTS

The Stem

Stems have buds closely associated with leaves or leaf scars. The stem is often erect but can be horizontal, and may be short, long, thin or thick depending on the particular plant. Xylem is important for the transport of water and dissolved salts from the roots to other parts of the plant, phloem transports sugars and other foods manufactured by the leaves to other parts of the plant. The potato is a stem tuber, the 'eye' of the potato being a bud which sprouts in the spring to form a new plant. Asparagus is a stem vegetable with a leafless stem. In older stems the vascular tissue can become woody or lignified and cause stringiness.

The leaf

Leaves are flat, usually green structures which have large surface areas, their primary function being to photosynthesise. Examples of leaf vegetables are cabbage, lettuce, spinach and parsley. In rhubarb and celery it is the leaf stalk which is eaten, and in rhubarb the leaf itself is poisonous due to the high content of ethanedioic (oxalic) acid.

Buds

Buds can be thought of as short shoots with closely packed leaves which develop in the leaf axil (the angle between the leaf and the stem). Brussels sprouts are buds which develop above ground level whereas bulbs, e.g. onions, shallots and garlic, are underground buds, which have fleshy leaves full of stored food.

Roots

Roots can be distinguished by the fact that they do not have leaves or buds. Examples of root vegetables include carrots, chicory and parsnips.

12.3.2 REPRODUCTIVE PARTS

Flowers

Cauliflowers and broccoli are flowers which are used by Man as foods. Flowers are the sexual parts of a plant and produce either pollen or ovules, or both pollen and ovules. The pollen is produced by the male part of the flower and has to be carried to the female part of the flower in a process known as pollination, utilising wind, insect or other transport. The ovules develop in ovaries from which extends a style divided at the tip into the stigma. The structure of a flower is shown in Fig. 12.1.

Fruits

Pollen landing on the stigma can fertilise the ovule which develops into a seed. A fruit is a matured ovary complete with seed (see Fig. 12.2) and this definition would include peas, beans, tomatoes and cucumbers which would not normally be classed as fruits in the kitchen.

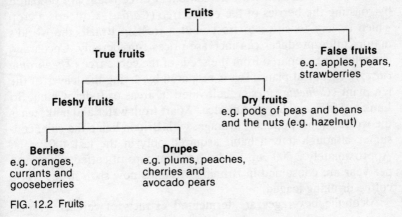

FIG. 12.2 Fruits

Fruits are divided into true and false fruits. In true fruits the ovary develops to form the fruit, in false fruits the edible portion is formed from some other part of the flower, e.g. apples, pears and strawberries which are formed from a swollen receptacle. True fruits are further subdivided into the fleshy fruits and the dry fruits (see Fig. 12.2).

Seeds

Seeds are the fertilised ovules of the flower and can germinate under suitable conditions to form new plants. They contain a reserve of food which is essential for the initial growth of the plant before it is able to produce its own food by photosynthesis. Seeds are important food sources for Man and include peas, beans and cereals. Peas and beans form an important protein source in vegetarian diets and some, e.g. soya beans contain more protein than the same mass of meat or fish, and are used as meat substitutes. Cereals are the seeds of grasses, e.g. rice, wheat, maize, oats and barley, and these form the basis of the diet in many parts of the world. It was the cultivation of grains for food which encouraged Man to end his nomadic existence of hunting for food and develop stationary communities. Cereals can be used whole or ground into flours. Not all flours are of cereal origin, e.g. sago which is obtained from the trunk of the sago palm, tapioca from the root of the cassava plant, and arrowroot from the tubers of the maranta plant. These are termed farinaceous non-cereals, i.e. flours not of cereal origin.

12.3.3 BEVERAGE PLANTS AND BEVERAGES

Cocoa, coffee and tea are widely consumed by Man, acting as mild stimulants due to their caffeine content. Coffee beans are prepared by roasting the berries of the coffee tree (*Coffea*). Coffee is a crop which is very sensitive to frost, and a frost in Brazil, the world's major coffee producer can increase prices considerably. Cocoa and chocolate are prepared from the seeds of the cocoa tree (*Theobroma cacao*), a tropical plant. Tea is prepared by drying the leaves of the tea plant (*Camellia sinesis*), cultivated in areas of India, China, Sri Lanka, Africa and South America. Apart from water and milk, tea is the world's most popular beverage, with Britain being the chief consumer although it is a habit acquired only in the last 100 years. Approximately 2 500 cups of tea and 750 cups of coffee per person per year are consumed in Britain. Britain is now sixth in the world coffee drinking league.

Alcoholic beverages are fermented extracts of cereals, grapes, apples and pears (beers, wine, cider and perry, respectively). Whisky, brandy, rum, gin and a whole range of liqueurs are produced by the concentration of alcoholic beverages by distillation.

12.3.4   HERBS AND SPICES

Herbs and spices have been important for centuries in the seasoning of food. Their aromatic qualities help to overcome the flavour of food which may otherwise be unpalatable. Herbs and spices have little nutritional value but can greatly enhance the flavour of a dish. A list of some of the important herbs and spices is shown in Table 12.3.

TABLE 12.3 Some important spices

Part of plant	Examples
Roots	Angelica
	Ginger
	Horseradish
	Sarsaparilla
	Turmeric
Bark	Cinnamon
Flowers	Cloves
	Saffron
Fruits	Peppers
	Paprikas
	Chillis
	Vanilla
Seeds	Caraway
	Cumin
	Cardamom
	Mustard
Leaves	Peppermint
	Sage
	Spearmint
	Thyme
	Basil

12.4   PLANTS AS THE PROVIDERS OF RAW MATERIALS

Apart from providing food, plants are useful in a variety of other ways. It would be impossible to list all their uses and only a few of their important commercial applications are outlined below.

Timber
Wood is a very strong material and can be used structurally and decoratively in buildings and for furniture. Wood is derived from the stems of gymnosperms and angiosperms (see Table 12.1), e.g. teak, pine, oak and mahogany.

Plant fibres
Vascular tissue which causes stringiness in plant foods can be extracted to give fibres. Fibres can be found in almost any part of the plant, e.g. cotton is obtained from the seed of the cotton plant, linen from the stem of the flax plant.

Plant dyes
In the dyeing of textiles the use of plant dyes has been almost superseded by modern dyes obtained from coal tar, but in the colouring of food, plant dyes are still of major importance, e.g. annatto extract used in the colouring of margarine.

Tannins
Tannins can be extracted from plants and are complex organic salts which combine with iron to form dark blue or greenish-black compounds which are used in inks. Tannins are also used in the preparation of leather. If tea is stewed then tannin is extracted from the leaves and gives a bitter taste.

Rubber and other latex products
Rubber is obtained from the phloem of certain woody plants as a milky juice and finds widespread use, e.g. in the production of car tyres.

Essential oils
Strongly aromatic extracts can be prepared from a number of different plants, e.g. mint, ginger, rose, cedar, etc. and can be used as perfumes and flavouring agents.

Gums and resins
Gums exude naturally from stems and many are used as adhesives. Gum tragacanth and gum arabic are used in catering as stabilising, emulsifying and thickening agents. Resins are usually solid, transparent substances which are produced by tree trunks. Many resins are obtained from fossilised tree remains, e.g. amber which is used for decorative purposes. Resins are used as lacquers and in the production of paints, inks, plastics and adhesives.

Waxes
Waxes are found on the outside of stems, leaves and fruits where they reduce the loss of water from the plant. Waxes can be used in the manufacture of soaps, candles, varnishes, etc.

Fuels
The fossilised remains of plants has given rise to fossil fuels, e.g. coal (see Sect. 2.4.2).

Medicines and drugs
Many of our modern medicines and drugs are based on the active ingredients contained in a wide range of herbal remedies. Foxglove leaves contain digitalis which is used in the treatment of heart conditions, quinine is used in the treatment of malaria and was originally obtained from the bark of the cinchona tree by Indians in South America. Drugs such as cocaine and opium are plant extracts and are useful for the relief of pain although they may become undesirable and habit-forming addictions.

Gelling agents
Jams are prepared with the aid of pectin which is a complex polysaccharide found in fruits. Some fruits, such as the apple, are particularly good sources of pectin and extracts of these fruits are often added to those with a low pectin content to help gelling during the production of jams and jellies.

QUESTIONS

1. Describe the ways in which caterers classify foods of plant origin and explain, with examples, how this differs from a scientific classification.
2. From which part of a plant do each of the following vegetables originate?
   (a) Brussels sprouts;   (e) potatoes;
   (b) cabbage;   (f) carrot;
   (c) onion;   (g) celery;
   (d) asparagus;   (h) broccoli.
3. Illustrate the structure of a typical flowering plant, discussing the importance of the parts above soil level and the parts below.
4. List three examples of seeds used as food sources. Explain the terms 'cereal' and 'farinaceous non-cereal'.
5. List with examples five non-food uses of plants.

13

THE ANIMAL KINGDOM

13.1 INTRODUCTION

The animal kingdom is divided into nine phyla and consists of organisms which range from the simple Porifera (Sponges) to the most complex organism of all, Man. Eight of these phyla can be grouped together as invertebrates (animals without backbones). One phylum, the Chordates, contains the vertebrates (animals with backbones). Fig. 13.1 shows the nine phyla with examples of

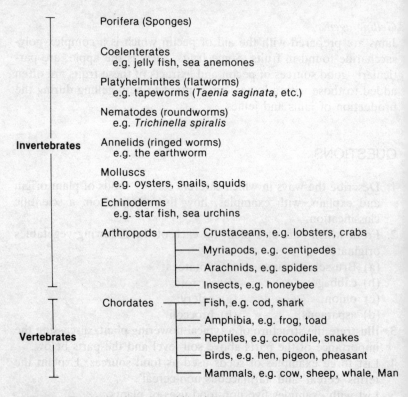

FIG. 13.1 The phyla of the animal kingdom

representative organisms, many of which are important to the food industry.

For caterers it is perhaps more useful to consider animals either as an aid or a detriment (harmful) to the food industry.

13.2   THE ANIMAL KINGDOM: HELPFUL TO THE FOOD INDUSTRY

Although animals can be useful to Man in many ways, e.g. the earthworm helps to fertilise and refine the soils, it is as providers of food that animals are mainly exploited. Some invertebrates are eaten but it is the vertebrates that are the most important food sources.

13.2.1   THE INVERTEBRATES

Of the invertebrate phyla used as food the molluscs, echinoderms and arthropods are the most important. Oysters, mussels, winkles, cockles, squids and snails are all molluscs consumed by Man, and are considered delicacies. More exotic dishes such as the starfish, sea cucumbers and sea urchins are echinoderms. As shown in Fig. 13.1 the arthropods consist of four classes, the crustaceans, myriapods, arachnids and insects. Important crustacean foods include lobsters, crabs, crayfish, prawns and shrimps. Myriapods, arachnids and insects are of little direct value as food as they are seldom, if ever, eaten in the United Kingdom, although in parts of Africa locusts are often consumed by Man in large quantities when no other food is available. The honeybee is an important insect to Man providing him with a valuable dietary commodity – honey.

13.2.2   THE VERTEBRATES

The vertebrates are divided into five classes (fish, amphibia, reptiles, birds and mammals) and provide a large proportion of our animal foods. With a few exceptions, such as frog's legs, turtle soup and crocodile or snakeskin handbags, the amphibians and reptiles are not of great importance and it is the fish, birds and mammals which are mainly exploited.

Fish
We eat a wide range of fish which provide a valuable source of protein and certain vitamins. Characteristics of fish are that they live

in water (either sea-water or fresh water), breathe through gills and are covered with overlapping scales. There are two sorts of fish, the cartilaginous fish (e.g. the shark and the dogfish) and the bony fish (e.g. the cod), whose bones are more brittle because they contain more calcium salts. In the kitchen, fish are divided into two different groups, the oily fish and the white fish. The flesh of oily fish contains about 20 per cent fat whereas white fish contains only about 3 per cent. White fish can be subdivided into round fish (e.g. hake, haddock and cod) and flat fish, which are found near the sea bed (e.g. skate, halibut, plaice and sole). Examples of oily fish include herring, mackerel, salmon and trout. Caviare is the salted roe (eggs) of the sturgeon and is considered a great delicacy. Fish liver oils are utilised as valuable sources of the vitamins A and D.

Although many fish are caught 'wild' Man has found that by providing the right conditions fish can be 'farmed', thus guaranteeing a steady supply. Trout are the most common farmed fish and they can be used for the artificial stocking of rivers and reservoirs.

Due to restrictions on traditional fishing grounds attempts are being made to introduce less well known fish species to the British diet.

Birds

Birds are vertebrates whose characteristics include forelimbs which are modified into wings (although not all can fly), skins covered in feathers and the laying of eggs from which their young hatch. Goose and duck feathers are used for bedding (pillows and quilts) and osprey feathers are much prized in millinery. As sources of food birds fall into two categories, 'domesticated' birds and 'game' birds. Domesticated birds, such as chickens, turkeys, ducks and geese, are used as meat or for their eggs which are collected for use directly as foods or as ingredients in a whole range of products. Flightless birds, e.g. hens and turkeys, have lighter coloured breast muscle (whiter meat) than flighted birds, e.g. ducks and geese, since less blood flows to the muscle. Force feeding of poultry produces the enlarged liver used to prepare paté. Game birds are usually only half wild, being managed on country estates ready for the shoot. Game birds include partridge, pheasant, quail and grouse.

Mammals

Mammals give birth to live young which they suckle, that is feed on milk produced by the mother. Some mammals have adapted readily to domestication, e.g. cows, horses, sheep, goats and pigs. Mammals are used for food including meat and dairy products, for clothing (leather, sheepskin and wool) and for transport (horses, cattle and elephants). Selective breeding has considerably improved specific aspects of food production (e.g. milk production). Friesian or Jersey cattle are high milk yielders, whereas Aberdeen Angus and Charollais are bred as beef cattle. Sheep and pigs are also 'improved' by selective breeding, e.g. in pigs the market value is determined by the 'red-white ratio', i.e. the relative amounts of meat and fat in the carcass, and a combination of breeding and nutrition seeks to improve this ratio.

Increasing demand for food has resulted in a trend towards intensive farming methods. Most of our pork is produced today by intensive or 'battery' farming where a close watch is kept on overall efficiency to ensure the maximum output of meat is achieved for the minimum input of feed. Intensive farming methods of this type often employ the use of a computer and are extremely cost effective. Similarly most of our hens are produced by battery farming. One delicacy which requires specific farming practice is the production of veal, the meat of calves. To produce the characteristic pale-pink meat the calf is fed on milk and kept in a confined space to restrict movement and minimise blood flow to the muscles.

As well as domesticated mammals, game mammals are also used as sources of food. Game mammals are divided into two groups: furred game, e.g. hares and rabbits; and hoofed game which in Britain is mainly deer yielding venison.

13.3   THE ANIMAL KINGDOM: HARMFUL TO THE FOOD INDUSTRY

A variety of organisms in the animal kingdom can be considered undesirable to the food industry and the caterer, i.e. as pests. These range from the invertebrate worms to the vertebrate rodents.

13.3.1   PARASITIC WORMS

Two groups of worms may cause problems to the food industry – the flatworms (platyhelminthes) (see Table 13.1) and the roundworms (nematodes) (see Table 13.2).

Both these types of worm are distinct from the common earthworm (annelids) which helps the farmer.

TABLE 13.1 Tapeworms and their animal hosts

Animal	Tapeworm
Fish	*Diphylobothrium latum*
Cattle	*Taenia saginata*
Pig	*Taenia solium*
Cats/dogs	*Diplidium caninum*
Sheep/dogs	*Echinococcus granulosum*

TABLE 13.2 Round worms and their animal hosts

Animal	Roundworm
Dog	*Toxacara canis*
Cat	*Toxacara cati*
Man/rat/pig	*Trichinella spiralis*
Man	*Ascaris lumbricoides*

Flatworms include the tapeworm group and a number of animals may harbour tapeworms. Tapeworms can be passed on to humans either indirectly via food which has been improperly cooked, e.g. fish, beef, lamb, pork, etc., or through direct contact, e.g. with cats and dogs.

The pork tapeworm (*Taenia solium*) infects pigs and can be passed on to humans where it may grow up to 4 m in length. The tapeworm has a long thin segmented body capable of producing large numbers of eggs (see Fig. 13.2).

Fortunately in the United Kingdom tapeworms are not a common problem and it is the job of meat inspectors working in abattoirs (slaughterhouses) to ensure that meat going to the butcher is free from such parasites.

Apart from tapeworms other platyhelminth worms may cause diseases in Man and animals, e.g. schistosomiasis which is spread in infected water and liver fluke of sheep which in rare cases is spread to humans via infected watercress.

Nematode (round) worms may be free living in soil but can also infect humans, other animals and plants. Direct infection can occur from cats, dogs and other pets, which should not be allowed in food preparation areas. As with tapeworms, proper cooking of food and good hygiene are essential to prevent the transfer of roundworms to humans. Proper food inspection is necessary to prevent infected food reaching the public. Trichinosis (caused by *Trichinella spiralis*) is the most important human roundworm infection spread in food and can occur after eating infected pork (called 'measly' pork because of its spotted appearance (see Fig. 13.3)).

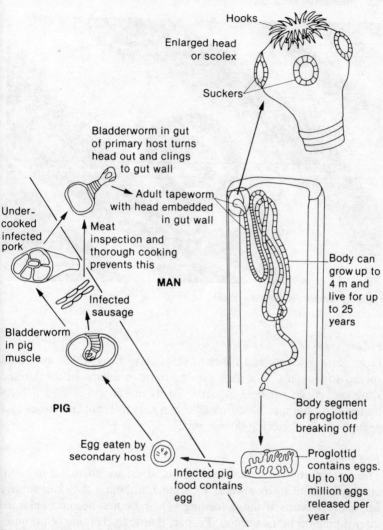

FIG. 13.2 Life cycle of a pork tapeworm

13.3.2 INSECTS

Insects may cause problems for the caterer in a number of ways: by irritating the guests (e.g. fleas and bed bugs); damaging furnishings (e.g. moths and carpet beetles); spreading or carrying diseases (cockroaches and house flies); spoiling stored foods (e.g. moths, weevils and mites); or their general nuisance value (e.g. silverfish, ants and wasps).

FIG. 13.3 *Trichinella spiralis* in meat

Fleas
Dogs, cats, rodents and other animals carry fleas which may then spread to humans. The flea causing most problems in the United Kingdom is the cat flea. Apart from its nuisance value as it bites humans to obtain a 'blood meal' it can also transmit infections (yet again pets and catering do not mix!).

Bed bugs
These are particularly unpleasant pests which are nocturnal in habit, emerging about once a week for a meal, although they can survive for many months without feeding. Their bodies become enlarged after dining on human blood. Proper, thorough cleaning of premises combined with frequent changing of blankets and linen helps to control this pest.

Clothes moth (*see Fig. 13.4*)
The adult moth lays eggs in or on clothes or fabrics and these develop into larvae which can then take up to 10 months to develop into pupae. The larval stage is the problem as it feeds mainly on the keratin content of wool thus leaving a tell-tale hole. The clothes moth may attack clothing, blankets, carpets and furnishings at most times of the year, but particularly in late spring, illustrating the need for spring cleaning. Moth balls can be used to deter moths from

entering wardrobes or slow-release insecticides, lasting about four months, can kill the moths after gaining access. Alternatively sprays containing pyrethrum can be used to proof garments so that larvae eating the garments will die soon afterwards.

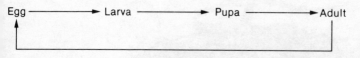

FIG. 13.4 Life cycle of the clothes moth

Carpet beetle (see Fig. 13.5)
Again it is the larval stage, the so called 'woolly bears', which causes the most damage. The larvae attack wool in carpets, curtains, blan-

FIG. 13.5 Adults and larvae (woolly bears) of the carpet beetle (*Anthrenus verbasci*) on damaged fabric (Rentokil Ltd.)

kets, fabric covers, etc. producing bare patches. Hairs from the larvae may also irritate people. This pest is increasing in importance and seems to be associated with increased use of fitted carpets and is more of a problem in the affluent south-east of the United Kingdom. Thorough vacuuming of carpets, especially under beds, settees, tables and other furniture is a good preventive measure.

FIG. 13.6a Female Black beetle (*Blatta orientalis*) (Rentokil Ltd)

FIG. 13.6b Wall-ceiling junction showing cockroaches congregating around a water pipe and electricity cables (Rentokil Ltd)

Insecticides containing permethrin can be used to proof clothing and carpets which are susceptible to attack all the year round. Previously low winter temperatures interrupted the insect's life cycle but central heating now provides suitable growth conditions in the colder months.

Cockroaches (see Fig. 13.6a–d)

Cockroaches are perhaps the most important insect pest infesting catering premises. Two species are relevant to the caterer, the oriental cockroach (or black beetle) and the German cockroach (or steam fly). These pests not only spoil stored foods but also carry disease, contaminate food with their moult cases and taint it with an unpleasant odour. Cockroaches occupy crevices in walls and floors in warm inaccessible places and may be a particular problem in bakeries and public houses. Methods of preventing infestations

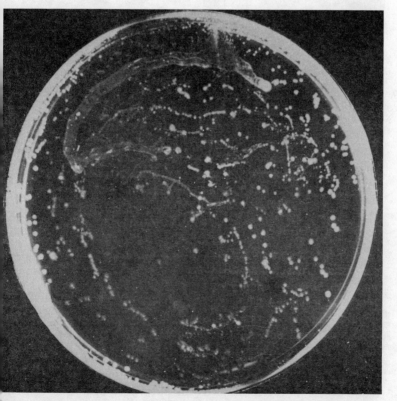

FIG. 13.6c An agar plate over which a cockroach has walked, inoculating the plate with potentially pathogenic bacteria. After incubation the bacteria grow to form large, easily visible colonies containing millions of individual cells (Rentokil Ltd)

FIG. 13.6d Application of insecticidal lacquer to metal stanchions of kitchen equipment where frequent washing may remove other applications of insecticide (Rentokil Ltd)

include the proper construction of premises and good hygiene. Infestations can be controlled by the use of insecticidal lacquers, sprays and baits (see Fig. 13.6d).

House fly (see Fig. 13.7a–d)
The adult house fly lays about 200 eggs which under ideal conditions may develop into adults within 10 days. Breeding grounds include food refuse and animal droppings. The problem with flies is that they contaminate food with harmful bacteria or the eggs of parasites (see Sect. 15.4.2). Contamination of food can occur in three ways: physical transfer on the body of the fly, contamination of the food with infected digestive juices or their droppings. Good hygiene and preventing access into buildings help to control fly populations. Once inside buildings flies can be killed by insecticidal sprays, slow release insecticides or electrocution (see Fig. 13.7d).

Electrocution is particularly useful in catering establishments as the flies are attracted towards an ultraviolet light which is surrounded by a charged cage. On touching the cage the flies are killed and their bodies caught in a tray.

FIG. 13.7a An adult common house fly (*Musca domestica*) (Rentokil Ltd)

Insects spoiling stored foods
Numerous types of insects are capable of spoiling stored foods and the two types most frequently involved are beetles and moths (see Table 13.3).

Mechanisms of control again include good hygiene and cleaning, rotation of stock, correctly designed containers and use of insecticides.

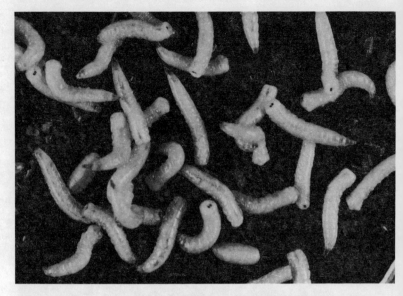

FIG. 13.7b Common house fly larvae, i.e. typical fly maggots (Rentokil Ltd)

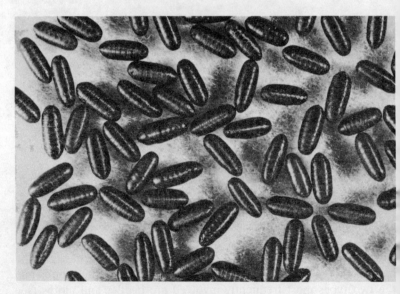

FIG. 13.7c Common house fly puparia (Rentokil Ltd)

FIG. 13.7d Electrocution unit consisting of an ultraviolet light which attracts flying insects to a charged cage and a tray to catch the dead flies (Rentokil Ltd)

TABLE 13.3 Insects spoiling stored foods

Insect	Example
Beetle	Larder beetle
	Confused flour beetle
	Biscuit beetle
	Saw-toothed grain beetle
Moth	Warehouse moth
	Mill moth
	Indian meal moth
Weevil	Grain weevil
Mite	Flour mite

13.3.3 RODENTS

Three types of rodent may cause infestations in catering premises (see Table 13.4).

Rodents are characterised by their gnawing habit and high breeding rate. Apart from the risk of disease spread by rodents they damage buildings, gnawing through wood, pipes and cables. They can spoil food and food packaging materials. A trained rodent operator can tell the type and approximate numbers of rodents causing an infestation just by inspecting the premises. Signs to look for include the frequency, distribution and type of droppings, the presence and position of grease marks, gnaw marks and footprints in dust and flour. Caterers can prevent infestation by correct building construction, cleaning of premises and correct storage of food and packaging materials. Control of established rodent infestations is usually best left to the experts. Measures a caterer may himself take include trapping (effective against small infestations only) or the use of a limited number of chronic rodenticides. Warfarin, the best known of these needs to be consumed by the rodent on repeated occasions over a period of about five days. Where serious damage to food occurs a caterer is legally obliged to report it to the authorities. In these cases trained rodent operators will use a variety of chronic or acute (single dose) rodenticides.

TABLE 13.4 Comparison of the three main types of rodent

Characteristic	Brown rat	Black rat	House mouse
Length (excl. tail)	25 cm	20 cm	6 cm
Average weight	340–400 g	230 g	Less than 30 g
Ears	Small, thick, with hair	Large, thin, no hair	Large furry
Muzzle	Blunt	Pointed	Pointed
Distribution	Urban/rural over UK	Large towns, ports	Any populated area
Habits	Burrows, swims, can climb	Non-burrowing agile climber	Climbs, sometimes burrows
Names	*Rattus norvegicus* Common rat Sewer rat	*Rattus rattus* Ship rat Roof rat	*Mus musculus*
Colour of coat	Brown/grey Lighter belly	Black/grey Lighter belly	Brown/grey
Specific notes	Problem in autumn, tries to enter buildings	More restricted distribution, more harmful as disease carriers	

13.3.4 OTHER ANIMAL PESTS

Birds, e.g. seagulls and pigeons, may pose problems in certain areas such as seaside resorts and large cities. The feeding of birds with scraps near catering premises is not to be encouraged. Birds spread certain types of diseases, roosting and nesting may damage roofs and the build-up of bird droppings beneath their perches looks unsightly and gives rise to unpleasant odours (see Fig. 13.8).

FIG. 13.8 Bird droppings damage and deface stonework, produce an unpleasant odour and favourable conditions for fly breeding (Rentokil Ltd)

Of lesser importance, a number of other animals may occasionally trouble the caterer. These include close relatives of the insects, e.g. woodlice and spiders. In general spiders are useful for trapping flies and other insects, but their appearance in the bath may disturb some guests!

QUESTIONS

1. What are the characteristics of fish? Explain the value of fish farming and name one type of fish which can easily be farmed.
2. Explain how increased food demands has resulted in a change in farming methods. Discuss these changes in detail with a named example.
3. Name four types of parasitic worm and list their animal hosts. State how they can be transmitted to humans and how good hygiene can prevent this.
4. List four ways in which steam flies may be a nuisance to the caterer. Discuss two ways of preventing infestations of steam flies in catering premises.
5. State three reasons why rodents are undesirable to the caterer. Compare and contrast the two main species of rat.

GROWTH AND TRANSPORT

14.1 INTRODUCTION

The term growth can be used to describe changes in a single cell or in a multicellular organism. Growth can also describe increases in the number of individuals within a population, e.g. the number of bacteria in food or the number of humans on the Earth. In discussing growth it is essential to understand the context in which the term is being used.

14.2 GROWTH IN AN INDIVIDUAL CELL

This may be measured by an increase in the cell volume or mass or both, although cell growth is really more than this and is best considered as a balanced increase in cell contents. Increases in volume or mass may occur without growth taking place, e.g. cells temporarily increasing in volume as a result of taking in water would not have grown (see sect. 14.5.2).

14.3 GROWTH IN MULTICELLULAR ORGANISMS

All organisms start life as a single cell, which itself grows, but then undergoes repeated cell division until the whole organism reaches its full size, i.e. growth in a multicellular organism must involve increase in the number of cells. It has been estimated that there are approximately 50 000 000 000 000 cells in the human body.

The increase in the number of cells per unit time is referred to as the growth rate. This can be calculated by taking frequent measurements (size, mass, etc.) of the whole organism at regular time intervals. For multicellular animals the growth rate increases steadily, reaches a maximum and then decreases (see Fig. 14.1). Plants show a slightly different pattern of growth (see Table 12.2). Growth in animals is determined by the availability of nutrients, including energy and protein.

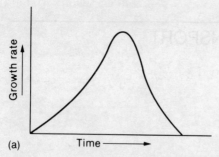

(a)

FIG. 14.1a Growth rate in a multicellular animal plotted against time

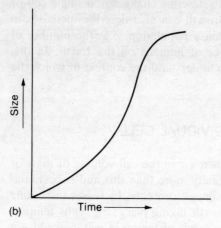

(b)

FIG. 14.1b Increase in size of an organism plotted against time

Plants show a slightly different pattern of growth (see Table 12.2).
Normal cell division in plants, animals and most protists is by a
process known as mitosis which involves enlargement of the nucleus
followed by duplication of the chromosomal material. Thus each
daughter cell contains identical genetic information. In addition the
cytoplasm of the original cell divides into halves and each half becomes associated with one nucleus (see Fig. 14.2). In multicellular
organisms these two new cells remain attached but grow individually
(size, cell contents, etc.) until their maximum size is reached when
they either stop growing or divide into two.

The maximum size of a cell is determined by the activity of the
particular cell and by the ratio of the external surface area to volume. In a young multicellular organism the rate of formation of new
cells is greater than the rate of death of the old cells (cells only have
a limited life span) hence the whole organism grows. As an organism
increases in age cell division becomes restricted to certain areas of
the body and the rate of new cell formation is balanced by the rate

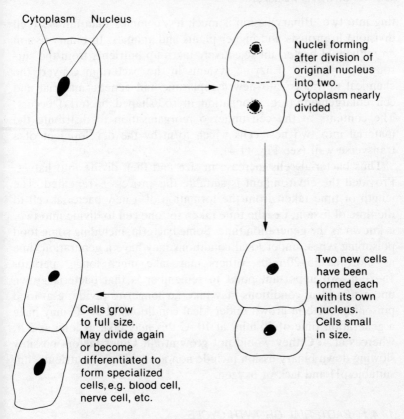

Cytoplasm   Nucleus

Nuclei forming
after division of
original nucleus
into two.
Cytoplasm nearly
divided

Two new cells
have been
formed each
with its own
nucleus.
Cells small
in size.

Cells grow
to full size.
May divide again
or become
differentiated to
form specialized
cells, e.g. blood cell,
nerve cell, etc.

FIG. 14.2 Successive stages of cell division

of cell death. Different cells have different life expectations, for instance skin and blood cells are constantly dying either through damage or wear and tear and thus need replacing by mitotic division. Cells of the gut wall live for about six days before being eroded by the passage of food along the gut and a red blood cell has a life span of about 100 days while others, e.g. some brain cells, have to last a lifetime.

14.4   GROWTH IN POPULATIONS OF BACTERIA

Growth of an individual bacterium may be defined as an increase in mass or size caused by a synthesis of cytoplasm. More frequently the term growth refers to changes in the numbers of cells rather than changes in the individual bacteria themselves.

Bacteria reproduce by a process known as binary fission. This is an asexual method of reproduction and involves the bacterium splitting into two. Binary fission is much less complex than mitosis (cell division) in protists and higher plants and animals. In binary fission an individual bacterium selectively takes up nutrients from the surrounding medium. Enzyme systems in the bacterium convert the chemical nutrients into new cytoplasmic and genetic material and cell enlargement (e.g. elongation in rod-shaped bacteria) occurs. The contents of the cell undergo reorganisation to distribute the material into two new cells which form by the development of a transverse wall (see Fig. 11.4).

Thus bacterial cells increase in size and then divide into halves. Provided the environment is suitable this process is repeated. The length of time taken from the formation of a new bacterial cell to the time of fission, i.e. the time taken for one cell to divide into two, is known as the generation time. Some bacteria, including some food poisoning types, under ideal conditions may have a generation time as short as 15–20 mins, others may take much longer perhaps 15–20 h. An important point to remember is that bacteria grown under non-ideal conditions may take far longer to divide, e.g. food poisoning bacteria grown under ideal conditions at 37 °C may have a generation time of 20 min, at 10 °C this may take as long as 6 h, whereas at 4 °C they would not grow at all. Other factors possibly slowing down binary fission include non-availability of nutrients, unsuitable pH and lack of oxygen.

14.4.1 BACTERIAL GROWTH CYCLE

When a liquid medium, e.g. milk, cream, soup or casserole, is inoculated with bacteria, perhaps transferred there from an unhygienic chef's finger, a characteristic series of events takes place. A knowledge of these will be very useful in understanding a number of food hygiene regulations and how food poisoning can occur (see Ch. 18).

Lag phase
Bacteria having been transferred from one environment to another have to undergo a phase of adjustment. During this period they become accustomed to the new environmental conditions; conditions on a chef's finger are quite different to those in a fresh cream trifle. During this phase the cells are very active physiologically and are synthesising new cell contents and taking in nutrients. Although the cells may increase in size there is no increase in the numbers of cells. The length of the lag phase will depend on how different the conditions are. If bacteria are transferred from one environment to a similar environment the lag phase is short, e.g. 10 min, if con-

ditions are very different the lag phase may last several hours. At the end of the lag phase the bacteria start to divide as fast as they can in those environmental conditions.

The exponential or logarithmic (log) phase
This phase is noted as being the phase of great increase of number of cells, and is called the logarithmic (log) phase because a graph of the logarithm of the numbers of cells plotted against time gives a straight line. During this phase all the cells are very similar in terms of chemical composition and size, and the cell number may be doubling every 15–20 min (see Table 14.1).

TABLE 14.1 Increase in cell numbers for a bacterial cell culture with a generation time of 20 minutes

Time (minutes)	(hours)	Number of cells
0		1
20		2
40		4
60		8
80		16
100		32
120		64
140		128
160		256
180	3	512
	4	4096
	5	32 768
	6	262 144
	7	2 097 152
	24	2 361 183 241 434 822 606 848

The stationary phase
The phase of logarithmic growth comes to an end after several hours and the cells pass into the stationary phase. This may be caused by lack of nutrient, by a build-up of toxic waste products or just by overcrowding. It is not difficult to see why this happens – having produced millions of bacteria each wanting more nutrients to grow it would seem inevitable that some nutrients become entirely used up. In some instances the build-up of toxic waste products prevents this from happening, e.g. the bacteria souring milk produce so much acid (by converting lactose to lactic acid) that the pH becomes un-suitable for further bacterial growth. Similarly yeasts converting sugar to alcohol may produce so much alcohol that their own growth

is inhibited, thus limiting the alcoholic content of fermented but undistilled beverages. In the stationary phase therefore the number of bacteria remains constant, either as a result of no growth or a balance between the rate of growth and the rate of death.

The death or decline phase

A stationary phase culture of micro-organisms if left too long passes into a death phase in which the majority of cells start to die and few, if any, new cells are formed. The actual cause of death is complex but may be simply imagined as the effect of old cells being present in unsuitable conditions. The actual rate of death will vary but in some cases may be quite rapid.

The growth cycle of bacteria in a liquid medium is summarised in Table 14.2 and Fig. 14.3.

TABLE 14.2 Bacterial growth cycle

Phase	Description
Lag	A period of adjustment to new conditions. No increase in numbers of cells
Logarithmic	A period of rapid increase in numbers of cells
Stationary	Period of no increase in total numbers. Numbers of cells formed equals the numbers dying
Decline	A period where the bacteria die

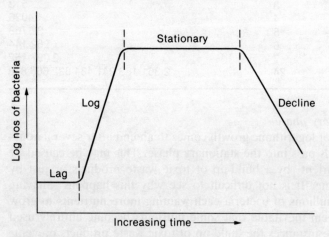

The culture proceeds gradually from one phase to another, i.e. not all the cells are in exactly identical condition towards the end of a given phase of growth.

FIG. 14.3 Growth of log. numbers of bacteria against time assuming suitable conditions for growth in a liquid medium

The importance of this bacterial growth cycle is that the caterer should realise that food having been contaminated and providing suitable conditions for the growth of bacteria **will rapidly become the home of millions of their descendants and food spoilage or food poisoning will result**. In **ALL** cases of food poisoning there will have been **an error in catering practice allowing undesirable bacterial growth**. Examples include food left on display in warm conditions or not refrigerated after cooking, resulting in log phase bacterial growth. For this reason many hygiene measures (see Ch. 18) are directed towards preventing this growth cycle from taking place, e.g. proper refrigeration of foods stops food poisoning bacteria from entering their growth cycle. Hygiene regulations state that hazardous foods (e.g. cream, meat, gravies) must not be stored between 10 °C and 62.7 °C (unless on display for sale) as this will allow growth of harmful bacteria or pathogens.

14.5   TRANSPORT IN AND OUT OF THE CELL

The cell is a constant hive of activity with complex chemicals being synthesised (built up) from simpler ones and others being degraded (broken down). Collectively these reactions are known as metabolism (anabolism – building up, catabolism – breaking down). In order for these reactions to keep taking place there must be a constant turnover of chemicals entering and leaving the cell. In spite of all this the cell manages to keep its contents in a more or less steady state (known as homeostasis) and it is important to examine the movement of these chemicals in and out of the cell. Four mechanisms may be involved; namely, cell diffusion, osmosis, active transport and phagocytosis.

14.5.1   DIFFUSION INTO CELLS

Some chemicals enter and leave the cell simply by diffusing (see sect. 6.7.1) in and out, e.g. potassium and calcium ions and oxygen diffuse in and carbon dioxide diffuses out. Chemicals may diffuse in or out of the cell independently of other chemicals and at a rate dependent on their size and type, and the temperature of the environment (diffusion is more rapid at higher temperatures). Diffusion occurs because the molecules in fluids (liquids and gases) are in a state of constant random motion when molecules move from a region of high concentration to a region of lower concentration (i.e. along a diffusion gradient) until they become evenly dispersed throughout the whole fluid. The speed at which molecules move is relatively fast (about 500 m s^{-1}), but they do not move very far before they collide with other molecules (about 10^{-7} m) and thus change direction. The net result is that movement of molecules over short distances is rapid but it can take several days for a molecule to cover a distance measured in centimetres. This can be illustrated by adding a crystal of copper sulphate to a beaker of water in which it may take several weeks for the blue colour of the copper sulphate molecules to diffuse throughout the beaker. The number of molecules which can enter a cell by diffusion is therefore limited and larger organisms have to have transport systems, e.g. xylem and phloem (see sect. 12.3.1) in plants, and blood in mammals which ensures that sufficient food and oxygen reaches all cells of the body.

14.5.2 OSMOSIS

In studying the structure of the cell (see Ch. 10) it was observed that cells have on the outside of their cytoplasm a cell membrane con-

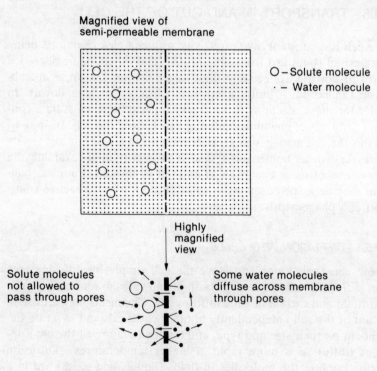

FIG. 14.4 Osmosis – diffusion through a semi-permeable membrane

sisting of a double layer of protein separated by a layer of lipid and possessing small pores. The cell membrane is semi-permeable, which means that it allows some chemicals to pass in and out unhindered but restricts the passage of others allowing the cell membrane close control of the chemicals passing in and out of the cell. The cytoplasm is a mixture of chemicals and if a cell is placed in water osmosis – the diffusion of water across a semi-permeable membrane – takes place (see Fig. 14.4).

The water molecules move from a region of low solute concentration (i.e. fewer dissolved chemicals) to a region of higher solute concentration (i.e. more dissolved chemicals). Cells placed in distilled water increase in volume (but this not growth) due to the passage of water into the cell by osmosis. Nature likes things to be equal and water passes into the cell in an attempt to 'dilute' the concentrated cytoplasm, since chemicals cannot pass out. Cells with a rigid cell wall (plants and some protists) take in so much water that eventually the rigidity of the cell wall limits any further increase in volume. An osmotic pressure – a force or pressure equal to that driving the water into the cell is exerted by the rigid cell wall. These cells are now turgid or stiff with water and this helps give them shape (see Fig. 14.5).

In times of water shortage they become limp and flaccid and the cytoplasm shrinks away from the cell wall – known as plasmolysis. Cells lacking a cell wall have devised other methods of controlling water content, *Amoeba*, for example, has contractile vacuoles to pump out excess water. Multicellular organisms have developed even more sophisticated methods; in the human body water levels are regulated by the blood and kidneys.

If cells are placed in very concentrated solutions osmosis takes place and water passes out of the cell; use can be made of this in food preservation (see Fig. 14.6).

For centuries Man has added chemicals, such as salt and sugar, to foods in order to prevent the growth of spoilage organisms. These traditional preservatives increase the osmotic pressure of the environment and literally dehydrate any spoilage organisms. Sugar is the main ingredient in jams, which by law must contain a minimum of 68.5 per cent sugar. This high sugar level is necessary to prevent spoilage by moulds. Cans of condensed sweetened milk also contain high concentrations of sugar, enabling them to be kept for a considerable time even when opened. Other foods in which sugar aids preservation include syrups and candies, fondant fillings in chocolate, honey, dates and sultanas. Addition of salt to foods is the basis of 'curing'. Curing of meats such as bacon and hams involves im-

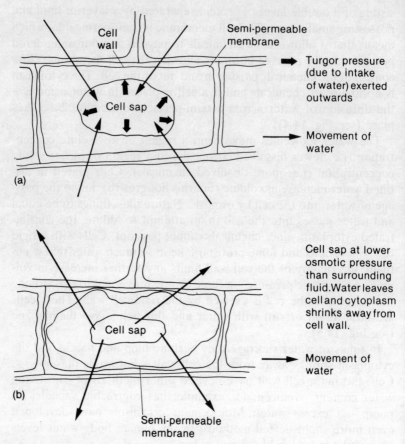

FIG. 14.5 Osmosis in plant cells (a) Cell becomes turgid (stiff) as water is taken in by osmosis (b) Flaccid cell

pregnating the meat with brine (see sect. 6.7.1) containing salt (sodium chloride) as the main ingredient with lesser quantities of potassium nitrate, sodium nitrite and possibly sugar. The meat to be preserved is either immersed in the brine or the brine is injected into the meat, a process called pumping. Addition of the curing mixture not only preserves the meat but helps to give it a desirable pink colour. Treatment of fish with salt solution is another traditional technique of preservation. Both meat and fish may be smoked after addition of the brine. This has an additional preservative effect as well as altering the flavour. Apart from acting as the principal preservative in the salting of meat and fish, much smaller quantities of salt exert a slight preservative effect in butter and cheese.

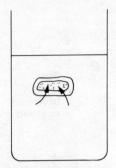
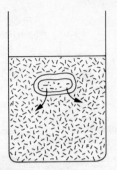

Spoilage bacterium
in distilled water.
Water passes *into* cell
by osmosis until rigid cell
wall prevents further uptake.

Spoilage bacterium
in sugar/salt solution.
Water passes *out* of cell
by osmosis, plasmolysis occurs.
Cell prevented from growing.

FIG. 14.6 Very concentrated solutions of sugar or salt can be used to prevent food spoilage

14.5.3   ACTIVE TRANSPORT

After studying cells scientists discovered that cells could absorb certain chemicals even when their intracellular concentration of that chemical was far higher than their extracellular concentration, i.e. against a concentration gradient, e.g. many cells have higher levels of magnesium than their surroundings. Such uptake against a concentration gradient requires energy and is termed active transport.

14.5.4   PHAGOCYTOSIS

The mechanisms of entry into the cell so far discussed will explain how small molecules gain access, but some cells take in much larger substances which involves a process of engulfment known as phagocytosis (which literally means cell eating). The cell membrane folds itself inwards around the particles enclosing it in a vesicle or vacuole. This vacuole then migrates into the centre of the cell where the particle is digested by enzymes. This process is important for feeding in *Amoeba* (see Fig. 14.7) and is also important in immunity in humans where phagocytic cells (certain white blood cells) engulf and destroy invading micro-organisms.

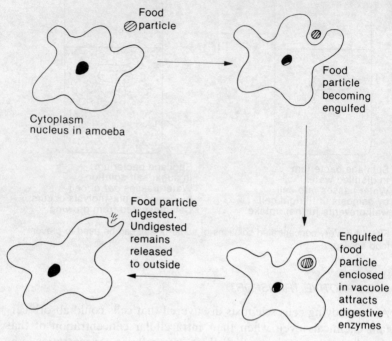

FIG. 14.7 Phagocytosis in amoeba

QUESTIONS

1. Distinguish between growth in an individual cell and growth in a multicellular organism.
2. Describe the chain of events which follow contamination of a bowl of trifle by an unhygienic caterer.
3. Define 'osmosis'. Explain the significance of osmosis in food preservation.
4. What is meant by the term 'generation time' of a bacteria. State the typical generation time of a food poisoning bacterium. How does refrigeration affect generation time.
5. Explain the importance of transport of materials into and out of a cell. Discuss the four methods of transport into cells.

MODES OF NUTRITION

15.1 INTRODUCTION

One of the characteristics of living things is that they feed (see sect. 10.2.2). Nutrition is the study of feeding and the chemicals (nutrients) that are required by a particular organism. Nutrients are required for growth, tissue repair and energy production. Although living things obtain their nutrients in a wide range of different ways they can be divided into two major groups, representing the major differences between plants and animals (see Table 12.2). These two major groups are autotrophs and heterotrophs.

15.2 AUTOTROPHS

Autotrophic (literally self-feeding) organisms have the ability to make their own organic nutrients from inorganic raw materials. Nearly all plants, some protists and some bacteria have an autotrophic mode of nutrition. This process of making food requires energy. Some autotrophic bacteria can utilise the energy released as a consequence of inorganic chemical reactions and are called chemoautotrophs, e.g. *Nitrosomonas* sp. in soil oxidise ammonium ions to form nitrites, as shown below:

$$4NH_4^+ \quad + \quad 7O_2 \quad \longrightarrow \quad 4HNO_2 \quad + \quad 6H_2O \quad + \quad \text{ENERGY}$$

ammonium ions — oxygen — nitrous acid — water

Most autotrophs use the energy obtained from sunlight in a process called photosynthesis and are called photoautotrophs. During photosynthesis, organisms with chlorophyll absorb light and use this energy to convert water and gaseous carbon dioxide into carbohydrate. This means light energy is trapped and converted into stable chemical energy. Although the whole process can be summarised into one simple overall equation, many different intermediate reactions are involved.

$$CO_2 \quad + \quad 2H_2O \quad \xrightarrow{\text{LIGHT}} \quad C(H_2O) \quad + \quad H_2O \quad + \quad O_2$$

| carbon dioxide from air | water from soil | | carbohydrate | | water | oxygen into air |

The green pigment chlorophyll used in the reaction to trap light energy is usually contained in cell organelles known as chloroplasts. Apart from light, water and carbon dioxide, plants also require certain minerals or inorganic elements as nutrients. These are normally obtained from the soil, some are required in relatively large amounts – macronutrients, e.g. nitrogen, phosphorus, etc. whereas others are required in much smaller amounts – micronutrients, e.g. copper, zinc, etc.

Autotrophs are of vital importance to all other living things. Chemautotrophs, such as *Nitrosomonas* contribute to soil fertility since the nitrites it forms are converted to nitrates and used by plants as a source of nitrogen. The photosynthetic autotrophs produce oxygen as a by-product and this is of paramount importance in replenishing atmospheric oxygen which is used by heterotrophic organisms in the release of energy from organic compounds during respiration (see sect. 9.9.2). Secondly, autotrophic organisms are producers, i.e. they act as a source of nutrients either directly or indirectly for all heterotrophic organisms. Without sunlight to provide energy for photosynthesis, neither photoautotrophs nor heterotrophs could exist.

15.3   HETEROTROPHS

The word heterotroph literally means fed by others. Most bacteria, some protists and all animals are heterotrophic and cannot make their food from inorganic material. They must obtain all their nutrients, with the exception of water and mineral salts, as preformed organic molecules, i.e. they are consumers, utilising organic molecules made by producers. Heterotrophs can be sub-classified into groups based on the source of their organic nutrients.

15.3.1   HERBIVORES

Herbivores, e.g. sheep and cattle, obtain their nutrients directly from plant material. Herbivores have problems in that nutrients in plant cells are contained within a strong cell wall of cellulose and lignin. To improve physical breakdown of the food herbivorous mammals have evolved teeth specialised for grinding up the food. Herbivorous insects have highly modified mouth parts.

15.3.2 CARNIVORES

Carnivores, e.g. cats and dogs, eagles, etc., obtain their nutrients from other animals which may be herbivores or smaller carnivores. Unlike herbivores, carnivores have the problem of catching their food and have evolved specialised mechanisms to facilitate this, e.g. the ability to run fast, stings and poisons to paralyse their prey or tentacles for grabbing. A few specialised carnivorous plants supplement their nitrogen supply by trapping and digesting animals, usually insects, e.g. the sundew plant which is found growing on moors and heaths, and the Venus fly trap.

15.3.3 OMNIVORES

Omnivores, e.g. humans, obtain their nutrients from both plant and animal sources, e.g. the Great British Hotel Breakfast which consists of foods of both plant and animal origin (see Table 15.1).

TABLE 15.1 The great British hotel breakfast

Plant origin	Animal origin
Cereal	Milk
Sugar	Butter
Tomatoes	Bacon
Bread	Sausage
Marmalade	Egg
Orange juice	
Tea	

15.4 TYPES OF NUTRITIONAL ASSOCIATION

Heterotrophs vary widely in their needs for organic nutrients. Some, e.g. certain bacteria, require only a few simple organic compounds whereas viruses require whole living cells for their growth. This could be described as the ultimate nutritional requirement. In their search for organic nutrients, organisms may enter into specialised types of nutritional association and heterotrophs can be categorised according to the type of relationship formed.

15.4.1 HOLOZOIC NUTRITION

Holozoic organisms, e.g. Man, feed on solid organic material which is ingested and then digested into a utilisable form.

15.4.2   PARASITIC NUTRITION

This is a mechanism of nutrition whereby the organism feeds on or in the body of another living organism (called the host). The host suffers in some way as a result of the relationship and in some cases may even die. When one looks at the whole field of infectious diseases one is really looking at the effects of parasitic organisms on their host (see Table 15.2).

TABLE 15.2 Diseases caused by parasitic organisms

Organism	Disease	Host
Bacterium	Tuberculosis	Man
Bacterium	Whooping cough	Man
Protozoan	Malaria	Man
Virus	Influenza	Man
Tapeworm	Taeniasis	Cattle/pig/man
Plant	Mistletoe	Apple trees

Some bacteria, animals, plants and protists are parasitic. Parasites may be ectoparasites, attacking the outside of their host, e.g. bed bugs, or endoparasites, attacking from within, e.g. tapeworm. Parasites may be transient, e.g. the mosquito bites a host and quickly moves on, whereas the malarial parasite transmitted by the mosquito remains almost indefinitely. Parasites vary in the damage which they inflict on their host. The mosquito is a mild irritant, the effects of the malarial parasite can result in death. It is in the parasite's own interest not to be too severe since it may kill the goose that lays the golden eggs!

15.4.3   SAPROPHYTIC NUTRITION

This literally means plant rot nutrition and features in the nutrition of some bacteria and fungi. Saprophytes obtain their nutrition from the remains of dead, organic material which they digest with extracellular enzymes. Saprophytic organisms are very important as decomposers in the recycling of organic material (see Figs 15.1 and 15.2). The distinction between parasites and saprophytes may not be absolute. Some organisms such as the food poisoning *Salmonellae* described as facultative parasites may be parasitic or saprophytic. *Salmonellae* can grow as saprophytes on the surface of food and once the food is consumed by an unsuspecting human can continue to grow as harmful parasites in the gut, the body tries to reject them, resulting in the symptoms of food poisoning, e.g. diarrhoea.

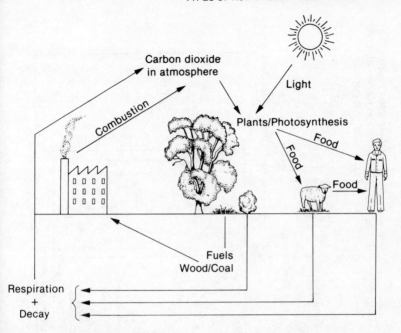

FIG. 15.1 The carbon cycle

15.4.4 COMMENSALISM

Close nutritional relationships between organisms need not always be destructive. A commensal lives in peaceful coexistence with and receives benefit from a host which is not normally adversely affected. Many of the bacteria inhabiting the gut, skin and other parts of the body fall into this category, although some, normally harmless organisms may under suitable conditions cause infection, and are termed opportunist pathogens. *Staphylococcus aureus* which is found on human skin with no ill effects can invade cuts, burns, and other breaks in the skin and cause infection. The same organism passing from hands to food may give rise to food poisoning hence the need for good personal hygiene in food preparation (see Ch. 18).

15.4.5 SYMBIOSIS

Symbiotic relationships involve an organism (a symbiont) and its host living together and receiving mutual benefit, i.e. the host also gains from the association. For example in Man certain bacteria in the gut make vitamins B and K which are absorbed and utilised. The bacteria in the gut are provided with a suitable environment for

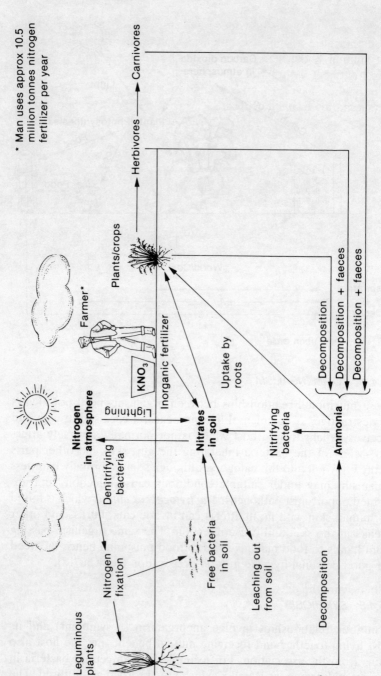

* Man uses approx 10.5 million tonnes nitrogen fertilizer per year

FIG. 15.2 The nitrogen cycle

growth (warmth, moisture, food) and thus both organisms benefit. The importance of this association to Man is underlined by the fact that vitamin K deficiency is rarely observed except following long-term treatment with antibiotics which destroy the gut bacteria.

Herbivores have problems in digesting cellulose, the structural polysaccharide of plant cell walls, owing to their inability to produce cellulase, the enzyme capable of breaking down cellulose. The ability to produce cellulase is limited to a few organisms, mainly bacteria, fungi and some protozoa. Herbivores form symbiotic relationships with cellulase producing bacteria and protozoa. Such organisms are found in the rumen (part of the digestive system) of the cow, which provides warmth, food and moisture for the protozoa and bacteria in return for having glucose released from the cellulose. Humans are not endowed with specialist herbivore digestion and cellulose passes through the gut unchanged and is important as dietary fibre or roughage (see sect. 16.4).

15.5   CHEMICAL CYCLES

Having seen how individual organisms obtain their nutrients and the relationships they form it is possible to take a broader look at the complex interrelationships which exist. Life on earth is a delicate balance between the building up of a whole range of complex organic chemicals followed by their breakdown and resynthesis. Two chemical elements important to life are carbon and nitrogen, both of which are involved in complex cycles.

15.5.1   THE CARBON CYCLE (see Fig. 15.1)

The amount of carbon dioxide in the atmosphere remains relatively constant at approximately 0.03 per cent. Carbon dioxide is absorbed during daylight by green plants for use in photosynthesis and is replaced in a number of ways including plant and animal respiration (see sect. 9.9), the burning of carbon fuels (e.g. coal, oil and petroleum) and the decomposition of organic remains.

15.5.2   THE NITROGEN CYCLE (see Fig. 15.2)

A similar cycle exists for nitrogen. Some autotrophic bacteria, either living on their own in the soil or in symbiotic relationship with the roots of leguminous plants (e.g. clover and beans), are able to convert atmospheric nitrogen into nitrites. Bacterial oxidation of nitrites yields nitrates which can be absorbed by plants and converted into amino acids and proteins. Omnivores and herbivores use plant proteins which are in turn consumed by other omnivores and carnivores. Omnivores, carnivores and herbivores on dying are broken down by saprophytes (decomposers) thus replacing nitrogen in the soil.

15.6   FOOD CHAINS AND WEBS

The nitrogen and carbon cycles illustrate the interdependence of living things since the essential chemicals of life pass from one organism to another. Food chains (see Fig. 15.3) begin with an autotroph (producer) which is consumed by a heterotroph (a primary or first-order consumer or herbivore), which is in turn consumed by another heterotroph (a secondary or second-order consumer or carnivore).

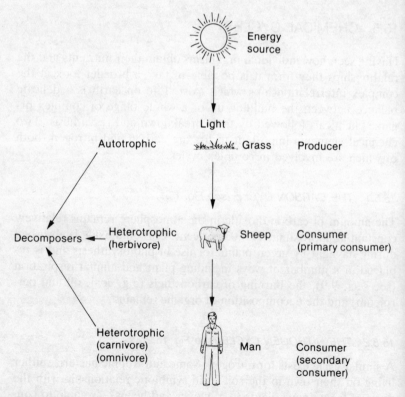

FIG. 15.3 A food chain

The organic remains of all three are decomposed by small insects and saprophytic bacteria and fungi. Energy flows through the food chain and organic substances are built up, utilised and then recycled.

Food chains, however, are really an oversimplification since herbivores usually eat more than one type of food, and one type of food is generally eaten by more than one type of herbivore. Further interaction between food chains occurs when herbivores are eaten by several different consumers. This complex situation is better described by a food web (see Fig. 15.4) which more accurately represents most biological communities.

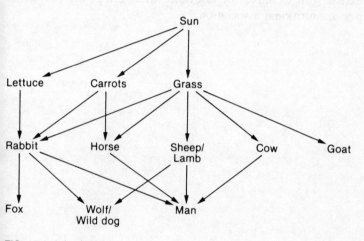

FIG. 15.4 A food web

Ecology is the study of individual organisms within the community and their relationships to their environment. Man has an important role to play in many food webs and his effect on the environment is significant and often harmful. Early human existence as hunters and gatherers of food meant a close interrelationship with many food webs. With the advent of civilisation and enormous technological innovation Man threatens to destroy the fine ecological balance of vast areas of the earth to a degree which may even jeopardise his own existence. Man has chopped down whole forests for timber, dug open-cast mines, dammed rivers and changed the ecology of large tracts of land. The production of toxic nuclear and chemical wastes and pollution by exhaust fumes, pesticides and fertilisers are at last attracting government attention.

QUESTIONS

1. Man is an omnivore. Explain this statement with reference to the typical British breakfast.
2. Distinguish between autotrophs and heterotrophs. Discuss the fundamental importance of autotrophs to all living things.
3. Illustrate the nitrogen cycle and discuss the role of leguminous plants.
4. Distinguish, with examples, between a food chain and a food web.
5. Discuss, with examples of relevance to catering, the five main types of nutritional association.

INTRODUCTION TO HUMAN NUTRITION

16.1 INTRODUCTION

To produce energy and to grow and repair tissues, all living things need a supply of chemical substances. Autotrophs (see sect. 15.2) are able to make all their organic chemicals from carbon dioxide, water and mineral salts. Heterotrophs (see sect. 15.3) are dependent, to varying degrees, on a range of preformed organic chemicals for their existence. These chemicals, which must be supplied in the food, are termed nutrients, the study of which is termed nutrition. As a large part of the catering industry is concerned with the provision of food, caterers need to be informed about human nutrition.

16.2 NUTRIENTS

The food which a person eats is termed the diet (a word which is often misunderstood as applying to slimming diets only). Regardless of the foods which make up the diet, whether they are of plant or animal origin, 'cordon bleu' or fish and chips, the diet must provide the complete range of nutrients in order to maintain health. A balanced diet is one which provides an individual with the correct amount of each nutrient. The nutrients needed in a balanced diet are divided into six groups:

Water	Lipids
Carbohydrates	Vitamins
Proteins	Minerals

Although all foods provide some or all of these nutrients, no one food contains all the nutrients in the optimum quantities. The best single food item is milk, but even milk does not provide adequate amounts of some nutrients, particularly iron and vitamin C. Before people can use the nutrients which are provided by their diet the food they have eaten has to be digested (see Ch. 17).

TABLE 16.1 Carbohydrates in foods

Carbohydrate group	Number of Sub-units	Examples	Constituent Sub-units	Occurrence	Taste	Solubility
Monosaccharide	1	Glucose	—	Found in grapes (Formed from maltose)	Sweet	Water
		Fructose	—	Found in fruit	Sweet	Water soluble
Disaccharide	2	Sucrose	Glucose/Fructose	'Cane' sugar	Sweet	Water soluble
		Lactose	Glucose/Galactose	'Milk' sugar	Sweet	Water soluble
		Maltose	Glucose/Glucose	'Malt' sugar (Formed from starch)	Sweet	Water soluble
Polysaccharide	over 10	Starch	Glucose	Potatoes, flour, rice	None	Water insoluble
		Glycogen	Glucose	Storage polysacc. in animals	None	Water insoluble
		Cellulose	Glucose	Structural polysacc. in plants	None	Water insoluble

16.3   WATER

In the body, biochemical reactions take place in an aqueous solution which must be maintained at the right concentration. Our bodies contain about 70 per cent water which means that if you weigh 60 kg you would contain approximately 40 litre of water. Water is lost continually from the body in three main ways, breathing, perspiring and urinating. Water vapour lost through breathing can be detected in a poorly ventilated bedroom by water vapour condensing on the window panes. We lose about one litre of water through the skin in 24 h without the skin becoming wet (insensible perspiration). Water lost in a 24-hour period by urination can vary from about 500 cm^3 to about 3 litre. To avoid dehydration water loss must be replaced by water gain. Sources of water include water itself or drinks, such as fruit juices, tea and coffee that contain water. In addition water is obtained from solid foods such as fresh fruits and vegetables.

16.4   CARBOHYDRATES

Carbohydrates are a group of substances which contain carbon, hydrogen and oxygen with hydrogen and oxygen in the ratio 2 : 1 (as in water, H_2O), hence the name carbohydrate. The simplest carbohydrates are monosaccharides (literally single sugar units) e.g. glucose, fructose and galactose which are isomers (see sect. 9.2.3) with the molecular formula, $C_6H_{12}O_6$.

Monosaccharides can be linked together to give a range of molecules consisting of two, three, four or more monosaccharide units. Of the carbohydrates found in food, monosaccharides (one sugar unit), disaccharides (two sugar units) and polysaccharides (many sugar units) predominate (see Table 16.1). Mono- and disaccharides are sweet, polysaccharides are not.

In order to be absorbed across the gut wall, disaccharides and polysaccharides must be broken down into their constituent monosaccharides as they pass along the digestive tract (see Ch. 17). Carbohydrates which can be broken down and absorbed across the gut wall are known as available carbohydrate. Carbohydrate is the primary source of human energy (see sect. 9.9.2) and is preferentially utilised before fats or proteins. **One gram of available carbohydrate can provide 16 kJ of energy.**

Cellulose is not broken down in the human digestive tract and therefore cannot be absorbed into the blood stream. Although cellu-

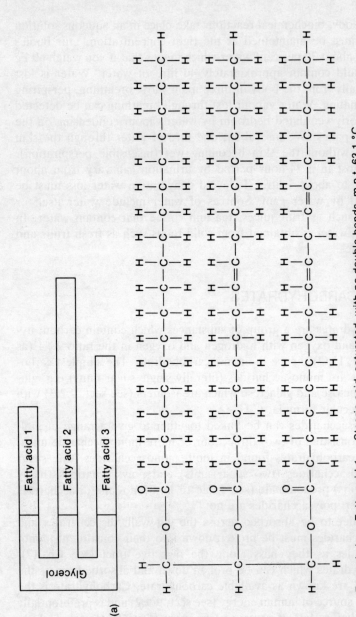

Formula has: Fatty acid 1 – Stearic acid, saturated, with no double bonds, m.p.t. 63.1 °C
Fatty acid 2 – Oleic acid, unsaturated, with 1 double bond, m.p.t. 13.4 °C
Fatty acid 3 – Linolenic, polyunsaturated with 2 double bonds, m.p.t. – 5 °C

FIG 16.1 A triglyceride (a) Schematic representation (b) Structural formula

lose contains glucose units, exactly the same as starch, they are linked in a different manner. Polysaccharides which cannot be broken down and absorbed across the gut wall are termed unavailable carbohydrate.

Although unavailable carbohydrate cannot be used for the production of energy it has an important role in the diet as 'roughage' or 'dietary fibre'. Fibre adds bulk to the unabsorbed material left after digestion and helps to hold water in the faeces making them softer and more easily voided. Dietary fibre helps to alleviate constipation and can help to prevent haemorrhoids (piles). Foods important in providing dietary fibre are bran, wholemeal bread, fresh fruit, vegetables and baked beans.

16.5 PROTEINS

Proteins are used primarily for the growth and repair of body tissues. Additionally, certain proteins are important as enzymes (see sect. 9.10). If there is inadequate energy supply from carbohydrate or fat in the diet then protein can be diverted from its primary role and used for the production of energy. **One gram of protein is able to provide 17 kJ of energy**.

All proteins are made up from amino acids (see sect. 9.3), of which there are about twenty naturally occurring ones. An amino acid is a molecule which contains an amino group (NH_2) and an organic (carboxylic) acid group (COOH) attached to the same carbon atom. The amino group of one amino acid can react with the acid group of another to form a peptide bond and proteins are long chains of amino acids linked by peptide bonds. The sequence of amino acids is important in determining the nature of a protein. Letters in the word CATERER can be arranged to give the words TERRACE and RETRACE. In the same way different blends of some or all of the twenty different amino acids give different proteins. The number of amino acid units in a protein can vary; insulin (a hormone controlling the level of sugar in the blood) has 51 amino acid units while others have many thousands. Other examples of proteins include amylase (a digestive enzyme), keratin (the structural protein of skin and hair), albumen (the protein in egg white) and myosin (the protein in muscles, e.g. steak).

The protein we eat is broken down into its constituent amino acids during digestion (see Ch. 17). Amino acids are absorbed into the blood stream and then either utilised or broken down and the nitrogen removed as urea in the urine. The body can transform some amino acids into others which do not have to be provided in the diet and are termed non-essential amino acids. There are eight amino acids which the adult human body cannot make (10 for children) and these have to be provided in the diet and are known as essential amino acids. If one essential amino acid is lacking from the diet proteins cannot be synthesised correctly.

Proteins, which provide enough of all the essential amino acids, are said to be of high biological value (HBV), e.g. milk, egg, soya and meat proteins. Proteins which are low or completely lacking is one or more essential amino acids are said to be of low biological value (LBV) and most plant proteins fall into this category. If a food low in one amino acid is eaten with a food low in another amino acid the body will obtain its overall requirement for both amino acids. This matching of low biological value protein foods is called **complementation** and is very important to a caterer planning a balanced menu, particularly a balanced vegetarian menu.

16.6 LIPIDS

Athough the term lipid can be applied to a whole range of fatty substances, such as waxes and cholesterol, most of the lipid in our diet is neutral fat or triglyceride. Triglycerides consist of a molecule of glycerol chemically combined with three molecules of fatty acids. In a simple triglyceride the three fatty acids are the same, in a mixed triglyceride the three are not the same (see Fig. 16.1).

All fatty acids consist of straight chains of carbon atoms with a –COOH group at one end. Fatty acids can be either saturated or unsaturated (see sect. 9.2). Animal fats tend to be saturated and have higher melting points, i.e. they are solids at room temperatures, whereas vegetable oils tend to be unsaturated and are liquid at room temperature. Fatty acids with more than one double bond are called polyunsaturated fatty acids. Linoleic and linolenic acids are two polyunsaturated fatty acids which cannot be made in the body and therefore have to be provided in the diet for normal health, i.e. they are essential fatty acids. The structure of linolenic acid with its two double bonds is shown in Fig. 16.1. Polyunsaturated fatty acids are found in many vegetable oils, especially sunflower seed oil and corn oil.

Lipids, especially cholesterol, are important in the structure of the cell membrane (see sect. 10.4.1) and fats can be used in the body as a secondary source of energy. **One gram of fat can provide 37 kJ of energy**. Their presence in food improves palatability and acts as a vehicle for the fat-soluble vitamins A and D (see below). Excess fat in the diet and fat made from any excess carbohydrate is stored under the skin in the subcutaneous layer (see sect. 10.6), acting both as an energy reserve and insulating the body, reducing the loss of body heat. Nutritionists today suggest that the British diet contains too much fat, especially saturated fat, and recommend that fat intake should be reduced.

16.7 VITAMINS

Vitamins are a collection of diverse organic substances which are required in minute amounts for normal health. If a particular vitamin is missing from the diet then a specific deficiency disease will arise, e.g. lack of vitamin C causes scurvy, lack of vitamin D causes rickets.

Vitamins are divided into two groups on the basis of their solubility – the fat-soluble vitamins (A, D, E, K) which can be stored in the body fat and the water-soluble vitamins (B-complex and C) which cannot be stored in the body to any great extent and thus need continual replacement.

Vitamins A and D are the two fat-soluble vitamins whose absence from the body have been commonly shown to cause deficiency diseases. Although vitamin K has a specific role in the clotting of blood in Man a deficiency is unlikely to occur as vitamin K is synthesised by the bacteria which live in the gut (see sect. 15.4).

Vitamin A is needed for the production of a light-sensitive pigment (rhodopsin) which allows vision in poor light conditions. Deficiency of vitamin A results in a condition called night blindness and vitamin A is also important for keeping healthy mucous membranes in the mouth and nose. Dietary sources of vitamin A are shown in Table 16.2. Fish liver oils are rich sources of vitamin A and may be taken as a vitamin supplement. Carrots contain an orange pigment called β-carotene which splits into two in the body to give two molecules of vitamin A.

Vitamin D is sometimes called the 'sunshine vitamin' because it is produced in the skin by the action of ultraviolet rays of sunlight. Vitamin D is important in controlling the deposition of calcium in the bones and a lack of vitamin D can cause malformation of bones leading to rickets in children and osteomalacia in adults.

The B-vitamin complex is not one single substance but several different vitamins: vitamin B_1 (thiamin), B_2 (riboflavin), B_3 (pantothenic acid), B_4 (niacin), B_6 (pyridoxine) and vitamin B_{12} (cyanocobalamin), sources of which are shown in Table 16.2. Deficiency of a particular B-vitamin results in a specific illness, e.g. a deficiency of B_1 leads to beriberi and of B_{12} leads to pernicious anaemia. All the B-vitamins act as coenzymes in metabolic reactions (see sect. 9.10).

Vitamin C (ascorbic acid) is the centre of much controversy, with

TABLE 16.2 Dietary sources of the vitamins

Vitamin	Dietary source
A	Milk, butter, egg yolk and some fatty fish
D	Margarine, butter, egg yolk or fatty fish liver oils
B-complex	Whole cereals, wheat germ, yeast extracts and meat, especially liver. B_{12} is found only in yeast extracts and meat
C	Fresh fruit and vegetables, especially citrus fruits, blackcurrants, cabbage, Brussels sprouts and potatoes

certain scientists believing that large doses of the vitamin are able to prevent virus infections and reduce susceptibility to the common cold. Deficiency of vitamin C results in scurvy, and although this is not a common problem in Britain today the average vitamin C intake of residents in certain institutions, e.g. hospitals and prisons, could fall below the recommended daily allowance of 30 mg per day.

16.8 MINERALS

As well as organic substances the body requires some inorganic substances, e.g. calcium and iron, for its normal functioning (see Table 5.3). A diet balanced with respect to the organic nutrients will normally provide the minerals required by the body.

In this country the most common mineral deficiency is of iron and results in anaemia. Iron is required for the production of a red, iron-containing protein called haemoglobin which contributes 90 per cent of the solid material in the red blood cell and is essential for the transport of oxygen in the blood. Meat, especially liver, and eggs are the best dietary sources of iron.

16.9 EFFECT OF COOKING ON NUTRIENTS

16.9.1 CARBOHYDRATES

Starch is stored in plant and animal cells in the form of granules (see 10.4.1). Granules from different plant sources have different shapes. The outer layer of the granule consists of closely packed starch molecules which are impervious to cold water. As a suspension of starch in water is heated, water diffuses into the granule causing it to expand in a process called gelatinisation, e.g. in the cooking of potatoes or in the preparation of sauces containing cornflour. The cooking of carbohydrate foods at high temperatures can lead to caramelisation and make many dishes more appetising, e.g. caramel creme, or grilling potatoes before serving, or the preparation of toast.

16.9.2 PROTEINS

Proteins are denatured during the cooking of foods, i.e. the shape of the protein molecule is disrupted. Egg white is denatured by heating and changes from a clear liquid to a white opaque solid. Freezing of foods can also damage proteins and meat which has been frozen and then thawed is often more stringy.

16.9.3 LIPIDS

Heating solid fats causes melting. Heating of fats and oils causes some decomposition of the triglyceride into glycerol and free fatty acids. Further heating causes breakdown of the glycerol to form acrolein, giving the characteristic unpleasant smell of burning fat.

16.9.4 VITAMINS

Two factors influence the effect of cooking on the vitamin content of foods, namely heat stability and solubility. Vitamins A and D are not water-soluble and are therefore not leached out by boiling of foods, although they are removed from meats during cooking. They are returned to the final meal by the preparation of the gravy if the meat juices are used. The water-soluble vitamins are leached out into the cooking water, the volume of which should be kept as low as possible. Again addition of the cooking water to the gravy helps to prevent their loss.

Vitamins B_1 and C are heat labile, i.e. they are broken down by the action of heat during cooking. In order to maintain as much of these two vitamins as possible in the final product, cooking times should be minimised.

QUESTIONS

1. List the six nutrient groups required in a balanced diet. State the function of each nutrient in the human body. List foods important for providing each nutrient.
2. What is meant by the term 'unavailable carbohydrate'. List foods important for providing unavailable carbohydrate and state the function of unavailable carbohydrate in the human diet.
3. Distinguish between essential and non-essential amino acids.
4. Describe the functions of lipids in the human body. What is the difference between a fat and an oil?
5. What are vitamins? Give examples of vitamins and state sources of each in the human diet.

DIGESTION

17.1 INTRODUCTION

The food that we eat cannot be utilised by the body until it has been digested, that is the large insoluble food molecules have to be broken down into smaller soluble molecules. Once swallowed, food passes along the digestive tract (also known as the gastrointestinal (GI) tract, alimentary canal or gut) as if on a conveyor belt. This movement is known as peristalsis and is due to rhythmic muscular contractions of the gut wall. In addition food is subjected to mechanical churning and the action of enzymes which are secreted from epithelial cells (see sect. 10.5.1) lining the gut wall and from digestive glands.

17.2 THE DIGESTIVE SYSTEM

The digestive system is a highly modified tube plus associated glands for the production of enzymes, running from the mouth to the anus. In Man it is between 8 and 10 m in length (24–33 ft), most of this length being coiled to enable it to fit into the abdominal cavity. Food passes from the mouth and is then forced by peristalsis through the pharynx, oesophagus, stomach, small intestine, large intestine and is finally voided through the anus. The structure of the digestive tract is shown in Fig. 17.1.

Food usually takes between 24 and 48 hours to pass through the gut although the actual time taken (called the transit time) varies according to the precise nature of the diet.

The three main functions of the digestive system can be summarised as follows:

1. *Digestion*. Large molecules, e.g. polysaccharides and proteins, are not able to pass across the gut wall into the blood stream and are of no value to the body until they have been broken down into smaller soluble compounds. Digestive processes are divided into two stages: primary digestion (the breakdown of food com-

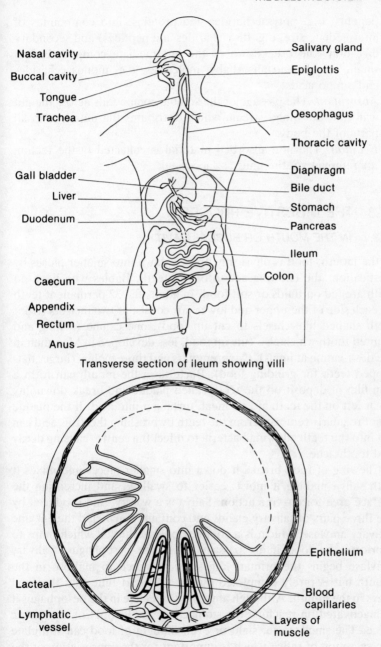

Nasal cavity

Buccal cavity

Tongue

Trachea

Salivary gland

Epiglottis

Oesophagus

Thoracic cavity

Gall bladder

Liver

Duodenum

Diaphragm

Bile duct

Stomach

Pancreas

Ileum

Colon

Caecum

Appendix

Rectum

Anus

Transverse section of ileum showing villi

Epithelium

Lacteal

Lymphatic vessel

Blood capillaries

Layers of muscle

FIG. 17.1 The human digestive system

ponents, e.g. polysaccharides and proteins, into compounds of intermediate size, e.g. disaccharides and peptides) and secondary digestion (the breakdown of the intermediate compounds into small, soluble and absorbable molecules, e.g. monosaccharides and amino acids).
2. *Absorption*. The passage of the soluble compounds across the gut wall into the blood stream which distributes the nutrients to all parts of the body.
3. *Egestion*. The non-absorbed material is collected in the rectum for removal via the anus as faeces.

17.3   THE DIGESTIVE PROCESS

17.3.1   IN THE MOUTH OR BUCCAL CAVITY

In the mouth, food is physically broken down into smaller pieces by mastication, the chewing action of the teeth. Babies who have no teeth are fed on fluids or soft food. In adults the 32 permanent teeth on each side of the upper and lower jaw consist of two incisors (front teeth shaped like chisels to cut up food), one canine (a long and pointed tooth which also cuts up food, less developed in Man than in the flesh-eating animals), two premolars and three molars (large, flat-topped teeth for grinding food). Bacteria in the mouth can form a thin film of deposit on the teeth called plaque and break down any sugar left on the teeth after a meal, turning it into acid. If the plaque is not regularly removed from the teeth by brushing then this acid can eat into the teeth allowing bacteria to infect the centre, causing decay and tooth-ache.

Chewing of food breaks it down into smaller pieces and mixes it with saliva making it moist, easier to swallow, and increasing the surface area for enzyme action. Saliva is a watery fluid produced by the three pairs of salivary glands and contains mucin and the enzyme salivary amylase. Mucin is a complex polysaccharide which helps to lubricate the food in its passage down the oesophagus. Salivary amylase begins the primary digestion of starch to maltose in the mouth but is rarely completed due to the short time that the food stays in the mouth. Although amylase is effective in the oesophagus it is inactivated on reaching the stomach by the low pH of the gastric juice. The smell, taste, sight or even thought of food can stimulate the secretion of saliva which is important for the appreciation of the flavour of food, since dry foods cannot be tasted until moistened. The taste buds are located on the upper surface of the tongue and are sensitive to four basic sensations, namely sweet, sour, bitter and salty. The range of flavours which we experience on eating food are caused by a blending of the basic sensations.

The tongue shapes the food in the mouth into a small ball or bolus which is swallowed and passed through the pharynx (throat) into the oesophagus (gullet). To prevent food being swallowed into the larynx (voice box) and lungs the hole in the larynx, the glottis, is covered by the epiglottis, a fleshy valve-like flap. Food which has 'gone down the wrong way' (i.e. passed into the larynx by accident) can be dislodged by coughing.

Peristalsis moves the food along the oesophagus. Peristaltic contractions are so strong that they can overcome gravity and move food along the gut of a person upside down. The oesophagus leads from the pharynx through the thoracic cavity (the chest) via the diaphragm (the sheet of muscle separating the thoracic and abdominal cavities) and into the stomach.

17.3.2   IN THE STOMACH

The stomach is a sac-like organ with sphincters (circular muscles) at each end controlling the entry and exit of food. The wall of the stomach is very thick and muscular and the inner surface is lined with a number of pits called gastric glands which secrete gastric juice. This is a mixture of pepsin (an enzyme for the primary digestion of protein into peptides) together with hydrochloric acid which lowers the pH of the stomach contents to about 2. Rhythmic contractions of the stomach wall mix the food with the gastric juice to liquidise it producing a semi-solid mixture called chyme. Pepsin works best at these very low pH values which also have the advantage of restricting the growth of bacteria in the stomach. Different foods are retained for different lengths of time in the stomach but most foods remain for between one and four hours. Some of the food will however pass on into the small intestine within 10 minutes while others, e.g. nuts, which have a high fat content may remain in the stomach for up to 30 hours.

17.3.3   IN THE SMALL INTESTINE

The small intestine is the longest part of the gut, being about 7 m in length. It is divided into three main sections; the duodenum, the jejenum and the ileum. The duodenum is the main site of digestion with chyme being mixed with secretions from three sources; the liver, the pancreas and the wall of the intestine itself. The liver and the pancreas produce enzymes important for the primary digestion

TABLE 17.1 Digestive enzymes and their influence on a meal of fish and chips and a glass of milk shake

Region	Source of secretion	Active ingredient	Nutrient digested	Products of reaction
Mouth	Salivary glands	Salivary amylase	Starch; (in potatoes and batter)	Maltose
Stomach	Stomach wall	Pepsin	Protein (from fish and milk)	Peptides
Small intestine	Liver	Bile salts (*not enzymes)	Fat (from fish and oil)	Fat droplets (Emulsification)
	Pancreas	Amylase	Starch	Maltose
		Trypsin	Protein	Peptides
		Lipase	Fat	Fatty acids and glycerol
		Maltase	Maltose	Glucose
		Peptidase	Peptides	Amino acids
	Intestinal wall	Sucrase	Sucrose (from milk shake powder)	Glucose and fructose
		Lactase	Lactose (from milk)	Glucose and galactose

of starch, protein and fat, the walls of the duodenum producing enzymes for the secondary digestion of disaccharides and peptides, a process which is continued in the jejenum and ileum (see Table 17.1)

1. *The liver.* The liver produces bile, a greenish-yellow liquid which is stored in the gall bladder before passing down the bile duct and into the duodenum. It contains bile salts which act on the globules of fat in the chyme, causing them to be emulsified. Bile is alkaline and neutralises the acid in the chyme to allow the action of intestinal enzymes.

2. *The pancreas.* The pancreas is a leaf-shaped organ which shares a common entrance to the duodenum with the bile duct. Pancreatic juice contains three enzymes, amylase (which converts starch to maltose), trypsin (which converts protein to peptides) and lipase (which converts fats to glycerol and free fatty acids).

3. *The wall of the intestine.* Glands in the wall of the intestine secrete enzymes which complete the digestion of food components. Maltose, sucrose and lactose (disaccharides) are broken down by enzymes into monosaccharides. Peptidases convert peptides into amino acids.

17.4 ABSORPTION

17.4.1 IN THE STOMACH

The stomach is not an important site of absorption although water, water-soluble components of food (such as salts and vitamin C) and alcohol can be absorbed across the wall of the stomach into the blood stream.

17.4.2 IN THE SMALL INTESTINE

Absorption of nutrients takes place mainly in the jejenum and the ileum. The surface area of these sections of the gut is greatly increased by finger-like projections called villi (singular – villus). It has been estimated that there are about 5 000 000 villi in the small intestine giving an absorptive area of about 10 m². The structure of a villus is shown in Fig. 17.1. Nutrients pass into the blood capillaries and are transported to the liver via the hepatic portal vein. Although some compounds enter the blood stream by diffusion, most are actively absorbed and therefore have a specific absorption site in the intestine. Fats, fatty acids, glycerol and the fat-soluble vitamins (A and D) are absorbed through the wall of the villus into the lymph vessel before ultimately reaching the blood stream. The absorption of vitamin B_{12} in the small intestine is facilitated by intrinsic factor, a protein produced by the stomach and secreted in gastric juice.

17.4.3 IN THE LARGE INTESTINE (CAECUM AND COLON)

The large intestine is the major site of water absorption. The unabsorbed remains of the chyme pass into the large intestine and water is removed as they move along. The drier remains, the faeces, are collected in the rectum prior to evacuation through the anal canal. Faeces are a residual mixture of water, dietary fibre (see sect. 16.4), bacteria, dead cells, bile pigments and salts. It is the bile pigments which give faeces their characteristic colour.

Under certain circumstances bacteria can multiply in and irritate the colon, leading to the production of a watery mucus. The reabsorption of water from the colon is impaired and water is lost from the body with the faeces, as diarrhoea. If diarrhoea is allowed to continue untreated for several days then large amounts of water can be lost and dehydration occurs.

17.5   THE ROLE OF THE LIVER

The liver is the largest organ in the body, weighing about 1.5 kg in a normal human adult. It is situated beneath the diaphragm at the top of the abdominal cavity. All the blood from the intestine passes straight to the liver, enabling it to monitor chemicals entering the body. Some desirable substances are stored in the liver; undesirable or toxic substances and any excess amino acids are metabolised before being excreted in the urine. The functions of the liver can be summarised as:

1. *Storage of desirable substances*. The liver can act as a store for glucose, glycogen, fats, vitamins and blood.
2. *Formation of urea*. Any amino acids surplus to immediate requirements are eliminated from the body by conversion to urea and excretion via the kidneys in the urine.
3. *Detoxification*. Toxic compounds entering the body are broken down in the liver prior to their removal from the body in the urine.
4. *Secretion of bile* (see sect. 17.3.3).

QUESTIONS

1. Using cod and chips as an example describe the action of digestive enzymes.
2. Draw a fully labelled diagram to show the regions of the digestive tract through which food passes.
3. State the major site of absorption of nutrients in the gut and describe the way in which this area is modified for absorption.
4. Explain the importance of the liver in the digestive system.
5. What are the functions of saliva in digestion?

18
BASIC FOOD HYGIENE

18.1 INTRODUCTION

Hygiene is to do with health, e.g. good oral hygiene means having healthy teeth and gums. Food hygiene deals with ensuring that food is *safe* or healthy to eat. It is important for any caterer to realise that not all the food that we eat may be good for us and could result in illness, including food poisoning and possibly even death. Food poisoning does not happen by accident but is usually caused by ignorance which can lead to mistakes in the safe handling of food. Food hygiene, therefore, covers all aspects of processing, preparing, storing, cooking and serving of food to ensure that it is safe to eat.

Food hygiene is more important today than at any other time in the past. Increasingly people are eating foods prepared outside their own home either in restaurants, canteens, cafes, hotels or take-away meals. Over 100 000 000 meals or snacks are purchased per week in the UK. The number of reported cases of food poisoning in England and Wales has climbed dramatically since 1972. Food poisoning has resulted in illness and lost working days (approximately 20 000 000 per year). It is wrong to think that good hygiene costs a lot of money, in fact the reverse is true, bad hygiene can be extremely expensive. Caterers who operate unhygienic premises are breaking the law and are liable to prosecution which can lead to fines or imprisonment and closure of premises. Court cases dealing with such offences often make newspaper headlines, and bad publicity leads to loss of trade and revenue. Caterers ignoring food hygiene run the risk of giving people food poisoning and victims of food poisoning can claim for compensation. Once again bad publicity associated with such outbreaks leads to loss of business. One recent outbreak of food poisoning aboard an airliner resulted in claims for compensation estimated in millions of pounds! *No caterer should have a customer's death on his conscience*. For these reasons students on food-related courses should learn the causes of food poisoning and it's prevention. It is an unfortunate fact that some poorly-trained staff do not understand the need for, or are prepared to ignore, good hygiene. This should not deter better informed food handlers from maintaining their own high standards and doing their utmost to ensure that all food is produced hygienically, if possible trying to improve the situation by educating less well informed people.

18.2   CAUSES OF FOOD POISONING

There are several causes of food poisoning but the prime cause in the UK is due to the growth of food poisoning bacteria in food. Bacteria (see sect. 11.3) are microscopic living organisms which cause food poisoning in one of two ways. Some food poisoning bacteria, e.g. *Salmonella* species grow in food and after several hours will be present in very large numbers (see Table 14.1). Consumption of large numbers (a minimum of 100 000) of such living bacteria enables the bacteria to become established inside the gut (see sect. 17.1) resulting in food poisoning of the consumer. Other bacteria, e.g. some strains of *Staphylococcus aureus*, grow in the food and produce toxins or poisons in the food. Consumption of these toxins can result in food poisoning.

18.3   SOURCES OF FOOD-POISONING BACTERIA

Bacteria, including those capable of causing food poisoning are widely distributed in nature (see sect. 11.3). Any meal causing food poisoning has to be investigated and the reasons for the food being contaminated (i.e. how they arrived in the food) investigated. It is convenient to consider contamination of food under three headings:
1. Food contamination by humans.
2. Food itself being contaminated.
3. Cross contamination.

18.3.1   FOOD CONTAMINATION BY HUMANS

Humans can be sources of food-poisoning bacteria. The gut, infected cuts and spots, and the nose are areas of potentially very heavy contamination (see Fig. 18.1). The whole purpose of personal hygiene is to prevent humans from acting as a source of food poisoning bacteria. Realising this should make every food handler concerned to maintain high standards of personal hygiene.

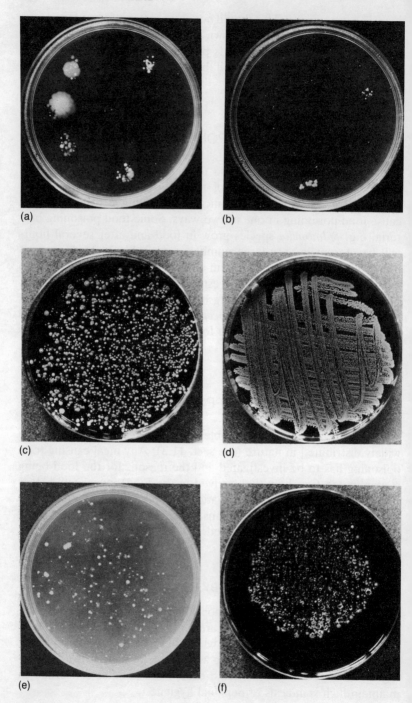

18.3.2 CONTAMINATED FOOD

Unfortunately many items of food arriving in a hotel or restaurant kitchen may already be contaminated with food-poisoning organisms. One recent survey showed that 79 per cent of frozen poultry was contaminated with *Salmonellae*. Providing the poultry is handled correctly and cooked thoroughly no problems will occur, if not then the chances of food poisoning are quite high. The contamination rate for other foods may not be so high but it is reasonable to suspect that many raw food products could be contaminated with food-poisoning bacteria before their arrival in a kitchen. This is really not so surprising when one of the first operations after the slaughtering of food animals is to remove their protective coats (hides, skin, etc.) making them susceptible to contamination from many sources (including their own intestines, air, contaminated equipment, human handling, etc.). Similarly, vegetables can be contaminated from soil and fish from water.

18.3.3 CROSS CONTAMINATION

This means the transfer of bacteria from contaminated material on to food. This can happen directly, if raw food is stored touching cooked food or if raw food is placed above and drips on to other food, e.g. defrosting poultry stored above cooked ham or trifle. Cross contamination can occur indirectly if a knife, chopping board, dish cloth, bowl, mixer or any other utensil or work surface touches contaminated food, e.g. raw meat, and is then used, without thorough cleaning, on other foods.

Preventing cross contamination requires correct organisation and layout of food preparation areas, well-designed equipment, good standards of cleanliness and correct food storage. Foods in catering establishments can also be contaminated by flies and other pests (see Ch. 13), domestic pets and by dust.

18.3.4 GROWTH OF FOOD POISONING BACTERIA

For cases of food poisoning to occur it is not just sufficient for the food to be contaminated – there must be a period when the harmful bacteria grow in the food. *Even if the initial contamination of the food with the food poisoning bacteria is not the caterer's fault –*

FIG. 18.1 Colonies of bacteria growing on nutrient media isolated from: (a) hands before washing; (b) hands after washing; (c) fingernails; (d) the nose; (e) cough; (f) dishcloth (the bacterial growth follows the pattern of the weave of the cloth)

allowing them to grow in food is! Foods that can support the growth of food-poisoning bacteria are termed 'high risk foods'. Before bacteria will grow in such foods they need the correct conditions for growth, e.g. the correct pH, moisture level and temperature (see sect. 14.4). Food poisoning bacteria normally grow between 10 °C and 45 °C with an optimum (i.e. best) temperature of 37 °C. This means that they will grow quite well at room temperature, especially during the summer when the ambient (surrounding) temperatures in a hot kitchen can approach 30 °C.

18.4 HOW FOOD HYGIENE WORKS

The aim of food hygiene is to ensure that food is safe to eat. To ensure this the caterer can use two strategies:
 i. to prevent contamination of foods;
 ii. to prevent the growth of bacteria in contaminated foods.

18.4.1 PREVENTING THE CONTAMINATION OF FOODS

To prevent food poisoning, bacteria need to be prevented from contaminating food. Good personal hygiene will ensure that the caterer himself does not contaminate the food. Good general hygiene, i.e. proper design and construction of premises and equipment coupled with thorough and regular cleaning, will minimise cross-contamination and decrease the numbers of contaminating bacteria in or on foods. Caterers should work on the common sense principle of '*clean as you go*'. This means that after handling raw food any equipment, work surfaces, etc. should be thoroughly cleaned, hands should be washed and only then should any other food be handled. Better still, reserve separate areas and equipment for handling raw foods. Proper cleaning does *not* just mean wiping down with a damp cloth so that the surface or equipment *looks* clean but it means a two or three stage process:

1. Remove food debris, i.e. the larger pieces or particles of residual food:
2. Wash down with hot water (50°–60 °C) and a detergent;
3. Either use an appropriate chemical disinfectant or germicide to kill any remaining 'invisible' micro-organisms or disinfect with very hot water or steam.

Sometimes, sanitisers (chemicals with a combined detergent and disinfectant action) are used, and thus stages 2 and 3 are combined. The use of such chemicals is not usually as efficient as the use of separate detergents and disinfectants. Good personal hygiene and general hygiene will minimise the number of bacteria contaminating food but unfortunately the food may be contaminated before entering the catering premises and therefore other controls are needed.

18.4.2 PREVENTING THE GROWTH OF BACTERIA IN CONTAMINATED FOOD

The other strategy to ensure food hygiene is to *assume that all 'high-risk foods' are contaminated* and to store or cook them in such a way that any contaminating bacteria will not grow or survive. Remember, food poisoning requires bacterial growth or growth plus toxin production in the food. Preventing microbial growth and survival is thus a vital part of food hygiene. Catering errors where food is stored at the wrong temperature for a period of time, which can be as short as 1–2 h, can result in bacterial multiplication and possibly food poisoning. The 'temperature danger zone' in which high risk foods must *not* be stored is between 10 °C and 63 °C. Below 10 °C food poisoning bacteria will not grow because there is insufficient warmth and the bacteria are inactive. Above 63 °C food poisoning bacteria are killed by the heat. In catering the rule is to keep foods hot or cold but *never* warm. Equipment used in catering to keep foods out of the 'danger zone' include refrigerators which operate between 1° and 4 °C and may be of the domestic type or the larger 'walk in' type (chilled or cold rooms). Refrigeration keeps food safe by preventing *food poisoning* bacteria from growing but it will not stop *food spoilage* organisms from growing. Perishable items deteriorate if left in refrigerators for more than a few days. Deep freezers (3 star) operate at −18 °C and completely inhibit microbial growth. Ovens of various types are used to cook food which if cooked correctly will be free of harmful micro-organisms. Food having been cooked or heated in ovens but which is not to be served immediately must either be cooled quickly or be kept hot. Hot cupboards with glass or metal sides can be used for plate warming or the short-term holding of hot foods, e.g. whole meals, pies or pasties. Similarly, *bains-marie* contain wells heated underneath by hot water or steam and can keep foods hot. Note *bains-marie* and hot cupboards must *not* be used for heating up cold foods but only for *keeping* hot foods hot. Cold foods placed in *bains-marie* and hot cupboards will only become warm and thus become a health risk.

18.5 RULES FOR PERSONAL HYGIENE

Any person going into catering should familiarise themselves with the rules of personal hygiene. These rules are easier to remember and obey if the underlying principles are understood (see Table 18.1).

TABLE 18.1 Rules for Hand Washing

Rules for Hand Washing	Why is it important
Wash hands before handling food.	Bacteria already on the hands could cause food poisoning.
Wash hands after visiting the toilet.	Potential food-poisoning bacteria from gut and faeces get on to the hands.
Wash hands after blowing the nose, coughing or sneezing. Never cough or sneeze over food.	Many people harbour a particular type of food-poisoning bacteria in their nose.
Wash hands after smoking. Never smoke in food preparation areas.	Bacteria from the nose and lips are transferred on to hands during smoking.
Wash hands between handling raw foods and cooked foods.	To prevent transfer of bacteria from heavily contaminated raw foods to uncontaminated cooked foods, i.e. to prevent cross contamination.
Wash hands after handling refuse or similar 'dirty jobs'.	To prevent cross contamination.

Hand washing should be thorough and involve the use of plenty of hot soapy water!

The most important part of the human body in personal hygiene is the hands because these come into contact with food most frequently. Special care must be taken to clean hands thoroughly, particularly the fingernails and forearms (see Fig. 18.1). After washing the hands they should be dried thoroughly with a hot-air drier, disposable towel or clean linen automatic roller towel. Hands washed frequently may need an antiseptic hand cream to keep the skin in good condition. Sinks used for hand-washing should not be used for any other purpose. Hand-washing even thoroughly carried out will only reduce, not eliminate bacteria from the hands (see Fig. 18.1) and therefore all the other rules of personal hygiene must be observed (see Table 18.2).

Remember it is a legal requirement for caterers to have good standards of personal hygiene.

TABLE 18.2 Rules for Personal Hygiene

Rule	Reason
Personal habits should be good, i.e. no nail biting, spitting, touching of ears, hair or nose, dipping of fingers into food, returning of licked spoons into food.	The human body can harbour food poisoning bacteria which can be transferred to foods.
Any cuts, spots, burns etc. to be protected by water-proof dressings.	Infected areas store potential food-poisoning bacteria in large numbers.
Fingernails must be short. Do not wear nail varnish.	Bacteria can be trapped under fingernails in large numbers.
Always wear clean, protective overalls and head coverings. Do not wear short-sleeved overalls over long-sleeved jumpers, etc. Outdoor clothing must be kept well away from food production areas.	Many bacteria can be trapped in the outer and inner layers of ordinary clothing which could contaminate food.
Do not wear hair clips, loose jewellery, rings (other than a plain wedding ring).	Jewellery can fall into foods. Large numbers of bacteria can be trapped next to the skin under jewellery and can be transferred on to food.
Tell your superior if you are suffering from a stomach upset (diarrhoea, vomiting, abdominal pain), skin or throat infection.	Any of these conditions can be caused by bacteria capable of causing food poisoning and therefore there is a greater possibility of food being contaminated with harmful organisms just by your presence.

QUESTIONS

1. During an interview for a job you are asked to explain the meaning of food hygiene. Describe fully the answer you would give.
2. Discuss the statement 'good hygiene can save caterers money'.
3. Explain the term cross contamination and illustrate your answer with practical catering examples.
4. Write short notes on the prevention of bacterial growth in food.
5. Construct a table of rules concerning handwashing for use by catering personnel.

APPENDIX OF PRACTICAL EXPERIMENTS

EXPERIMENT 1   MEASUREMENT OF THE DENSITY OF SOLIDS

1.1   INTRODUCTION

Density is mass/volume (m/v) and all density measurements involve weighing the sample to find the mass. Different techniques are involved in volume determination, depending on the particular food-stuffs examined. The methods outlined below involve different ways of finding the volume of the sample.

1.2   APPARATUS AND REAGENTS

Callipers
Displacement can
Top pan balance (reading to two decimal places)
Measuring cylinders (50 and 100 cm³)
Glass trough
Wide-necked filter funnel
Sheet of paper

Samples of food
e.g. potato,
carrot,
bread,
flour,
cheese.

1.3   METHODS

SOLIDS WITH A DEFINITE GEOMETRIC SHAPE

For example, cheese cubes, bread cut into cubes, etc.
(a) Cut as large a cube as possible from the sample.
(b) Determine the mass of the sample using the top pan balance.
(c) Measure the length (l), breadth (b), and height (h) of the sample and calculate the volume of the same.

   volume = length × breadth × height.

Results

Mass of sample (m_s) = ———————————— g

Volume of sample (v_s) = ———————————— cm³

Density = $\dfrac{m_s}{v_s}$

Density = ———————————— g cm⁻³.

IRREGULARLY SHAPED SOLIDS NOT AFFECTED BY WATER – THE DISPLACEMENT CAN METHOD

For example, potatoes, carrots

(a) The displacement can is filled to the brim (initially placing a finger over the spout) then allowed to overflow into a sink until the level reaches that shown in Fig. A1(*a*).

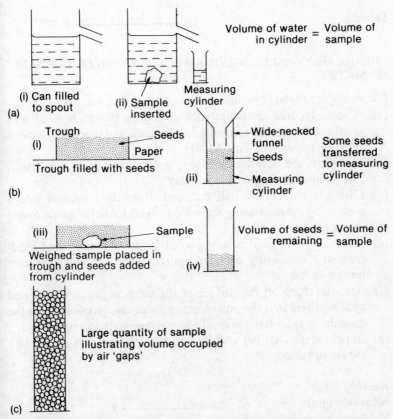

FIG. A1 Measurement of densities of solids (a) Displacement can method (b) Method of seeds (c) Bulk density

(b) A suitably-sized sample of food is weighed, i.e. one which will fit into the can!
(c) A measuring cylinder is placed under the spout and the sample is gently lowered into the water.
(d) The volume of water displaced and collected in the measuring cylinder equals the volume of the sample.
(e) Repeat steps (a), (c) and (d) taking the average of the two readings obtained for the volume of the sample.

Results

Mass of sample (m_s)   = _____ g
Volume of water displaced (1)   = _____ cm^3
                          (2)   = _____ cm^3
Average volume (v_s)   = _____ cm^3
Density   = $\dfrac{m_s}{v_s}$
Density   = _____ g cm^{-3}.

IRREGULARLY SHAPED SOLIDS AFFECTED BY WATER – METHOD OF SEEDS

For example, bread, biscuits
(a) A suitably-sized container such as a glass trough is filled with small seeds, e.g. rape, mustard or linseed, and placed on a clean sheet of paper (see Fig. A1(b)).
(b) The seeds are 'levelled off' using a flat object such as a ruler.
(c) The sample of foodstuff is weighed.
(d) Carefully pour about half the seeds from the container into a measuring cylinder using the wide-necked funnel to avoid losing any seeds.
(e) The sample of food is now placed in the container and seeds from the measuring cylinder poured back into the container until it is full.
(f) After levelling off the surface of the seeds in the container and pouring them into the measuring cylinder the excess seeds in the measuring cylinder represent the volume of the sample.
(g) Repeat steps (d), (e) and (f) and take the average of the two values obtained.

Results

Mass of sample (m_s)   = _____ g
Volume of sample (1)   = _____ cm^3
                  (2)   = _____ cm^3

Average volume (v_s)   =   _____ cm³

Density   = $\dfrac{m_s}{v_s}$

Density   =   _____ g cm⁻³

DENSITY OF POWDERS – 'ONE TAP' METHOD

For example, flour.
(a) Weigh a clean, dry 100 cm³ measuring cylinder.
(b) Fill the measuring cylinder to just above the 100 cm³ mark with the powder and reweigh.
(c) Gently tap the base of the cylinder on the bench and read the volume of the powder directly, ensuring first that the surface is reasonably level.

    This method is really a measure of the bulk density since there are air gaps between the particles of the sample. These air spaces are more obvious with larger particle sizes, see Fig. A1(c).

Results

Mass of cylinder (m_1)	=	_____ g
Mass of cylinder + flour (m_2)	=	_____ g
Mass of flour (m_f)	= $m_2 - m_1$	g
	=	_____ g
Volume of flour (v_f)	=	_____ cm³
Density	= $\dfrac{m_f}{v_f}$	
Density	=	_____ g cm⁻³

EXPERIMENT 2   MEASUREMENT OF RELATIVE DENSITY

2.1   INTRODUCTION

Relative density is the density of a substance relative to that of water (see sect. 1.4). The methods outlined below involve the use of a relative density bottle (a container of known accurate volume), the construction of a 'test-tube' hydrometer and the use of commercial hydrometers.

2.2   APPARATUS AND REAGENTS

Relative density bottle with ground glass stopper
Top pan balance
100 cm³ measuring cylinders
Thin-walled test-tube
50 cm³ measuring cylinder
Selection of small masses (e.g. 1, 2, 5 g)
Series of hydrometers ranging from 0.700 to 1.200

Alcohol
Brine
Sugar solutions
Glycerine (or glycerol)
White sticky labels
Pencil

2.3   METHODS

USING A RELATIVE DENSITY BOTTLE (SEE FIG. A2)

(a) Weigh the bottle and stopper.
(b) Fill the bottle with liquid and insert the stopper. Wipe away any excess liquid with a soft tissue.
(c) Reweigh the bottle and liquid.
(d) Empty the bottle and wash thoroughly with water. Refill the bottle with water and replace the stopper.
(e) Wipe away excess water and reweigh the bottle and water.
(f) Record the temperature of the liquids.
(g) **Note**: Take care not to hold the bottle in the palm of the hand as this will cause expansion and loss of liquid.
(h) Record your results in the table below:

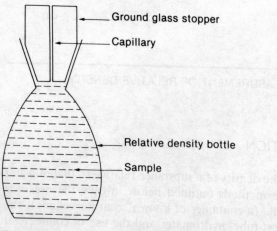

FIG. A2 Measurement of relative density using relative density bottle

Mass of empty bottle and stopper (m_B)	=	_____ g
Mass of bottle and liquid (m_L)	=	_____ g
Mass of bottle and water (m_W)	=	_____ g

$$\text{Relative density (RD)} = \frac{\text{mass of any volume of liquid}}{\text{mass of same volume of water}}$$

$$= \frac{m_L - m_B}{m_W - m_B}$$

$$= \underline{\hspace{3cm}}$$

CONSTRUCTION OF A 'TEST-TUBE' HYDROMETER (see Fig. A3)

(a) Fill a 50 cm³ measuring cylinder with water.
(b) Attach a white label to one side of the test-tube. This will be used to mark a scale on the side of the tube. Use a pencil to mark the scale as ballpoint pen and felt-tip pen marks are soluble in certain solvents.
(c) Place the tube in the measuring cylinder and carefully add the small weights until the tube floats vertically and is approximately

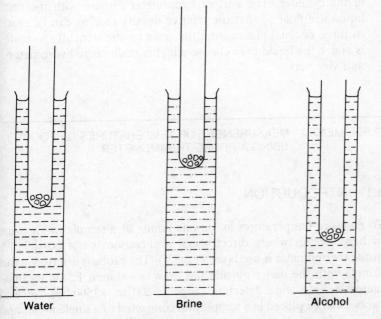

Water   Brine   Alcohol

FIG. A3 Construction of a test-tube hydrometer

half immersed. Hold the tube at an angle when adding the weights to avoid breaking the bottom of the tube. Mark the level of the liquid on the white label.

(d) Fill a 50 cm³ measuring cylinder with the test liquid and place the test-tube (and weights) in the liquid. Mark the level of the liquid.

(e) Measure the distance from the bottom of the tube to each of the two marks, i.e. the depth of the tube in the water and the depth in the test liquid.

(f) Record your results in the table below:

Depth of the tube in the water (d_W) = _____ cm

Depth of the tube in the liquid (d_L) = _____ cm

$$\text{Relative density (RD)} = \frac{\text{depth of tube in water}}{\text{depth of tube in liquid}}$$

$$= \frac{d_W}{d_L}$$

$$= \underline{\hspace{3cm}}$$

USE OF A COMMERCIAL HYDROMETER

(a) Fill the measuring cylinder with the test liquid.

(b) From the range of hydrometers select any hydrometer and place in the cylinder. The correct hydrometer for use with the test liquid will float so that the relative density reading can be read to three decimal places from the scale on the stem. If the scale is above the liquid then choose a higher scale range hydrometer, and vice versa.

EXPERIMENT 3   MEASUREMENT OF TEMPERATURES OF FOODS USING A PROBE THERMOMETER

3.1   INTRODUCTION

To measure temperatures at various points of a sample in an oven or blast freezer where direct visual observation is not possible, a probe thermometer is used (see Fig. 3.3). The probe is inserted in the sample with the meter outside the oven or cabinet. Probe thermometers have a wide detection range (-200 to $+1500$ °C). Several probes can be placed in a sample and connected to a single meter and using a multiswitch temperature at different parts of the sample can be measured.

3.2   APPARATUS AND REAGENTS

Probe (thermocouple) Ice
Meter – calibrated in °C Boiling water
Food samples, e.g. steam puddings, custard, meat pie, large potato heated in boiling water, etc..

3.3   METHOD

(a) Connect the probe to the meter terminals and check the calibration by immersing the probe in ice/water at 0 °C and boiling water at 100 °C.

(b) The probe is inserted into the foodstuff (solid or liquid) and the temperature recorded from the meter in °C. Check the temperatures of tinned puddings which have been reheated in boiling water and note the time taken for the sample to achieve the required temperature. Similarly note the time taken for large potatoes and pies to reach temperature at the centre during cooking. Measure samples of custard, pies, omelettes and meats as they are frozen in a blast freezer. If the probe is used in an oven or a blast freezer fold wires carefully so that they give good door seals. Check temperatures of foods stored in pie cabinets and *bains-marie*.

EXPERIMENT 4   TO DEMONSTRATE OHM'S LAW

4.1   INTRODUCTION

Ohm's law states that the ratio of the current flowing through a conductor (I) to the potential difference (V) across the conductor is a constant, known as the resistance of the conductor.

i.e. $\dfrac{V}{I}$ = a constant, R

where R is resistance of the conductor (measured in ohms)

The current flowing through a length of wire is adjusted by means of a variable resistance (rheostat) and the potential difference across the wire measured using a voltmeter.

4.2 APPARATUS AND REAGENTS

0–12 V d.c. power supply
Ammeter (0–5 A)
Voltmeter (0–5 V)
Variable resistance
Length of wire
Connecting leads

4.3 METHOD

(a) Set up the circuit as shown in Fig. A4.
(b) Adjust the rheostat to give an initial current of 0.5 A and note the reading of the voltmeter.

Circuit diagram

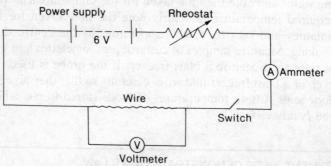

FIG. A4 To prove Ohm's Law

(c) Vary the current in 0.5 A stages (1.0, 1.5, 2.0 A) and record the corresponding voltages.
(d) Record your results in the table shown below:

Current (I) (A)	Potential difference (V) (V)	V/I Ω
0.5		
1.0		
1.5		
2.0		

(e) The ratio of V/I should be a constant, proving Ohm's Law. A graph of V against I will be a straight line with a slope of R (resistance).

EXPERIMENT 5 ELECTRICAL CONDUCTIVITY OF MATERIALS

5.1 INTRODUCTION

This experiment is designed to indicate whether a material will conduct electricity at low voltages, i.e. whether it is an insulator or a conductor.

5.2 APPARATUS AND REAGENTS

0–12 V d.c. power supply
Milliammeter (0–1000 mA)
Lamp holder
Thick copper wire
Thin copper wire
Glass rod
Wooden ruler
Tea spoon
Rubber tubing
Torch bulb
Switch

Connecting leads
Crocodile clips
Nichrome wire
Aluminium strip
Plastic strip
Water
Saturated salt solution
Dilute acid
200 cm³ beakers

5.3 METHOD

(a) Connect the circuit as shown in Fig. A5(a) and attach the sample using crocodile clips.

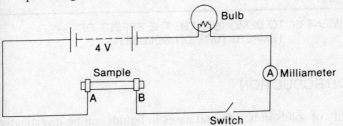

FIG. A5a To demonstrate conductivity of materials

(b) Close the switch and observe if the bulb glows.
(c) Note the current on the milliammeter and feel if the sample becomes heated.
(d) Solutions can be tested by placing the terminals A and B into the solution as shown in Fig. A5(b).

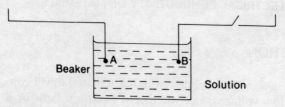

FIG. A5b Modified circuit for solutions

(e) Record your results in the table shown below:

Sample	Bulb glows Conductor	Bulb does not glow Insulator	mA	Sample becomes hot
Thick copper wire				
Thin copper wire				
Thin Nichrome wire				
Strip of aluminium				
Teaspoon				
Water				
Saturated salt solution				
Dilute acid				
Human body				
Wood				
Glass rod				
Plastic				
Rubber tubing				

Indicate response using a tick

EXPERIMENT 6   TO DEMONSTRATE THE EFFECT OF TEMPERATURE ON SOLUBILITY

6.1   INTRODUCTION

Solubility of solids in liquids and gases in liquids can be investigated using sugar in water and carbon dioxide in water respectively.

6.2   APPARATUS AND REAGENTS

Top pan balance
Bunsen burner
Tripod
Test-tube with delivery tube
Thermometer
Glass stirring rods
Water baths at 20 °C, 30 °C and 50 °C.
500 cm³ beakers
Measuring cylinder 50 cm³
Stop watch

Sugar
Limewater
Carbonated drinks

6.3   METHODS

SOLUBILITY OF SOLIDS IN LIQUIDS

(a) Weight 10 g of sugar into 90 g of water at 20 °C and stir to dissolve.
(b) Add a further 5 g of sugar and stir again.
(c) Repeat the additions in 5 g portions till no more sugar will dissolve, i.e. a saturated solution of sugar is produced. Record the amount of sugar added.
(d) Repeat the experiment at 30 °C and 50 °C.
(e) Plot a graph of the maximum amount of sugar dissolved at each temperature and deduce a relationship between the solubility of sugar and temperature.

SOLUBILITY OF GASES IN LIQUIDS

(a) Place 30 cm³ of a carbonated drink into a test-tube.
(b) Quickly fit the cork and delivery tube leading to a beaker of limewater.
(c) Immerse the test-tube in a water bath at 20 °C.
(d) Observe the time taken for the limewater to turn milky.
(e) Repeat the experiment at 30 °C and 50 °C.
(f) Plot a graph of the time taken for the limewater to turn milky against temperature and deduce a relationship between the solubility of gases in liquids and temperature.

EXPERIMENT 7 MEASUREMENT OF THE pH OF LIQUIDS AND SOLIDS

7.1 INTRODUCTION

The pH values of some common substances used in catering may be determined using universal indicator paper or solution, or a pH meter (see sect. 8.4.1).

7.2 APPARATUS AND REAGENTS

Universal indicator paper (pH 1–14)
Colour comparison chart
Universal indicator solution
Colour comparison chart
100 cm³ beakers
Clock glasses
Spatulas
pH meter and electrode

Samples (to include those in Table A1)
pH 4 and pH 9 buffer solutions

7.3 METHODS

USING A pH METER

(a) A pH meter can be used for all liquids. The meter is standardised by immersing the electrode in a buffer solution of known pH, e.g. pH 4, adjusting the scale reading so that it coincides with the pH value of the buffer and checking the scale using a buffer of a second value, e.g. pH 9.
(b) Wash the electrode in distilled water. Wipe carefully with a very soft tissue.
(c) Half fill a 100 cm³ beaker with the sample, stir. Immerse the electrode in the solution and note the pH reading on the scale. The readings are accurate to 0.1.

USING UNIVERSAL INDICATOR (pH) PAPER OR SOLUTION

(a) pH paper is moistened and then placed in the sample. The colour obtained is compared with the standard colour chart. Readings are accurate to one unit of pH.

(b) For solids, pH paper is moistened and the solid is then smeared on.

(c) For some powders etc. a small amount of the sample can be placed on a clock glass and a few drops of universal indicator solution added. The colour is again compared with standard pH colour chart.

EXPERIMENT 8   USE OF A COMPOUND MICROSCOPE

TABLE A1 pH of liquids and solids used in catering

Sample	Measured pH	Method used for measurement of pH
Distilled water		
Tap water		
Pure unsweetened orange juice		
Pure unsweetened lemon juice		
Vinegar		
Oranges		
Lemons		
Butter		
Cheese		
Bread		
Flour		
Jam		
Potato		
Carrot		
Meat		
Fish		
Gravy		
Milk		
Double cream		
Ice cream		
Sour milk		
Ice cream		
Yogurt		
Egg yolk		
Egg white		
Stale egg		
Fresh egg		

8.1   INTRODUCTION

The human eye cannot see objects that are smaller than 0.1 mm in diameter and many studies in biology require the use of a microscope. A magnifying glass is an example of a simple microscope and would enable some larger micro-organisms and cells to be observed. To obtain more detail or to examine most micro-organisms a compound microscope is used. This consists of two magnifying lenses, one magnifying the enlarged image of the other. There are many different types and makes of compound microscope on sale in the UK and students should follow the manufacturers instructions. The following therefore are only guidelines to assist the student.

8.2   APPARATUS AND REAGENTS

One monocular compound microscope
Lens tissue
Immersion oil

8.3   METHOD

(a) Students should familiarise themselves with the main component parts of the microscope, comparing their actual model with the diagram in Fig. A6.

Beneath the stage is a built-in lamp to illuminate the object. An iris diaphragm controls the amount of light entering the condenser. The condenser concentrates the beams of light passing through the object.

On the stage the object is mounted on a 2 × 1 in glass slide and held in position by two metal clips.

Above the stage the lenses are held in position by a hollow tube known as the body tube. At the top of the body tube is the eye-piece which magnifies the image produced by the objective lens. At the base of the body tube is a revolving nosepiece which holds the objective lenses. Screwed into the nosepiece are two, three, or four objective lenses which are of different magnifying power and produce a magnified image of the object.

The knob beneath the stage, attached to the condenser mechanism, adjusts the beam of light entering the object and controls the clarity of the image. The larger knob attached to the main frame is the coarse adjustment control and is used to roughly focus the object. The smaller separate knob, or sometimes the central part of the coarse adjuster, is the fine focus control used to precisely focus the image.

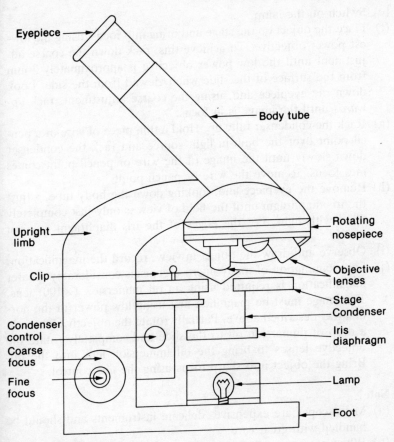

FIG. A6 A monocular compound microscope

The total magnification of the microscope is calculated for each objective by multiplying the eyepiece magnification by the objective magnification.

i.e. eyepiece × objective = total magnification
e.g. (×10)   (×40)   (×400)

Note: Always focus using the low power objective first, then go to high power. The coarse adjustment control must *never* be used when the high power objective is in use.
(b) Check that the objective lenses are clean.
(c) Check that the eyepiece is free from dust.
(d) Check that the condenser is in the correct position, i.e. about 1–2 mm below the stage.

(e) Switch on the lamp.

(f) Place the object on the stage and bring into focus, using the lowest power objective. To achieve this, rack down the coarse adjustment until the low power objective is approximately 3 mm from the surface of the slide when viewed from the side. Look down the eyepiece and, using the coarse adjustment, rack *upwards* until the image is in focus.

(g) Rack the condenser fully up. Hold a thin piece of wire or a pencil point over the built-in light source and rack the condenser down slowly until the image of the wire or pencil point comes into focus. Remove the wire or pencil point.

(h) Remove the eyepiece and, looking down the body tube, adjust the iris diaphragm until the field of view is only just completely filled with light, i.e. the edges of the iris diaphragm are just visible.

(i) Observe and draw the object in view, record the magnification.

(j) For examination of many micro-organisms considerably greater magnification is required using an oil immersion (×100) lens. The image must be magnified first using low power in the normal way described above. Partially rotate the objective lens, add a drop of immersion oil to the slide and completely rotate the objective lenses to bring the oil immersion lens into the oil. Bring the object into sharp focus using the *fine* control.

Note

(a) Microscopes are expensive, delicate instruments and should be handled with great care.

(b) When not in use, the microscope should be protected by a box or dust cover.

(c) Clean any immersion oil from the lenses completely using *lens tissue*.

(d) Do not allow low power, or any other non-oil objectives to come into contact with the immersion oil.

(e) If the microscope has to be moved lift by the upright limb and NOT by the body tube.

(f) Do not examine wet preparations unless they are protected by a cover slip.

EXPERIMENT 9 EXAMINATION OF CELLS USING MICROSCOPY

9.1 INTRODUCTION

A number of differences between cells can be observed by using a light microscope. Cells consist mainly of clear protoplasmic material which makes a detailed examination of their structure difficult. This problem is partially overcome by staining the cells.

9.2 APPARATUS AND REAGENTS

Compound microscope
Microscope slides
Coverslips
Dissecting needles
Knife
Blotting paper
Spatula/spoon
Bunsen burner

0.1% methylene blue
Dilute iodine solution (1.0 g iodine + 2.0 g potassium iodide in 300 cm^3 distilled water).
Natural yoghurt.
Yeast suspension (1.0 g bakers's yeast suspended in 100 cm^3 distilled water).

9.3 METHODS

EXAMINATION OF ANIMAL-TYPE CELL

(a) Gently scrape the inside of your cheek with a blunt instrument such as a clean spoon or spatula.
(b) Transfer the scrapings to a drop of water on a clean microscope slide.
(c) Carefully cover with a cover slip, avoiding air bubble formation.
(d) Examine under low and high power using the microscope. It should be possible to observe the nucleus and the cytoplasm in the cells, although many cells may be crumpled and irregular in outline. More detail is visible by irrigating the slide with methylene blue (see Experiment 10).

EXAMINATION OF PLANT CELLS

(a) Take a small onion and cut it into two vertically.
(b) Lift out one of the inner leaves.

(c) Break the leaf into two and peel off a small piece of the epidermis.
(d) Mount the epidermis in dilute iodine on a glass slide and add a coverslip.
(e) Observe under low and high power. Note the cell wall, nucleus, cytoplasm and vacuole.

EXAMINATION OF YEAST CELLS

(a) Transfer a drop of yeast suspension on to a microscope slide. Cover with a cover slip and examine.
(b) Transfer a drop of yeast suspension to a second microscope slide, allow to dry to form a smear.
(c) Heat-fix the smear by passing the slide several times through a Bunsen burner flame.
(d) Allow the slide to cool and stain with methylene blue for 5 min.
(e) Wash off the stain and blot dry.
(f) Examine under low power, then high power using the oil immersion lens.
(g) Observe and record (see Fig. 11.8). Look for yeast cells in the process of budding.

EXAMINATION OF BACTERIA IN YOGHURT

(a) Place a drop of sterile saline on a microscope slide.
(b) Transfer a small quantity of natural yoghurt to the slide and mix in with the saline. This is best carried out with a sterile wire loop.
(c) Allow to dry to form a smear.
(d) Heat-fix the smear.
(e) Allow to cool and stain with methylene blue for 3 min. Wash off excess stain and blot dry.
(f) Examine under low power, then high power using an oil immersion lens.
(g) Observe and record (see Fig. 11.5). Look for approximately equal numbers of Streptococci (round bacteria in chains) and Lactobacilli (long, rod-shaped bacteria).

EXPERIMENT 10   TO ILLUSTRATE THE EFFECT OF OSMOTIC PRESSURE ON CELLS

10.1   INTRODUCTION

Osmosis is the passage of water from a region of low concentration to a region of higher concentration across a semi-permeable membrane. Cells must be maintained within an osmotically correct environment otherwise they will gain or lose water, so swelling or shrinking. Use is made of the latter effect in the preservation of food by means of sugar or salt solutions.

10.2   APPARATUS AND REAGENTS

Rhubarb leaf stalk   30% (w/v) sucrose solution
Coverslip   5% (w/v) sodium chloride solution
Glass slides
Microscope (see Experiment 8)
Blotting paper

10.3   METHOD

(a) Strip a small piece of the epidermis of the rhubarb petiole (leaf stalk) and mount in water on a slide. Cover with a cover slip.

(b) Observe under low and high power using the microscope.

(c) Place a drop of sugar or salt solution against one edge of the coverslip. Against the opposite edge of the coverslip hold a small piece of blotting paper. This soaks up the water from underneath the cover slip and draws the sugar or salt solution under the cover slip. This technique is known as irrigation.

(d) Repeat the irrigation procedure at least once to ensure that the water is fully replaced.

(e) Leave for 10 min and re-examine the cells under the microscope. Look for plasmolysis (shrinkage of the pink cytoplasm away from the cell wall).

(f) Find out if plasmolysis is reversible by repeating the irrigation, this time replacing the sugar or salt solution with distilled water.

EXPERIMENT 11   IDENTIFICATION OF CHEMICAL GROUPS IN FOOD

11.1   INTRODUCTION

The main organic chemical constituents of food can be classified as carbohydrates, lipids, proteins or vitamins. Carbohydrates are relatively easily identified by giving a positive Molisch test, and can be further identified by more specific chemical tests, e.g. Benedict's test for reducing sugars, iodine test for starch, etc. Proteins can be detected either by using reactions involving individual amino acids, e.g. Millon's test, or by the presence of peptide linkages joining the amino acids together, e.g. biuret reaction. Lipids are a more diverse group of compounds but it is mainly the fats and oils, solid and liquid triglycerides, that caterers encounter. Lipids all share the property of being relatively insoluble in water but soluble in organic solvents such as acetone, ether, etc. Vitamins are also a diverse group of chemicals, their only common property being that they are required in minute amounts in the diet. The easiest vitamin to identify is vitamin C.

11.2   APPARATUS AND REAGENTS

Bunsen burner
Test-tubes and racks
Pipettes (1 cm³ and 5 cm³)
500 cm³ beaker (for use as a boiling water bath)
Burette (10 cm³)

1% (w/v) glucose solution
1% (w/v) sucrose solution
Starch suspension
Egg albumen
Butter
Milk
Cooking oil
Suspensions of food ground up in water, e.g. pea, bread, etc.
Orange juice (fresh and tinned)
Molisch reagent
Sudan III
Millon's reagent
2M copper sulphate
2M sodium hydroxide
2,6-dichlorophenolindophenol solution (0.41 g l⁻¹)
Dilute iodine solution (see Experiment 9)
Concentrated sulphuric acid

11.3   METHOD

In each experiment use the test solutions and a control consisting of distilled water.

TESTS ON CARBOHYDRATES

1. Molisch test
   (a) To 2 cm^3 of test solution in a test-tube add a few drops of Molisch reagent and mix well.
   (b) Add *carefully* down the side of the test tube 1–2 cm^3 of concentrated sulphuric acid; this forms a layer beneath the aqueous solution. A purple ring appears at the interface of the liquids if a carbohydrate is present.
2. Iodine test
   (a) Place 2 cm^3 of test solution in a test-tube and add three drops of dilute iodine solution. Starch, a polysaccharide, gives a blue-black colour.
   (b) Repeat the test applying iodine to the cut surfaces of foods, e.g. bread and potato.
3. Benedict's test for reducing sugars (e.g. glucose)
   (a) To 3 cm^3 of Benedict's solution in a test-tube add 2 cm^3 of test solution.
   (b) Boil in a boiling water bath for 4 min. The production of a green, yellow or red precipitate indicates the presence of reducing sugar in the test solution. The commonest non-reducing sugar is sucrose (cane sugar).

TESTS FOR PROTEINS

1. Millon's test
   (a) Add three drops of Millon's reagent 2 cm^3 of test solution in a test-tube.
   (b) Boil in a boiling water bath for 5 min. A pink-red coloration indicates the presence of protein. This reaction only works in neutral or slightly acid solutions.
2. Biuret test
   (a) To 3 cm^3 of test solution in a test-tube add 3 cm^3 of 2M sodium hydroxide. Mix and add three drops of 2M copper sulphate solution. Remix. A violet colour indicates the presence of protein.

TEST ON LIPIDS (FATS AND OILS)

1. The grease spot test
   (a) Rub a small quantity of fat, oil or fatty food on to a piece of filter paper. The filter paper becomes translucent as the grease spot is formed. The grease spot will wash out with acetone but not with water.
2. The Sudan III test
   (a) Add 1 cm³ of oil to 1 cm³ of water in a test-tube.
   (b) Add a few drops of Sudan III and shake. On standing, the oil separates from the water and will have taken up the red dye.

TEST FOR VITAMIN C

(a) Place 1 cm³ of 2,6-dichlorophenolindophenol solution in a test-tube and using a burette add either orange squash, fresh or canned orange juice to the dye in the test tube.
(b) Note the amount of each orange drink required to decolorize the dye. The less orange added to decolorize the dye the more vitamin C it contains.

EXPERIMENT 12   TO SHOW THE DIGESTIVE EFFECT OF SALIVARY AMYLASE ON STARCH

12.1   INTRODUCTION

Salivary amylase is an enzyme which catalyses the breakdown of starch to maltose, a disaccharide giving a positive Benedict's Test.

12.2   APPARATUS AND REAGENTS

Test tubes and racks	Starch suspension
Pipettes	Saliva
Water bath at 37 °C	Benedict's reagent
Clock	Dilute iodine

12.3 METHOD

(a) Place two test-tubes each containing 1 cm³ of saliva and 3 cm³ of starch solution in a water bath at 37 °C.

(b) Remove one of the tubes after 1 min and divide the contents between two test-tubes.

(c) Test one half with iodine, the other with Benedict's reagent (as described in Experiment 11).

(d) Remove the second tube after 30 min and divide the contents between two test-tubes.

(e) Test one half with iodine, the other with Benedict's reagent.

(f) Record and explain your results. This experiment can be repeated using boiled saliva. Explain any difference in the results.

INDEX

Absorption, 196, 199–200
Accelerated freeze drying (AFD), 79
Acellular, 119
Acrolein, 193
Active transport, 173
Additives,
  Effect of boiling point, 30
  Effect on freezing point, 30
Adenine, 100, 101
AFD *see* accelerated freeze drying
Aflatoxin, 135
Air, Composition of, 84
Alcoholic beverages, 142–3
Alcohols, 99, 100, 102, 103–4, 105, 109–10
Aldehyde, 102
Algae, 113, 118, 125, 133
Alkanes, 98, 99
Alkenes, 101
Alkynes, 101
Amines, 102
Amino acid, 103, 188
Amoebic dysentery, 133
Amphibia, 147
Angiosperms *see also* flowering plant, 137
Animal kingdom, 112–13, 147–61
Annelids, 147
Arachnids, 147
Aroma, 106
Arthropods, 147
Ascorbic acid *see* vitamin C
Asparagus, 140
Atmospheric moisture, 36
Atomic number, 65
Atoms, 64–79

Size, 64
Structure, 64–5
Autoclaves, 29
Autotrophs, 131, 138, 175–6

Bacillus, 129
Bacteria, 113, 118–19, 125, 128
  Colonies, 132, 156, 204
  Micrographs of, 129, 132
Bacterial growth cycle, 166–9
Bacteriophage, 126
Bain-marie, 207
Bed bugs, 153
Benzoic acid, 88, 104
Beri-beri, 191
Berry, 141
Beverage plants, 142–3
Beverages, 142–3
Bile, 199, 200
Binary fission, 130–1, 165–6
Biochemistry and energy production, 108–10
Biological world, 112–13, 114
Biology, 112
Bird, 147, 149, 161
Blatta orientalis, 155
Bleaching, 84–5
Bonds,
  Covalent, 71–2
  Double, 85, 100–1
  Ionic (electrovalent), 68, 70–1
  Triple, 101
Botanical, 138
Bouquet, 106
Brine, 77–8, 171
Brownian motion, 76
Bryophyte, 137

Bud, 141
Budding, 135
Buffers, 93
Butane, 98, 99
Butanol, 99, 100, 102

Caecum, 195, 200
Calories, 30
Capsule, 129–30
Carbohydrates, 185, 186–8
Carbon,
  Chain, 97
  Cycle, 179, 181
  Tetravalent carbon atom, 97
Carbon compounds, 97–108
  Cyclic, 101
Carbon dioxide, 79, 80–1, 84, 91,
  108, 109, 110
Carbonate radical, 97
Carboxylic acids, 99, 102, 104, 105
Carnivores, 177, 182
Carpet beetle, 153–4
Catalysts, 83
  Biological *see also* enzymes, 110
Cell, 117–21
  Examination of, 227–8
Cell membrane, 17–19
Cell types, 117–20
  Coenocytic, 118
  Multicellular, 117
  Unicellular, 117
Cell wall, 118, 119, 172
Cellular differentiation, 120–1
Cellulase, 181
Cellulose, 118, 181, 186–8
Cereals, 138, 142
Champagne, 110
Chemical changes, 57, 58
Chemical reactions, 80–6
  Rate of, 81–3
Chemoautotrophs, 175
Chloroplast, 118, 138
Chordate, 147
Chyme, 197
Circuits, 43
  broken, 43
  open, 43
  short, 43, 54
Citric acid, 89, 104, 106
Class, 112
Clostridium, 129
Clothes moth, 153
Cockroaches, 154–5
Cocoa, 142
Coelenterate, 147
Coenzymes, 110
Cofactors, 110
Coffee, 142
Colloids, 61–2
Colon, 195, 200
Commensal, 179
Compound, 59
Condensation, 28–9
Conduction, 30, 31, 41
Conductivity, 31
  Determination of, 219–20
Conductors, 41
Contamination, 203–5, 206–7, 208
Convection, 31, 32, 33
  Forced, 32–33
  Natural, 32–33
Conversion factors, 2, 23
Cooking,
  Effect on nutrients, 192–3
  microwave, 35
Corrosion, 84–5
Cow, classification of, 113
Cross contamination, 203, 205, 206
Crustaceans, 147, 148
Crystal structure, 72–4
Culinary, 138
Curing, 77, 172
Current electricity, 40, 41–2
Cyanide, 110
Cyclisation, 100
Cytoplasm, 117–19

Dalton's atomic theory, 64
Death (or decline) phase, 168
Dehydration, 79, 116–17
  And freezer burn, 79
Density, 4
  experiments on, 210–13

Deoxyribosenucleic acid, 100, 107, 114, 118
Dermis, 121, 122
Diarrhoea, 200, 209
Dicotyledon, 137
Diet, 185
Dietary fibre, 188
Diffusion, 76–8, 169–70, 199
Digestion, 194–201
Digestive process, 196–9
Digestive tract, 194–200
Drugs, 145
Drupes, 141
Duodenum, 195, 199
Dyes, 144

Earth, 54–5
Earthworm, 147
Echinoderm, 147
Electrical current, 41–2
  Heating effect of, 47–8
Electrical symbols, 42
Electricity, 40–56
  Cost of, 49–50
  Current, 41–2
  Potential hazards of, 54–5
  Static, 40–1
Electromagnetic spectrum, 33–4
Electromagnetic waves, 33
Electron, 40, 65
  Shells, 66
Electronic configuration, 65–7, 68
Elements, 57–9
  Metallic, 58–9
  Non-metallic, 58–9
Emissivity, 35
Energy, 8, 12
  Chemical, 14
  Conservation of, 18
  Conversion of, 16–18
  Electrical, 15
  Heat, 15, 21–39
  Kinetic, 14, 21
  Light, 13
  Magnetic, 15
  Measurement of *see also* Joule, Calorie, 30

Nuclear, 15
Potential, 14
Value of foodstuffs, 30
Entamoeba histolytica, 133
Enzymes (biological catalysts), 133
Epidermis, 121, 122
Equations, 80–1
  Balancing, 80–1
ERH *see also* humidity, equilibrium humidity, 36
Essential amino acid, 188–90
Essential fatty acid, 190
Essential oil, 144
Esters, 104–5, 106
Ethanol, 99, 102, 103–4, 105, 109–10
Eukaryotic, 118, 119
Evaporation, 35–7, 78
  and cooling effect, 36–7
  and humidity, 35–6
Excretion, 115
Expotential phase, 167

Fabrics, 108
Facultative anaerobe, 109, 116
Facultative parasite, 131, 187
Family, 112
Farinaceous non-cereals, 142
Farming, intensive, 150
Fibres, 108
  Dietary, 188
  Natural, 108
  Plant, 144
  Regenerated, 108
  Synthetic, 108
Fish, 147, 148–9
Flagella, 129
Flat worm, 147, 150–2
Flavouring agents, 105–6
Flea, 153
Flower, 141
Flowering plant, 138–42
Food, 116
  Chains, 182–3
  Energy value of foodstuffs, 30
  Webs, 183
Food Poisoning, 202, 203
Food poisoning bacteria, 207

Food spoilage, 125, 129, 131, 135–6, 207
Force, 8–11
  Frictional, 9
  Gravitational, 10
Forced convection, 32
Freezer burn, 79
Fruit, 138, 141–2
  False, 141–2
  True, 141–2
Fuel, 14, 145
Functional groups, 99, 101, 102
Fungi, 113, 118, 125, 133–6
Fusel oils, 104
Fuses, 50–3

Gastrointestinal (GI) tract, 194
Gelling agent, 145
Generation time, 166
Genus, 112
Giardia lamblia, 133
Glucose, 100, 101, 108–9
Glycerol (or glycerine), 37, 100, 103–4, 189, 190
Glycerol monostearate (GMS), 105
Growth, 115, 163–74
  In individual cells, 163
  In Multicellular organisms, 163
  In populations of bacteria, 165–9
  Rates, 165–9
Gum, 144
Gut, 194
Gymnosperm, 137

Half life, 75–6
Hand washing, rules for, 208
Heat, 21–39
  Calculations of heat energy, 27
  Latent, 27
  Sensible, 28
Hepatitis, 127
Herb, 143
Herbivore, 176, 182
Heterotrophs, 131, 138, 176–7
Homeostasis, 169
Homologous series, 98–9
House fly, 156–9

Humectant, 37
Humidity, 35–7
  Absolute, 36
  Applications, 37
  Equilibrium relative (ERH), 36
  Relative, 36
Hydrocarbons, 98
Hydrogen carbonate radical, 97
Hydrogenation, 82, 85
Hydrometers, 5–7, 215–16
  Gay-Lussac hydrometer, 7
  Lactometer, 6, 7
  Saccharometer, 6, 7
  Sikes hydrometer, 7
  Test tube, 215–16
Hydrometry, 5, 215–16
Hygiene, 127, 202–9
Hygrometers, 37

Ileum, 195, 197–200
Inclusions, 118
Insect, 147, 152–9
Insulators,
  Electrical, 41
  Heat, 31
Intestine,
  Large, 195, 200
  Small, 194, 195, 197, 198, 199
Intrinsic factor, 200
Invertebrate, 147, 148
Iron, 192
Isomerism, 98–9, 100
Isotopes, 65–6

Jejenum, 197, 199
Joule, 11, 26, 38

Ketone, 102
Kilocalories, 30
Kilojoules, 30
Kinetic theory, 76–9
  Effect of pressure, 78
  Effect of temperature, 78
Kingdom, 112

Lactic acid, 89, 104, 106, 109
Lag phase, 166–7, 168

Latent heat, 27
Latex, 144
Leaf, 140
Leaf axil, 139, 141
Leeuwenhoek, Antonie van, 125
Life,
  Characteristics, 114–15
  Conditions for, 115–17
  Effect of temperature on, 116
Lignin, 138
Linolenic acid, 189, 190
Lipids, 190–1, 193
Liver, 195, 199, 200
Liverwort, 137
Logarithmic (log) phase, 167, 168

Malic acid, 88, 106
Mammal, 147, 149–50
Mass, 2, 10–11
Mass number, 65
Medicine, 145
Melamine, 107
Metabolism, 108
Methane, 98, 99
Methanol, 103
Microbiology, 125
Micro-organisms, 113, 125–36
  Importance to food industry, 131,
    133, 135–6
Microscope, 225
  Use of, 223–6
Microwave cooking, 35
Minerals, 192
Mitochondria, 118, 119
Mitosis, 164–5
Mixtures, 59–63
Molecular formulae, 69
Molecules, 68
Mollusc, 147
Monocotyledon, 137
Monomer, 106
Moss, 137
Moulds, 131, 134–5
  Micrographs of, 134
Mouse, 160
Movement, 115
Multicellular organisms, 163

Mus musculus, 157–60
Mycotoxin, 135
Myriapod, 147

Nematode, 147, 150, 152
Neutron, 65
Newton, 3, 10–11
Nitrogen cycle, 180, 181–2
Nomenclature (naming) of chemical
    compounds, 101–3
Non-conductors see also
    insulators, 31, 41
Nucleus (atomic), 65, 75
Nucleus (cell), 118
  Akaryotic, 119
  Eukaryotic, 118
  Prokaryotic, 118
Nut, 141
Nutrients, 185–193
  Identification, 230–3
Nutrition, 115
  Holozoic, 176
  Modes of, 175–83
  Parasitic, 178
  Saprophytic, 178
Nutritional association, 177–81
Nylon, 108

Ohm's Law, 47
  Demonstration of, 217–19
Omnivore, 177, 182
Order, 112
Organ, 121
Organelle, 117–18, 119
Organic chemistry, 97–108
Osmosis, 170–2
Osmotic pressure, effect of, 229
Ovary, 139, 141
Ovule, 139, 141
Oxidation and reduction, 83–6
Oxygen, 83–6, 80, 116
  in air, 84

Pancreas, 195, 199
Parasite, 131, 176
Parsitic worm, 150–2
Pasteur, Louis, 125

Pectin, 145
Penicillium, 134, 135
Peristalsis, 194
Pernicious anaemia, 191, 200
Personal hygiene, 203, 208–9
  Rules for, 209
pH, 91, 92, 93, 110, 156
  Experiment, 222–3
  Measurement of, 92, 222–3
Phagocytosis, 173–4
Phenols, 100, 104
Phloem, 139–40
Photoautotrophs, 175–6
Photosynthesis, 13, 116, 117, 118, 175–6
Phylum, 112
Physical changes, 57, 58
Plant kingdom, 112–13, 137–46
Platyhelminth, 147
Polio, 127
Polymer, 106–8, 186, 188, 190
Polysaccharides, 107
Polythene, 83, 101, 107, 108
Polyunsaturated fatty acids, 190
Porifera (sponges), 147
Potential difference, 42–4
Power, 19–20, 48–50
Pressure,
  Cooker, 29
  Effect on boiling point, 29
Prokaryota, 113, 118–19, 125, 128
Propane, 98, 99
Propanoic acid, 89, 99, 104
Proteins, 107, 110, 188–90
Protista, 113, 118, 125
proton, 65
Protozoa, 125, 133
Pteridophyte, 137

Radiation, 31, 33
Radicals, 69, 70–1, 97
Radioactivity, 75–6
  Applications to food industry, 76
Rancidity, 79, 83, 84–6
Rat, 160
  Black (*Rattus norvegicus*), 160
  Brown (*Rattus rattus*), 160

Redox reactions, 86
Refrigeration, 37–8, 169, 207
Relative density (RD), 4–5
  Experiments on, 213–17
Reproduction, 114
Reptile, 147
Resins, 40, 144
Resistance, 44–8
  Applications of, 48
  Parallel, 45–6
  Series, 45–6
Resistivity, 44
Respiration, 108–10, 115
  Aerobic, 108
  Anaerobic, 109–10
  And energy production, 109–10
Rhubarb, 140, 229
Rodenticide, 158
Rodents, 159–60
Root, 138, 139, 141
Rope, 130
Round worm, 147, 150, 152
Rubber, 107, 144

Saccharomyces, 135
Salmonella, 32, 178, 203, 205
saprophytes, 131, 176
saturated fats, 101
Saturation, 99–101
Scurvy, 191–2
Seed, 142
Sensible heat, 28
Sensitivity, 115
Shoot, 138, 139
SI (Systeme Internatinale), 1
Skin, structure and function of, 121
Solubility, 62–3
  determinatin of, 220–1
Solutions, 60–3
Sorbic acid, 89, 104
Soy sauce, 135
Species, 112
Specific heat capacity, 26–7
Spermatophyte, 137
Spice, 143
Spores, 129
Staphylococcus, 128–9, 179, 203

State, 27–8
 changes of, 27–9
 of matter, 78
Static electricity, 40–1
Stationary phase, 167–8
Stem, 140
Stigma, 139, 141
Stomach, 194–9
Streptococcus, 128–9
Style, 139, 141
Sublimation, 28, 79
Sulphurous acid, 89
Sunlight, 117
Symbiosis, 179–81
Symbols, 65
Systems, 121

Taenia saginata, 147
Tapeworm, 147, 150–2
Taxonomy, 112
Tea, 142
Temperature, 21
 Common catering, 23
 Conversion factors, 23
 Danger zone, 207
 Effect on life, 116
 Measurement of (thermometry), 2
 Scales of, 22–5
Thermal capacity, 26–7
Thermometer, 22
 Bimetallic, 24
 Thermocouple, 24–6, 216–17
 Types of, 22–5
Timber, 144
Tissues, 120–1
 Blood, 121
 Connective, 121
 Epithelial, 121, 194
 Muscular, 121
 Nervous, 121
 Skeletal, 120
Trichinella spiralis, 147

Triglycerides, 189, 190
True solutions, 61–2
Tuber, 139–40

Units, 1–3
 Derived, 3
 Imperial, 1
 Practical, 3
 Prefixes, 3
 SI, 1–3
Unsaturated fats, 101

Vacuole, 118, 138
Valency, 67
Vapour pressure, 29
Vascular tissue, 139, 140
Vegetable, 138
Vertebrate, 147, 148–50
Villus, 195, 199
Viruses, 113, 119–20, 125–7
Viscosity, 33, 57, 61
Vitamin A, 191, 192
Vitamin B-complex, 93, 110, 179,
  191–2
Vitamin C, 29, 88, 157, 193, 232
Vitamin D, 123, 191–2
Vitamin K, 179–80, 191–2
Vitamins, 110, 191–2, 193

Water, 116–17, 185, 196
Waxes, 145, 190
Weight, 10–11
Wiring,
 Code, 53
 Plug, 52, 53–4
Work, 11–12
 Useful and non-useful, 18–19

Xylem, 139–40

Yeast, 119, 131, 134–5